CliffsNotes®

NCLEX-RN®

CRAM PLAN™

CliffsNotes®

NCLEX-RN®
CRAM PLAN™

Michael Reid, MSN, RN, CCRN

Houghton Mifflin Harcourt
Boston • New York

About the Author

Michael Reid, MSN, RN, CCRN, is the founder and director of an NCLEX® test-prep company (The NCLEX Cure) specializing in individuals who are looking to pass the NCLEX® exam and become registered or practical nurses. Michael has worked for prestigious hospitals such as The Johns Hopkins Hospital and Northwestern Memorial Hospital. He currently works as a critical care nurse in a Chicago hospital ICU, in addition to teaching students from across the United States and abroad.

Dedication

To all the hard-working future and current nurses out there. You are crucial to society and provide grace at a very difficult time in people's lives. I applaud you.

Editorial

Executive Editor: Greg Tubach
Senior Editor: Christina Stambaugh
Production Editor: Jennifer Freilach
Copy Editor: Lynn Northrup
Technical Editors: Dr. Marcia Stout, DNP, APN, FNP-C, CWON, CHSE; Amteshwar Singh, MBBS, MD
Proofreader: Susan Moritz

CliffsNotes® NCLEX-RN® Cram Plan™

Library of Congress Control Number: 2018938540
ISBN: 978-1-328-90083-8 (pbk)

Printed in the United States of America
DOC 10 9 8 7 6 5
4500810424

For information about permission to reproduce selections from this book, write to trade.permissions@hmhco.com or to Permissions, Houghton Mifflin Harcourt Publishing Company, 3 Park Avenue, 19th Floor, New York, New York 10016.

www.hmhco.com

Table of Contents

Introduction

About the NCLEX

This board exam is created by the National Council of State Boards of Nursing (NCSBN). It is updated roughly every 3 years, most recently in 2016. The table below shows the breakdown of the NCLEX in the major subject areas that are tested. This book focuses strongly on prioritization, as well as safety and infection. From there, an overview on independent med-surg topics are covered, including other popular areas of the NCLEX, such as delegation. There is also a strong chapter on pharmacology, an important subject area, as shown in the following breakdown.

Major Subject Areas	Percentage of Each Subject Area
Management of Care (Priority, Delegation)	17%–23%
Safety and Infection Control	9%–15%
Health Promotion and Maintenance	6%–12%
Psychosocial Integrity	6%–12%
Basic Care and Comfort	6%–12%
Pharmacological and Parenteral Therapies	12%–18%
Reduction of Risk Potential	9%–15%
Physiological Adaptation	11%–17%

The above percentages adapt to each person throughout the exam. The NCLEX is a computer-adaptive exam. If certain questions within the above subjects are poorly answered, the exam will adapt to further test this area for aptitude.

The NCLEX Itself: Exam Format

The NCLEX has the possibility of 75 to 265 questions, with a total testing time of 6 hours for RN and 5 hours for PN. The exam will continue on until the decision to pass or fail the student based on the passing standard has been decided. The passing standard is unknown to anyone outside the NCSBN. It is the general idea of a shifting line the board has decided on every 3 years that indicates sufficient proficiency to work in the field of nursing.

There are a wide variety of question types, with the vast majority being Select One Multiple Choice and Select All That Apply. There may also be hot-spot questions, for which you must click on the area of the picture in question. The NCLEX can incorporate sound and/or video in questioning (common for lung sounds). Ordered questions may also pop up, such as which order a nurse performs suctioning.

For students unfamiliar with the overall NCLEX format and testing, the NCSBN website (www.ncsbn.org) provides in-depth instruction on what to expect for the exam itself and how to schedule your examination.

What to Think After the Exam

Most people who shut the exam down at 75 questions either nail it or bomb it. This exam is not easy, so if you have taken the NCLEX previously and the exam shut down at 75 questions, do not take that as a huge disappointment. Focus on areas where you struggled and apply yourself into truly understanding the disease. Many students have problems with anatomy and physiology before ever beginning to study for the NCLEX. Perhaps that is an area that needs additional study aside from this book.

When 265 questions is reached, statistically speaking the student has an 80% chance of passing on average. If the student fails at 265 questions, it is very likely he or she was close to passing and only requires some slight tweaking to previous knowledge and test-taking strategy to pass the next time.

About This Book

I wish you the best of luck studying through your specific Cram Plan and for the NCLEX. This book really is *the* CliffsNotes for the NCLEX. There is no line that I did not look at and think how I could make it easier to learn and apply to an NCLEX question. I tell my students at The NCLEX Cure all the time that it is impossible to memorize everything about everything. It is important to focus on the hard-hitting areas that are most likely to come up on the board exam.

Do not take the approach of studying more for the sake of studying more. Many students have a tendency to over-learn multiple topics; but remember, you went to nursing school, not medical school. Ask anyone who has ever taken the NCLEX, and they will tell you the same thing. There is simply too much knowledge for any one person to know straight out of school. This book will show you what is important. The purpose of the NCLEX is not to make you a robot. The purpose is to make sure you can operate as a safe nurse. Use that mentality when you approach these questions. Many of the authors of the NCLEX questions use this as a benchmark for what they are trying to get out of you.

Good luck!

Michael Reid, MSN, RN, CCRN
Founder and Director of Nursing Development
The NCLEX Cure
www.thenclexcure.com

Determining Your NCLEX Cram Plan

Take the following steps to determine which of the three cram plan study calendars best fits your needs:

1. Take the Diagnostic Test.
2. Use the answer key to find your baseline percentage.
3. Pay attention to which types of questions you got wrong.
   a. Prioritization
   b. Safety and Infection
   c. Individual med-surg areas (Cardiology, Respiratory, etc.)
   d. In the chart below, check the box that works within your schedule: two-month, one-month, or one-week.

Determining Your NCLEX Cram Plan			
Test Section	**Your Score**	**Your Cram Plan**	
Prioritization		❑ Two-Month Cram Plan	❑ One-Month Cram Plan	❑ One-Week Cram Plan
Safety and Infection		❑ Two-Month Cram Plan	❑ One-Month Cram Plan	❑ One-Week Cram Plan
Med-Surg topics		❑ Two-Month Cram Plan	❑ One-Month Cram Plan	

The cram plan calendars appear on the next few pages. Once you determine which cram plan calendar to follow, stick with that time frame. If you choose a two-month prep period, utilize this full book as described on pp. 2–3. If you choose a one-month prep period, utilize the suggestions in that cram plan (p. 4).

A one-week cram plan, as you can see in the chart above, does not include the med-surg topics as a full review. If you only have one week, it is far more important to utilize that time studying Prioritization and Safety and Infection. These are the two most important sections on the NCLEX, and if you have only one week, your time should be spent there.

The three different cram plans appear on the following pages. Each will detail what material to study week by week (and day by day in the one-week plan). Do not be concerned if the material in some weeks appears longer than that in others. Many of the chapters are short and can be reviewed quickly. Each week of the study plans is built with this is mind.

On your final days before the NCLEX exam, follow what to do on p. 5. There are some recommendations for final prep and what to do on the day of the exam.

Two-Month Cram Plan

Two-Month Cram Plan	
8 weeks before the exam	**Study Time: 2–3 hours a day** ❑ Read "Prioritization." ❑ Read "Safety and Infection." ❑ Read "Scope of Practice – RN" (or "Scope of Practice – PN," if that is the licensure you're seeking). ❑ Read "Delegation." ❑ Read "Basic Care and Comfort." ❑ Read "ADPIE (Nursing Process)." ❑ Read "Leadership and Management." ❑ Read "Cardiovascular." ❑ Read "Critical Care." ❑ Read "EKG Interpretation." ❑ Study "Cardiovascular Medications" (pp. 195–199). ❑ Apply prioritization for medical emergencies (pp. 27–29) to the areas studied this week.
7 weeks before the exam	**Study Time: 2–3 hours a day** ❑ Read "Respiratory." ❑ Read "O_2 Supplementation." ❑ Read "Lung Sounds." ❑ Read "Arterial Blood Gases (ABGs)." ❑ Read "Fluid and Electrolytes." ❑ Study "Respiratory Medications" (pp. 200–201). ❑ Apply prioritization for medical emergencies (pp. 27–29) to the areas studied this week.
6 weeks before the exam	**Study Time: 2–3 hours a day** ❑ Read "Lab Values." ❑ Read "Endocrinology." ❑ Read "Gastrointestinal." ❑ Study "Endocrine Medications" (pp. 202–203) and "Gastrointestinal Medications" (pp. 204–205). ❑ Apply prioritization for medical emergencies (pp. 27–29) to the areas studied this week.
5 weeks before the exam	**Study Time: 1–2 hours a day** ❑ Read "Hematology." ❑ Read "Immunology." ❑ Read "Genitourinary." ❑ Study "Hematology Medications" (p. 208) and "Immunology Medications" (pp. 205–207). Note: There is no genitourinary pharmacology to study. ❑ Apply prioritization for medical emergencies (pp. 27–29) to the areas studied this week.

4 weeks before the exam	**Study Time: 1–2 hours a day** ❑ Read "Musculoskeletal." ❑ Read "Neurosensory." ❑ Read "Oncology." ❑ Study "Musculoskeletal and Pain Medications" (pp. 208–209), "Neurology Medications" (pp. 210–211), and "Oncology Medications" (p. 208). ❑ Apply prioritization for medical emergencies (pp. 27–29) to the areas studied this week.
3 weeks before the exam	**Study Time: 1–2 hours a day** ❑ Read "Psychiatry." ❑ Read pp. 193–195 and pp. 213–214 in "Pharmacology." ❑ Study "Psychiatry Medications" (pp. 211–213). ❑ Apply prioritization for medical emergencies (pp. 27–29) to the areas studied this week.
2 weeks before the exam	**Study Time: 1–2 hours a day** ❑ Read "Pediatrics." ❑ Read "Obstetrics/Gynecology." ❑ Read "Neonatology." ❑ Apply prioritization for medical emergencies (pp. 27–29) to the areas studied this week. Note: No pediatric medical emergencies present in themselves; they are similar to those in adults.
1 week before the exam	**Study Time: 2 hours a day** ❑ Read "Genetics." ❑ Read "Motor Neurons and Glands." ❑ Read "Positioning." ❑ Study "Motor Neurons and Glands" pharmacology (p. 200). ❑ Review pharmacology information for all chapters. ❑ Review medical emergencies for all chapters and on pp. 27–29.
Final days before the exam	**Study Time: 1–2 hours a day** ❑ **Take the Practice Exam.** ❑ Review answers and explanations. ❑ For any questions you answered incorrectly, review the appropriate chapter.

One-Month Cram Plan

One-Month Cram Plan	
4 weeks before the exam	**Study Time: 2–3 hours a day** ❑ Read "Prioritization." ❑ Use the list of medical emergencies in the "Prioritization" chapter as a checklist (pp. 27–29). ❑ Begin reviewing roughly 10 emergencies. ❑ Focus on the following sections: "Pathophysiology," "Signs and Symptoms," and "Interventions." ❑ Read "Safety and Infection." ❑ Read "Scope of Practice – RN" (or "Scope of Practice – PN," if that is the licensure you're seeking). ❑ Read "Delegation." ❑ Scan "Cardiovascular," "Critical Care," and "EKG Interpretation" for areas of weakness and then review those areas. ❑ Scan "Respiratory," "O_2 Supplementation," "Lung Sounds," and "Arterial Blood Gases (ABGs)" for areas of weakness and then review those areas. ❑ Review "Cardiovascular Medications (pp. 195–199) and "Respiratory Medications" (pp. 200–201).
3 weeks before the exam	**Study Time: 2–3 hours a day** ❑ Read "Basic Care and Comfort." ❑ Read "ADPIE (Nursing Process)." ❑ Read "Leadership and Management." ❑ Read "Fluid and Electrolytes." ❑ Read "Lab Values." ❑ Scan "Endocrinology," "Gastrointestinal," "Hematology," "Immunology," and "Genitourinary" for areas of weakness and then review those areas. ❑ Review "Endocrine Medications" (pp. 202–203), "Gastrointestinal Medications" (pp. 204–205), "Hematology Medications" (p. 208), and "Immunology Medications" (pp. 205–207). Note: There is no genitourinary pharmacology to study. ❑ Apply prioritization for medical emergencies (pp. 27–29) to the areas studied this week.
2 weeks before the exam	**Study Time: 2 hours a day** ❑ Scan "Musculoskeletal," "Neurosensory," "Oncology," and "Psychiatry" for areas of weakness and then review those areas. ❑ Review "Musculoskeletal and Pain Medications" (pp. 208–209), "Neurology Medications" (pp. 210–211), "Oncology Medications" (p. 208), and "Psychiatry Medications" (pp. 211–213). ❑ Read pp. 193–195 and pp. 213–214 in "Pharmacology." ❑ Continue reviewing "Medical Emergencies" (pp. 27–29), focusing on areas of weakness.
1 week before the exam	**Study Time: 2 hours a day** ❑ Scan "Pediatrics," "Obstetrics/Gynecology," and "Neonatology" for areas of weakness and then review those areas. ❑ Scan "Genetics," "Motor Neurons and Glands," and "Positioning" for areas of weakness and then review those areas. ❑ Review "Motor Neurons and Glands" pharmacology (p. 200). ❑ Do a final review of "Medical Emergencies" (pp. 27–29). ❑ **Take the Practice Exam.** ❑ Review answers and explanations. ❑ For any questions you answered incorrectly, review the appropriate chapter.

One-Week Cram Plan

One-Week Cram Plan	
4–7 days before the exam	**Study Time: 3–4 hours a day** ❏ Read "Prioritization." ❏ Use the list of medical emergencies in the "Prioritization" chapter as a checklist (pp. 27–29). ❏ Begin reviewing a minimum of 30 to 40 medical emergencies you may not understand. ❏ Focus on the following sections: "Pathophysiology," "Signs and Symptoms," and "Interventions." ❏ Read "Safety and Infection." Review infections you may not understand. ❏ Read "Scope of Practice – RN" (or "Scope of Practice – PN," if that is the licensure you're seeking). ❏ Read "Delegation." ❏ Read "Basic Care and Comfort." ❏ Read "ADPIE (Nursing Process)." ❏ Read "Leadership and Management." ❏ **Take the Practice Exam.** ❏ Review answers and explanations. ❏ For any questions you answered incorrectly, review the appropriate chapter.
1–4 days before the exam	**Study Time: 3–4 hours a day** ❏ Continue reviewing chapters associated with questions that you answered incorrectly. ❏ Finish reviewing the list of medical emergencies (pp. 27–29). ❏ Review any weak areas in "Safety and Infection." ❏ If you have extra time, scan through the individual med-surg topics.

The Night Before and the Day of the NCLEX

The Night Before and the Day of the NCLEX	
The night before the exam	**What to do:** ❏ Do not do any heavy studying; if anything, brush up on some medical emergencies. ❏ Go to bed early. ❏ Do not drink alcohol or take any stimulants.
The day of the exam	**What to do:** ❏ Eat breakfast. ❏ Listen to classical music on the way to the NCLEX. Research shows that listening to classical music increases memory recall. ❏ Take breaks during the exam if needed. They count against time, but it is better to lose a little time than to feel flustered.

30 Questions

1. The charge nurse in the emergency department (ED) is alerted via a paramedic call that four patients in a motor vehicle accident are being brought in. Which of the following patients should the charge nurse delegate to a new nurse in the ED who just finished orientation?

   A. A toddler with ecchymotic areas around the right arm, who has a strong radial pulse and is guarding the arm
   B. An adult with unknown injuries and changing levels of consciousness
   C. A child crying with an obvious compound fracture
   D. An adult having some difficulty breathing after being thrown into the steering wheel

2. During evening rounds, a nurse has assessed four patients. Which of the following would require **priority** focus?

   A. An 82-year-old patient diagnosed with pneumonia 2 days ago who has been receiving IV antibiotics
   B. A 68-year-old patient on warfarin admitted 4 hours ago after a fall and hit to the head
   C. A 22-year-old patient with a BMI of 22 complaining of frequent urination and thirst
   D. A 50-year-old patient with chronic obstructive pulmonary disease and a pulse oximeter reading of 89%

3. After finishing morning rounds on a med-surg floor, the nurse decides to care for which client **first**?

   A. A 1-day post-op patient with serosanguinous drainage after a transurethral resection of the prostate (TURP)
   B. A 2-day post-op knee replacement patient who is being processed for discharge and requires a final dressing change of the surgical site
   C. A patient previously diagnosed with hypothyroidism who is complaining of neck tightness with visibly dry mucous membranes
   D. A patient with pneumonia who has a cough, sore throat, and purulent expectorant

4. While working on a general med-surg floor, the nurse is updated by the unlicensed assistive personnel (UAP). Based on the information shared about the following four patients, which patient would the nurse want to assess **immediately**?

   A. A patient with hepatitis A who is complaining of fatigue, with a temperature of 101.5°
   B. A patient diagnosed with pancreatitis who is complaining of severe worsening pain
   C. A patient with a blood pressure of 115/75 receiving IV ciprofloxacin and who has developed a rash on both arms
   D. A patient diagnosed with cholecystitis whose skin appears to have turned light yellow

5. A patient with moderately advanced Alzheimer's is prescribed donepezil. When the patient returns for a follow-up appointment, what would the nurse hope to find if the drug has been effective?

   A. The patient's family states activities of daily living (ADLs) are easier.

   B. The disease has improved to minor Alzheimer's.

   C. The patient remembers things he or she previously did not.

   D. The patient has been experiencing nausea and vomiting on and off for a week.

6. The nurse on a telemetry unit has recently assessed rhythms of four patients. Which of the following patients would require a follow-up assessment by the RN?

   A. A patient on digoxin with a pulse of 60 bpm

   B. A patient who appears to be in third-degree heart block

   C. A patient who underwent cardioversion for ventricular tachycardia 4 hours ago

   D. A patient with new onset of 4 PVCs every minute

7. A pregnant patient and her physician have decided to induce labor. The patient has a history of cesarean section in a previous pregnancy. Which of the following findings during the induction would the nurse find **most** concerning?

   A. Anxiety and lower back pain

   B. Changes in fetal position and maternal tachycardia

   C. Fetal tachycardia with findings of early deceleration

   D. Slow progression of contractions and cervical dilation

8. A charge nurse working on a post-surgical unit is expecting four patients to return to the unit within the next 2 hours. Which of the following patients would the charge nurse want to assign to the staff nurse with the **least** experience?

   A. A patient returning from a bifemoral popliteal bypass graft

   B. A patient who had a trach placed after prolonged endotracheal intubation

   C. A patient who had an appendectomy

   D. A patient with lung cancer who underwent a partial lobectomy

9. The nurse on an oncology floor is preparing to transfer a patient for a magnetic resonance imaging (MRI) scan for analysis of a brain tumor. Which of the following is important for the nurse to review before handing off the patient to the transport team? **Select all that apply.**

   A. Review the history for allergies to iodine or seafood.

   B. Review the history for medications that have been held for the past 8 hours.

   C. Review the history for a pacemaker.

   D. Review the history for anxiety or panic disorder.

   E. Review the patient's ability to remain in a standing position.

10. A nurse is triaging four patients in an emergency department (ED) who all walked in at the same time. Which of the following patients should the nurse see **first**?

    A. A patient who is diaphoretic and complaining of severe flank pain radiating to the groin area
    B. A patient with nausea, vomiting, and rebound tenderness in the right upper quadrant .
    C. A patient vomiting blood who is clearly under the influence of alcohol ✔
    D. A patient with a compound fracture of the right femur who is screaming in pain

11. A nurse is assessing the risk of complications in a patient diagnosed with peripheral artery disease (PAD). Which of the following statements by the patient requires **further education**?

    A. "I try to walk 15 minutes a day on a treadmill or outside."
    B. "I use lotion on my feet daily."
    C. "I am working with a smoking cessation therapist to stop smoking."
    D. "I place a heating pad on my feet when they are cold."

12. A patient admitted the previous day for a myocardial infarction has medications due at 1400. The nurse reviews recent vital signs and lab values before administration (see the two charts below). Which of the following medications should the nurse hold for clarification by the health care provider (HCP)? **Select all that apply**.

Vital Signs at 1300	
Temperature	98.8 F
Blood Pressure	110/70 mm Hg
Heart Rate	56/min
Respirations	16/min

Laboratory Results at 1200	
Sodium	137
Potassium	5.1
Calcium	9
Creatinine	1.3
BUN	15
Glucose	110

    A. Docusate
    B. Metoprolol
    C. Captopril ✓
    D. Lovastatin
    E. Bumetanide

13. A nurse is giving a presentation to a large group of people at a community center about Legionnaires' disease and how to prevent it for themselves and their children. Which statement made by one of the attendees does the nurse recognize as correct understanding of the disease?

    A. "I should be careful to cook meat at the recommended temperature to destroy all bacteria."
    B. "I should teach my family the importance of washing their hands after playing with animals."
    C. "I should be careful to not let my children play in small ponds."
    D. "This is a viral disease and often cannot be prevented."

14. A nurse on the med-surg floor is receiving reports on four patients. Which of the following patients should the nurse see **first**?

    A. A patient with suspected angina scheduled for coronary angiography
    B. A patient diagnosed with *pneumocystis jiroveci* pneumonia with a productive cough of yellow sputum
    C. A patient receiving continuous bladder irrigation post–transurethral resection of the prostate (TURP) who does not show signs of output
    D. A patient diagnosed with post-streptococcus glomerulonephritis. Current findings indicate a blood pressure of 148/88 and proteinuria.

15. A male nurse in the medical intensive care unit (MICU) is caring for an intubated patient diagnosed with septic shock due to an infected central venous catheter (vas-cath) utilized previously for chemotherapy. Which of the following interventions is the **most** important to prevent further infection to this patient?

    A. Handwashing before and after care of the patient
    B. Utilizing alcohol swabs before accessing any IV site
    C. Wearing personal protective equipment (PPE)
    D. Hanging ordered antibiotics as ordered

16. The nurse is discharging a patient with a new diagnosis of heart failure. Understanding that heart failure patients have a high chance of readmission, the nurse pays close attention to the patient's understanding of the discharge instructions. The patient is being discharged on captopril, spironolactone, and an order for a low-sodium diet. Which of the following statements by the patient displays understanding of the instructions?

    A. "I will be sure to eat more fruits and vegetables like bananas and apples."
    B. "I will avoid processed and canned foods."
    C. "I will use a salt substitute instead of sea salt."
    D. "It is important I monitor for a cough and call the doctor immediately if it occurs."

17. The nurse is reviewing voicemail messages at an outpatient clinic. Which patient should the nurse prioritize as being the **most** important to call back first?

    A. A 73-year-old male complaining of watery diarrhea after taking polyethylene glycol for bowel prep
    B. A 56-year-old female with diabetes who said she lost her insulin pen
    C. A 43-year-old male complaining of an erection lasting longer than 4 hours after use of sildenafil
    D. A 62-year-old female complaining of nausea after being discharged home from a cataract removal

18. A wound care nurse assigned to an intensive care unit (ICU) is rounding on a patient who requires a dressing change for an infected surgical incision and a patient with a Stage 3 pressure ulcer. How should the wound care nurse approach these tasks?

    A. Wear sterile gloves, a gown, and a mask when removing the soiled dressing.
    B. Remove the soiled dressing wearing sterile gloves, then apply another pair of sterile gloves.
    C. Wear clean gloves for the removal of the soiled dressing and another pair of clean gloves for the reapplication of a new dressing.
    D. Wear clean gloves for the removal of the soiled dressing and sterile gloves for the application of the new dressing.

19. An ambulance calls into the emergency department as the nurse picks up the phone. The paramedics explain to the nurse that a man roughly 45 years old is suspected of having a myocardial infarction. They began oxygen on the scene and were able to administer one sublingual dose of nitroglycerin before the man became unconscious. Upon admission to the emergency room, the nurse understands which of the following tasks is the **most** important to do first?

    A. Assess vital signs.
    B. Administer nitroglycerin sublingual.
    C. Assess an EKG.
    D. Draw labs for cardiac markers as ordered.

20. A nurse in the emergency department of a pediatric hospital has a surge of new arrivals. Which of the following patients should the nurse see **first**?

    A. A 4-year-old with a small, unknown object lodged in the left nostril
    B. A 10-year-old with second-degree burns to both arms
    C. A 6-month-old with a fever of 100.5 with vomiting and diarrhea for 2 days
    D. A 12-month-old who has a bulging anterior fontanelle when crying

21. During physician rounds and analyses of recent x-rays, the team has decided to perform a thoracentesis to correct a pleural effusion. They request the nurse to assist in the procedure. The nurse must be aware of potential complications of the procedure. Which of the following would be symptoms of a complication in this procedure? **Select all that apply.**

    A. Decreased effort of breathing
    B. Dyspnea
    C. Tracheal deviation
    D. Radiating pain to the left shoulder
    E. Tachypnea

22. While rounding on a patient, the nurse witnesses this rhythm (see EKG strip below). Which of the following orders would the nurse anticipate the physician to potentially order **immediately**? **Select all that apply.**

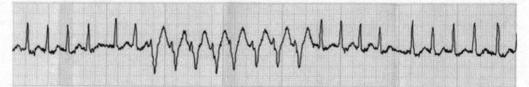

   A.   Amiodarone IV
   B.   Adenosine IV STAT
   C.   Lidocaine IV
   D.   Blood cultures
   E.   Chemistry panel
   F.   Immediate defibrillation

23. A patient diagnosed with chronic kidney disease (CKD) was admitted to the emergency department (ED) 1 hour ago. The family states he was complaining of heart palpitations at home and that the patient recently had surgery for an AV fistula placement in the left upper extremity. Upon assessment, the patient was found to be having frequent premature ventricular contractions (PVCs), a potassium level of 7.0, and a creatinine level of 3.8. The patient's lower extremities have +2 pitting edema bilaterally. The ED physician would like to immediately correct the problem. What would be the best **immediate** intervention?

   A.   Assess the fistula for potential use.
   B.   Administer regular insulin and D5 IV.
   C.   Administer sodium polystyrene sulfonate.
   D.   Administer furosemide.

24. A nurse on a post-surgical unit is charting when an alarm goes off down the hall. Upon entering the room, the nurse finds the patient in pain and anxious. Upon walking closer to the bed, the nurse finds the surgical dressing peeling off with dehiscence of the wound. While calming and reassuring the patient, what does the nurse anticipate as the **next** intervention?

   A.   Remove the dressing, apply sterile gloves, and place a new dressing.
   B.   Reinforce the current dressing and call the health care provider (HCP).
   C.   Close the wound by applying hard pressure.
   D.   Leave the room to obtain pain medication.

25. During a central line placement procedure, a patient begins to experience shortness of breath. An air embolism is suspected. In which of the following positions does the nurse expect to place the patient?

   A.   High Fowler's
   B.   Supine
   C.   Trendelenburg to the right
   D.   Trendelenburg to the left

26. The nurse is assessing a patient diagnosed with cardiovascular disease and hypertension. The patient has been receiving metoprolol around the clock. Which of the following would **most** cause the nurse to follow up?

    A.   Heart rate changing from 75 bpm to 63 bpm
    B.   Urine output of 120 mL in the last 3 hours
    C.   Headache and epistaxis
    D.   LDL (lipid) of 220

27. A type 2 diabetic mellitus (DM) patient was recently started on glyburide. During a follow-up appointment, the nurse is assessing the patient. Which of the following would be **most** important to mention to the health care provider (HCP)?

    A.   Recent A1C of 6.8%
    B.   Retinal changes from previous visit
    C.   Nausea
    D.   Weight gain of 5 lbs. since previous visit

28. During assessment of a new admission in the emergency department (ED), the nurse notices nuchal rigidity, a temperature of 101.5° F, and petechiae. Which of the following would be the **most** important to do first?

    A.   Initiate seizure precautions.
    B.   Request IV antibiotics.
    C.   Initiate droplet precautions.
    D.   Request IV antivirals.

29. During discharge teaching for a patient diagnosed with type 2 diabetes mellitus, the nurse is utilizing the "teach-back" method. Which of the following statements by the patient would require **further education**?

    A.   "I will check my blood sugar before I eat."
    B.   "I will adjust my sliding scale NPH dose accordingly."
    C.   "I will eat less simple sugars."
    D.   "I will take my scheduled doses at the same time every day."

30. Which of the following events would be considered as sentinel and require an incident report?

    A.   Administering nitroglycerine IV to a patient with hypertension
    B.   Administering insulin followed by dextrose to a patient with a potassium level of 7.5 mEq/L
    C.   Restricting fluids to ice chips for a patient post stroke with dysphagia
    D.   Restraining a patient with dementia using a Posey vest due to fall risk

Answer Key

1. A	7. B	13. C	19. A	25. D
2. B	8. C	14. C	20. A	26. C
3. C	9. A, C, D	15. A	21. B, C, E	27. B
4. D	10. C	16. B	22. A, C, E	28. C
5. A	11. D	17. C	23. B	29. B
6. B	12. B, C	18. D	24. B	30. D

Answer Explanations

Question 1

Answer: A
Review chapter: Delegation

When delegating to a new nurse or a nurse who has floated, it is best to give him or her the patient you would also think of giving to an LPN: one that is stable without complications. The most stable patient on the list here is the toddler, choice A. There are no ABC (airway, breathing, circulation) issues, no medical emergencies, and stable signs and symptoms. Guarding implies pain in the area. Delegation does not change based on age, and this does not sound like an abuse case; different stages of previous healing wounds would be a red flag for that. Therefore, choice A is correct.

Acute changes (getting worse) in level of consciousness (LOC) is always considered an unstable patient, choice B. A child who is crying is a child who is awake and breathing, choice C. An easy way to look at this case is that a compound fracture does carry a risk of fat embolism or loss of distal blood flow, but until signs and symptoms are presented, it remains just a risk. This patient would require a more experienced nurse to evaluate these risks. The adult having breathing difficulties, choice D, can be immediately eliminated for the obvious ABC involvement. There is a risk here for flail chest and/or pneumothorax as well since his chest hit the steering wheel during impact.

Question 2

Answer: B

Review chapter: Prioritization; Pharmacology

The word "**priority**" in the question should stand out. Priority strategy can be found in the "Prioritization" chapter. The most unstable patient here is the 68-year-old admitted after a fall, choice B. Warfarin and other blood thinners increase the risk for bleeding. With the trauma to the head, the risk for intracranial bleeding puts this patient very close to a potential medical emergency. Close monitoring of vital signs and level of consciousness is needed by the RN. Therefore, choice B is correct.

The 82-year-old, choice A, is currently receiving treatment for pneumonia. As long as the infection is not getting worse, which is not implied in the question, approach the situation from the standpoint that this patient has been evaluated, diagnosed, and is receiving treatment. It makes this patient lower on the priority totem pole. The 22-year-old, choice C, is very likely the secondary priority with what appears to be potential hyperglycemia. Since the question does not say whether the patient is diabetic or not, this could be untreated diabetes. The 50-year-old, choice D, is presenting with expected signs and symptoms of the disease. Patients with COPD typically saturate between 88% and 92%. Do not worry about things you expect to see unless they are ABC-oriented. An emergency is still an emergency, whether you expect it or not.

Question 3

Answer: C

Review chapter: Prioritization; Endocrinology

Hashimoto's Thyroiditis is an autoimmune condition in which the immune system attacks the thyroid, often leading to hypothyroidism. Myxedema is caused by insufficient production of thyroid hormones and is characterized by swelling of the hands, face, feet, and periorbital tissues, possibly leading to a coma. A myxedema coma is a term used to denote severe hypothyroidism and is a medical emergency. It is characterized by progressive swelling of the skin and soft tissue, creating swelling in the tongue or larynx. Immediate intubation is often needed. Therefore, choice C is correct.

Serosanguinous (pink) drainage is an expected finding post TURP. What you DO NOT want to see is sanguineous (red) drainage; this could indicate a hemorrhage. The patient described in choice A is not the priority. A patient scheduled for discharge, choice B, is very low if not at the bottom of the rankings for prioritization, even if you have people pushing you to discharge. The patient with pneumonia, choice D, is showing signs and symptoms expected with pneumonia. As long as there are no ABC issues or decreasing oxygen saturation, the patient is considered stable.

Question 4

Answer: D
Review chapter: Prioritization; Gastrointestinal

Life-threatening complications of cholelithiasis and cholecystitis are choledocholithiasis and acute cholangitis. Both of these complications are medical emergencies and require immediate intervention. The nurse would want to confirm the UAP's description of jaundice, choice D. Upon confirmation, the physician should be immediately notified. Therefore, choice D is correct.

Fatigue and a low-grade to moderate fever, choice A, are expected with viral hepatitis. Pancreatitis, choice B, is, unfortunately, very painful for patients. It would be an expected finding here. Maslow's hierarchy of needs also dictates that physiological and safety needs outweigh the importance of psychological needs such as pain, unless the pain is associated with a medical emergency (e.g., heart attack). The assessment of a localized rash on the arm or chest is not a great concern for anaphylaxis. If the rash is described as generalized or diffuse (over all the body), THIS is the larger risk and should be prioritized. As described, though, the patient in choice C is not the one who needs immediate assessment.

Question 5

Answer: A
Review chapter: Psychiatry; ADPIE (Nursing Process)

We are looking for signs of improvement such as ADLs becoming easier, choice A. Under ADPIE, evaluation is looking for the positive improvement in the patient. We NEVER expect to treat the patient and have them get worse. Therefore, choice A is correct.

Medications that are prescribed for Alzheimer's will not cure or reverse the disease that is already present, making choices B and C incorrect. The goal is to maximize the patient's ability to function. Given that the disease is moderately advanced, the patient will already have memory problems; the focus now is on preservation of ADLs. Nausea and vomiting, choice D, could be a potential side effect of the medication, but this is NOT what the question is asking.

Question 6

Answer: B
Review chapter: EKG Interpretation

Third-degree heart block (choice B) is NOT a safe rhythm for people to survive in. These patients require a permanent pacemaker. If the rhythm worsens, the patient may require transcutaneous pacing. Therefore, choice B is correct.

A heart rate of 60 is technically at the bottom of normal (60–100 bpm), but it would be expected with someone who is on digoxin, choice A. The medication acts by slowing down the heart rate, which is why we do not give digoxin if the heart rate is below 60. Time proximity strategy can apply to things that say occurred "4 hours ago." If you were going to be worried about the ventricular tachycardia (V. Tach), choice C, you should have been worried 4 hours ago. You cannot hypothesize what may or may not be happening right now. Take questions at face value. Choice D, 4 PVCs per minute, is stable enough. If a patient is at 6 PVCs per minute or more, you must follow up with the physician.

Question 7

Answer: B
Review chapter: Obstetrics/Gynecology

A vaginal birth after cesarean (VBAC) is not always successful. Many of these labor attempts fail, and a c-section is advised. The uterus may not be able to sustain a successful delivery of the fetus. If the fetus moves into an undesirable position, the mother and fetus may begin to show signs of compromise. This is the most concerning since it could result in fetal death and potentially maternal death if complications ensue. Therefore, choice B is correct.

Anxiety and lower back pain, choice A, are both symptoms of normal labor. Fetal tachycardia, choice C, while it should be monitored, is not necessarily a sign of something going wrong. Acceleration and early deceleration are completely normal and expected in labor. It is much more concerning to see fetal bradycardia with late or variable deceleration. A slow progression of contractions and cervical dilation, choice D, should be monitored, but it does not necessarily mean that a c-section is needed. As long as the baby and the mother are all right, you will continue to induce labor. However, if the labor begins taking many hours with no progression or if there are signs of infant distress, the physician may recommend a c-section.

Question 8

Answer: C
Review chapter: Prioritization

Appendectomy, choice C, is a rather simple surgery with a low incidence of post-op complications. It is best to delegate to the least experienced nurse those patients with no ABC issues and no previous medical emergencies—essentially, the most stable patients. Therefore, choice C is correct.

The patient post-bifemoral bypass, choice A, would require constant neurovascular exams and is potentially a large bleeding risk. It would not be advisable to assign this patient to the staff nurse with the least experience. The patient post-trach, choice B, would qualify as a potential airway concern after surgery. The patient would also require in-depth knowledge of care regarding the trach itself (suctioning, rotating out the inner cannula, site assessment, evaluating airway status, etc.). Once the trach is confirmed stable and the patient remains stable by vital signs, this patient would become a far lower risk. The patient post-lobectomy, choice D, would be a potential breathing risk and, therefore, would require a nurse with a higher level of experience to effectively assess pulmonary status.

Question 9

Answer: A, C, D

Review chapter: Basic Care and Comfort

An MRI may include the use of contrast dye, so an allergy to iodine or seafood, choice A, as well as risks for kidney disease, kidney failure, or transplant, are also contraindications for using contrast for the scan. MRIs for pacemaker patients, choice C, are never routine. Any metal present in the patient is a contraindication for an MRI. Foreign metal objects within the body can get moved or heated during an MRI (bullets, pellets, shrapnel, aneurysm clips, unknown fragments of metal in an eye or cochlear implants in the ear, etc.; even Swan-Ganz catheters may malfunction during scanning), so MRIs are generally avoided. An MRI can be traumatizing for patients who have a history of claustrophobia, anxiety, or other panic disorders, choice D. Therefore, choices A, C, and D are correct.

Medications do not need to be held for an MRI unless there is a specific risk, so choice B does not apply. Before a test that uses an IV contrast material, have your patient stop taking the following medications: Metformin should not be taken the day of the test or for 2 days after the test when the contrast has cleared. NSAIDs such as ibuprofen should not be taken 2 days before and 2 days after the test because they add to the risk of nephrotoxicity in addition to the contrast. Diuretics should be avoided for 24 hours before the test for obvious reasons. It is generally easier to think of holding medications for any procedure that involves general anesthesia or an upper and lower GI series or colonoscopy. This would fall under NPO rules for procedures and surgeries. An MRI is performed lying down. A patient's ability to stand would not interfere with the scan, so choice E does not apply.

Question 10

Answer: C

Review chapter: Prioritization

Vomiting blood, choice C, is an immediate emergency, as is any form of hemorrhage. Hemorrhage is typically classified as any bleeding at 100 mL per hour or more; however, in a case of a patient walking into the emergency room, you are not necessarily able to measure it. Given the use of alcohol, it is possible that this case could involve a perforated peptic ulcer or ruptured esophageal varices. Therefore, choice C is correct.

The diaphoretic patient, choice A, is displaying signs of a kidney stone (nephrolithiasis) working its way down through the ureter. This leads to pain associated with passing of a stone, but this case has no ABC issues. The patient with nausea and vomiting, choice B, is displaying possible signs and symptoms of cholelithiasis, cholecystitis, or hepatitis; however, there are no active ABC issues. The patient with the compound fracture, choice D, has a risk for compartment syndrome or a fat embolism, but until there are definitive signs and symptoms, it remains a risk, NOT an active problem.

Question 11

Answer: D
Review chapter: Cardiovascular

It is important to understand vascular issues for the NCLEX. Do NOT confuse arterial pathology with venous pathology. It is crucial for a person with peripheral artery disease (common in diabetics) not to place direct heat or cold on the extremities affected, choice D. In peripheral artery disease (PAD) there is decreased circulation and sensation, so hot or cold treatments may burn or cause frostbite to an extremity if one is not careful. This is why it is important for the nurse in a hospital to monitor the skin when using such treatments on all patients. Do not leave hot or cold therapies on for too long (15 minutes on, 15 minutes off), and always have a towel layer between the pack and the patient's skin, even in a patient with no vascular issues. The elderly are particularly prone to skin damage because of the thinning subcutaneous tissue. Therefore, choice D is correct.

Gentle exercise is a good idea, but NOT strenuous exercise such as running. Walking, choice A, is generally a good exercise with multiple benefits and minimal adverse effects, as is swimming. It is considered a low-impact sport protecting the joints and preventing future injuries. Lotion, choice B, is okay in this question. Skin products can occasionally be confusing. Soap and warm water is generally a good thought process. Lotion is okay if a person is not at risk for sensitivity of the skin (radiation burn). We like lotion for this patient to prevent any cracking of the skin, opening the patient up for infection risk. This is one of the very few times lotion would be a correct answer; it typically is not. The same rule applies for powders; do NOT use them except to prevent skin breakdown in a PAD patient. Smoking is a large risk factor for PAD, as it further constricts the vessels. Lifestyle changes such as smoking cessation (choice C), weight loss, and diet are important components to the management of PAD.

Question 12

Answer: B, C
Review chapter: Pharmacology

The heart rate of this patient is already low, so the next dose of metoprolol, choice B, should be held for clarification by the HCP. If administered, it is possible the patient may become hypotensive. The potassium level of this patient is elevated at 5.1. The nurse should also hold the captopril, choice C, to clarify. ACE inhibitors and ARBs carry a risk for hyperkalemia. It is possible the HCP would dismiss the risk because of the co-administration with the loop diuretic (bumetanide), but the nurse does NOT know unless clarified by the physician. Always stay within your scope of practice. Therefore, choices B and C are correct.

Giving a stool softener like docusate, choice A, is a good idea to help in preventing any bearing down with a bowel movement by the patient. It may trigger a vasovagal response of the body. A cardiac patient such as this should avoid the Valsalva maneuver or actions that may cause a vasovagal response; this can dramatically decrease the cardiac output, something that should be avoided in a post-MI patient. There are no clinical reasons why a statin, such as lovastatin (choice D), cannot be administered. There is no information in the question on liver enzyme levels that may make you question the administration, as the drug can potentially harm the liver. Remember, you cannot assume anything on the NCLEX. If the information is not provided, you CANNOT make it up. The loop diuretic bumetanide, choice E, can be administered here. The patient is not hypokalemic, which may warrant a hold. If anything, it is a good idea to help lower the patient's already-elevated potassium. Blood pressure is also stable in this patient, but you would still want to continue to monitor it closely. Diuretics can cause a problem with BP down the line.

Question 13

Answer: C

Review chapter: Safety and Infection

Legionnaires' disease is spread by the inhalation of contaminated water droplets containing bacteria called *Legionella,* which cause a form of pneumonia. It is important to note the bacteria are NOT transmitted by swallowing contaminated water. Public fountains and small ponds are breeding grounds for these bacteria, which thrive in warm water. Remember, bacteria love to grow in warm, dark places. Therefore, choice C is correct.

Cooking meat thoroughly, choice A, is a good way to prevent food poisoning. Animals certainly are carriers for a multitude of bacteria; however, *Legionella* is not one of them, choice B. Legionnaires' disease is caused by a bacterium, NOT a virus, choice D. The disease can also be prevented by appropriate teaching and national public health guidelines for prevention of Legionellosis.

Question 14

Answer: C

Review chapter: Prioritization; Genitourinary

In choice C, performing continuous bladder irrigation, the key word here is *continuous*. What goes in must come out. The bladder does expand, but it is possible to rupture the organ. A rupture of anything is a medical emergency, so the fact that there is no output puts this patient dangerously close to the possibility of a medical emergency. Symptoms of a ruptured bladder include sudden relief of pressure or pain followed by excruciating suprapubic pain, hematuria, hypotension, and eventually shock. Therefore, choice C is correct.

The patient scheduled for angiography, choice A, is going through the physician work-up to determine how severe the potential diagnosis is. There are no signs and symptoms of ABC compromise. Remember, patients scheduled for things and/or discharge are rarely the correct answer, if ever. The patient with pneumonia, choice B, is showing signs of the disease, which is expected. This type of pneumonia tends to be more common in those who are immunosuppressed, but the patient is not showing ABC compromise. The patient with glomerulonephritis, choice D, is showing signs and symptoms consistent with the disease.

Question 15

Answer: A

Review chapter: Safety and Infection

The single most important thing healthcare workers can do to prevent the spread of infection is handwashing, choice A. No matter the story, no matter the diagnosis, no matter the presentation of the patient, handwashing will be the **most** important. Therefore, choice A is correct.

Using alcohol swabs (choice B), wearing PPE (choice C), and administering antibiotics (choice D) are all important practices to prevent the spread of infection to this patient; however, the foundation of prevention is in handwashing.

Question 16

Answer: B

Review chapter: Cardiovascular; Pharmacology

Processed and canned foods, choice B, are incredibly high in sodium. This person will burn through his daily allotment of sodium if he eats these foods. Lifestyle changes are hard for people to recognize and agree to change; it is important for nurses to stress these changes at discharge. Therefore, choice B is correct.

Bananas, choice A, are high in potassium. ACE inhibitors carry a risk for hyperkalemia, as does spironolactone, a potassium-sparing diuretic. The risk of hyperkalemia exists and is compounded by the use of both of the prescribed medications. You want to be clear about monitoring the intake of foods with potassium and notifying the HCP for any signs of heart issues, such as palpitations, cardiac arrhythmias, or abnormal pulse. A salt substitute, choice C, is high in potassium, so it will need to be avoided. A dry cough, choice D, is a very common side effect of ACE inhibitors and should dissipate over time. It is NOT a reason for the HCP to change the medication. Explain to the patient that the cough should go away over time.

Question 17

Answer: C

Review chapter: Prioritization

An erection lasting longer than 4 hours, choice C, is called priapism. It is also a medical emergency that falls under a "loss of limb" concern. If immediate medical treatment is not initiated, it is possible that the male may lose the appendage. Therefore, choice C is correct.

Watery diarrhea is expected with bowel prep, choice A. The nurse would be more concerned if the patient was NOT having watery diarrhea and would need to question why the drug is not working. Remember, we call this an "expected" finding. The female who lost her insulin pen, choice B, is of concern given the risk for hyperglycemia, but it is just a risk, NOT an actual problem. If she was also complaining of symptoms in line with diabetic ketoacidosis (DKA), the nurse would become much more concerned. Nausea, choice D, is not a significant problem. The sensation of nausea is a common occurrence that has diverse causes. It is often a benign side effect or symptom related to something else such as a drug, post-operative nausea, chemotherapy-induced nausea, or motion sickness. Nausea is a symptom that acts as a precursor to vomiting. Vomiting would be more concerning, given the fluid and electrolyte results; however, nausea is simply a symptom. Acute nausea is easier to control than chronic, unexplained nausea. Nausea does not pose any immediate threat to patients; no one dies from nausea.

Question 18

Answer: D
Review chapter: Safety and Infection

Because the wound is infected, dressing changes need to be performed using sterile technique. The first dressing change post-op is performed by the surgical staff. If 24 hours have passed, you can assume the post-op dressing has occurred (NCLEX specific). The goal is to avoid introducing more bacteria into an already-infected wound. If the surgical wound is clean and open to air, clean technique may be used. Therefore, choice D is correct.

Gloves, gown, and a mask (choice A) would be appropriate personal protective equipment (PPE) if the wound has excessive drainage, which increases the risk of potential splatter onto the nurse. Established droplet precautions, which is not mentioned in the question, would also require masking. Sterile gloves (choice B) are not needed if the first thing you are going to touch that was once sterile is now contaminated; it defeats the purpose. This is also why you never need to wear sterile gloves for a gastrointestinal issue; the GI is already full of bacteria. As mentioned above, the wound is infected, but the nurse should still switch to sterile gloves after the soiled dressing is removed. Do not apply another dressing with clean gloves (choice C). Sterile technique is needed.

Question 19

Answer: A
Review chapter: ADPIE (Nursing Process); Cardiovascular

ADPIE strategy dictates that we assess before we perform an intervention. It is very plausible that this man is indeed experiencing a heart attack, but that does not change the general work-up that must be performed in a situation such as this or for any new patient coming into the emergency department. Vital signs are always the very first thing that you do, choice A. It dictates how you focus the rest of your immediate assessment. For example, if a nurse chooses any of the other three actions here, who is to say the patient is not already in cardiac arrest if the pulse check is not performed? The NCLEX could also just say to assess for a pulse; do not get tripped up on the words if they imply the same action. ADPIE says start at the beginning and follow nursing process. Therefore, choice A is correct.

If the patient is unconscious, as this man was in the ambulance, administering nitroglycerin sublingual is not a possible route, choice B. This patient may require nitroglycerin IV, but that will be ordered by the physician. Only sublingual is within the nurse's scope of practice to administer without an order. Morphine, oxygen, nitrates, and aspirin, known collectively as MONA, are no longer considered the preferred interventions for chest pain. Having said that, the NCLEX still lags behind in some content. Keep an open mind when reading questions. Advanced knowledge on MI treatment would be past the expected knowledge of an NCLEX candidate. When in doubt; keep it simple. An EKG will absolutely be performed to assess (choice C) if there is an ST elevation or not; however, it is not the first thing you should do. The EKG will be pointless if the person is already in a Code Blue and requiring CPR. Cardiac marker labs will be drawn (choice D), but again, this is not the immediate priority. It is a lot quicker to see an ST elevation than wait for labs to come back.

Question 20

Answer: A
Review chapter: Prioritization

While an object lodged in an adult's nose may not pose a large risk, in a young child, and especially a toddler or preschooler, this poses an immediate airway risk and will be the priority among these patients, choice A. Since none of these patients are experiencing any active issues of an ABC nature or other medical emergencies, the priority moves to risks. A risk for an airway becomes the most important thing on the list. If the object were to fall farther into the child's airway, the child could choke. Remember to ask yourself "what can kill the patient the quickest?" Therefore, choice A is correct.

No matter the type of burn (choice B), albeit some are worse than others, a medical emergency does not exist unless 30% of the body is burned using the rule of nines. The other exceptions include burns to the face potentially affecting the airway or electrical burns affecting cardiac rhythm. Most new NCLEXers would select choice C as the correct answer, and often it would be the absolute correct train of thought. The 6-month-old is at the greater risk for dehydration and hypovolemia, a potentially life-threatening circulatory issue. Remember, though, airway is worse than breathing, which is worse than circulation (ABCs). A bulging fontanelle on an infant, choice D, is expected when the infant is crying; it would be worrisome if the bulging was occurring at rest (ICP).

Question 21

Answer: B, C, E
Review chapter: Respiratory

The complication the nurse is on the lookout for is a pneumothorax (collapsed lung). The goal of the procedure is to remove the fluid in the pleural cavity; however, you do not want air to get into that space, which might collapse the lung. There are quite a few signs and symptoms of a pneumothorax, so be sure to review the "Respiratory" chapter to learn the spectrum. Dyspnea (shortness of breath, choice B), tracheal deviation (choice C), and tachypnea (choice E) are a few symptoms of a pneumothorax. Therefore, choices B, C, and E are correct.

The nurse would witness an increased effort of breathing, NOT a decreased effort (choice A). Radiating pain to the left shoulder (choice D) sounds like a myocardial infarction (heart attack). An MI is not a potential complication of a thoracentesis. Remember, this is a needle entering the pleural space, often guided by an ultrasound.

Question 22

Answer: A, C, E
Review chapter: EKG Interpretation

It is important to recognize certain EKGs for the NCLEX. It is not required to know every rhythm, but the strips pointed out in the "EKG Interpretation" chapter will give you an overview of what the NCLEX requires from a basic knowledge standpoint. This strip can be identified as sinus tachycardia with a run of ventricular tachycardia (V. Tach) or what could be called eight premature ventricular contractions (PVCs). One PVC here and there is not an immediate problem; however, when they start to group together, it is called a run of V. Tach, and this could potentially become a full Code Blue if there is no intervention. You are encouraged to reach out to The NCLEX Cure for additional questions on content.

Amiodarone IV (choice A) and lidocaine IV (choice C) are used for ventricular dysrhythmias. The goal is to minimize or eliminate the PVCs. The physician will also want to run a complete metabolic panel (CMP) to look at the potassium level, choice E. As the nurse is aware, hypokalemia, and especially hyperkalemia, can have a huge impact on the heart rhythm. Therefore, choices A, C, and E are correct.

Adenosine (choice B) is most commonly used in supraventricular tachycardia (SVT). It can also be used for ventricular tachycardia, but far less commonly. In this case there is a run of V. Tach, not technically a full Code Blue ventricular tachycardia. Underlying infections could potentially lead to a disruption in the heart rhythm; however, the priority at this moment is to stabilize the patient. If an underlying infection is suspected, that will involve a number of other assessments, not just blood cultures (choice D). Defibrillation (choice F) is reserved only for patients in Code Blue situations having ventricular tachycardia or ventricular fibrillation, both considered to be shockable rhythms. Again, this patient had a run of PVCs or run of V. Tach, not a full Code Blue situation. It would, however, not be a bad idea to keep a crash cart close by in anticipation of the possibility that this patient may get worse.

Question 23

Answer: B
Review chapter: Genitourinary; Pharmacology

This patient is experiencing extreme hyperkalemia, which explains the palpitations and PVCs. The creatinine level of 3.8 is relatively expected given the CKD; however, this is not the immediate priority. The best immediate intervention is to administer regular insulin and D5 IV, choice B. Insulin causes the potassium in the blood to move into the surrounding cells, thereby reducing the level in the blood. It is followed by D5 to prevent hypoglycemia. This immediately corrects the problem. Avoiding a full Code Blue is the goal. Therefore, choice B is correct.

An AV fistula for hemodialysis takes months to mature. The word *recently* implies that the fistula is not likely to be ready for use, choice A. This is something the healthcare team would want to assess moving forward after the immediate problem is corrected. The ED physician would not waste time by assessing it right now, not to mention it takes time to get a patient to dialysis. Sodium polystyrene sulfonate, choice C, is an oral medication that induces the release of potassium in the stool with likely diarrhea to follow. This process takes time, which the nurse does not have in this situation. Giving furosemide, choice D, requires working kidneys to excrete. The patient's kidneys are not effective, as explained by the CKD and elevated creatinine.

Question 24

Answer: B
Review chapter: Safety and Infection

Dehiscence of a wound is when the suture lining is opening up, causing a breach in the integrity of the skin. One cause of dehiscence is an increase in pressure at the surgical site. It is important to reduce anxiety and tension of your patient as well as explain to them not to cough until the physician can come in and suture the wound closed. The nurse cannot fix this problem within the scope of practice; a higher license is required to suture. In the meantime, the nurse wants to ensure that the problem does not get worse. The nurse should reinforce the dressing and wait for the HCP. Therefore, choice B is correct.

Placing a new dressing (choice A) will not fix the underlying problem. The wound needs to be closed. It is also important to note that an RN or LPN does not do the first dressing change after surgery; that will be performed by the surgical team. They want to see their work. It is quite possible that applying hard pressure (choice C) would make the wound open up more. The nurse should reinforce the dressing and hold it in place if need be. Pain (choice D) is not the priority here. The immediate risk is the complete opening of the surgical site, furthering the complication. Remember Maslow's hierarchy of needs: Physiological needs come first, safety needs next, and lastly psychological needs.

Question 25

Answer: D
Review chapter: Positioning

Air rises in a liquid—in this case, blood. Placing the patient head down (Trendelenburg) will assist in diverting the air away from the pulmonary vasculature; the same applies for the left side over the right. Since you are dealing with the right side of the heart and pulmonary bed, you need to position on the left side, choice D. The easiest way to conceptualize this is to close your eyes and picture the anatomy you are dealing with. Remember, air rises in liquid. This positioning helps to prevent air from traveling through the right side of the heart into the pulmonary arteries. If CPR is required, put the patient in a supine and head-down position. CPR may also serve to break up large air bubbles into smaller ones, forcing air out of the right ventricle into the pulmonary vessels, improving cardiac output. Therefore, choice D is correct.

Question 26

Answer: C
Review chapter: Prioritization

There are a few risk factors for this patient, including hypertensive crisis, stroke, and myocardial infarction. A headache may be a sign of an extremely elevated blood pressure, as well as the nose bleed in this patient, choice C. Remember, you may not worry about these things in a normal patient, but this person is already diagnosed with CVD and hypertension and has multiple risk factors. Hypertensive crisis is characterized as a systolic blood pressure above 180 mm/Hg. At this point, it is possible for a person to stroke out. Therefore, choice C is correct.

The nurse would expect to see a decreasing heart rate, choice A. The beta blocker will cause this. The urine output listed is adequate, choice B; anything above 30 mL/hr is considered acceptable for adults (neonatal urine output is different). The LDL here is elevated, choice D; normal is less than 150. The healthcare team would need to follow up on this value because it's possible the patient requires medication for this risk, but at this time it is NOT the priority.

Question 27

Answer: B
Review chapter: Prioritization; Endocrinology

Remember, a "loss of sensory organ" is considered a lower-level medical emergency. Since a diabetic is already at increased risk of retinopathy, it is important that the healthcare team pay close attention to changes in vision, choice B. Early detection and treatment can prevent blindness; unfortunately, fewer than half of all diabetics receive the recommended yearly eye exam. Nurses are not experts in this field, but if any vision change is noted, they should make the retinal scan a priority for the patient. Therefore, choice B is correct.

An A1C of 6.8%, choice A, would be expected with a patient started on an oral antidiabetic agent. The higher the number, the likelier the patient is either noncompliant with the oral medication regimen and ADA diet or may require insulin. Nausea, choice C, is a relatively common side effect of the medication. This expected finding would not be a priority. Remember to think of prioritization as "what can kill your patient the quickest?" No one dies from nausea. Weight gain, choice D, is common in type 2 DM. Too much weight gain too quickly could be of concern, but no information is given on the date of the previous visit. Do not make assumptions on the NCLEX. An active problem is more important than a risk for a problem, such as weight gain.

Question 28

Answer: C
Review chapter: Safety and Infection; Prioritization; Neurosensory

The patient likely has meningococcal meningitis, a droplet precaution (choice C). Maslow's hierarchy of needs prioritizes this safety of the patient above immediate treatment since it is NOT a medical emergency. Bacterial meningitis is very serious (choice B), but until there are signs and symptoms of a "loss of life" medical emergency, safety here will take priority. Therefore, choice C is correct.

Meningitis may lead to seizures (choice A), but until then this is a risk, not an actual problem. Petechiae are the big distinguisher between the two types of meningitis. Petechiae and purpura are classically associated with meningococcal meningitis. Since the patient is showing petechiae, this is not viral meningitis (choice D).

Question 29

Answer: B
Review chapter: Endocrinology; Pharmacology

Remember to pay close attention to negative questions. When they say "further education," or "needing clarification," or other negative signal phrases, it is important you pay close attention to click on the negative answer. You are looking for what is wrong with the answer choices, NOT what is right.

In this case, when the patient is stating an NPH sliding scale dose (choice B), this is incorrect. NPH is not a sliding scale insulin; it is a basal dose of insulin that does not change in amount due to glucose (Accu-Chek) numbers. The most commonly used sliding scale insulin is aspart. Therefore, choice B is correct.

Patients should always check their blood sugar before eating (choice A); otherwise, the sugar from the meal will elevate the number, making it impossible to treat accordingly. Eating less simple sugars (choice C) is also a good thing for a diabetic; it prevents drastic increases in glucose since simple sugars can be easily absorbed by the body. Simple sugars come in the forms of fruits, candies, etc. Simple sugars are used to quickly increase the blood sugar in a hypoglycemic patient, but that is not what we are talking about here. Scheduled doses (choice D) should always be taken at the prescribed time every day. The same could be said for any scheduled medication, not just insulin.

Question 30

Answer: D

Review chapter: Psychiatry

The Joint Commission characterizes a sentinel event as "an occurrence involving death or serious physical or psychological injury or risk." These events can come in many forms and do not necessarily have to be from an action; they could also occur from a lack of action. In the case of this question, restraining a patient who does not fit the criteria for restraints may be considered a sentinel event risk, choice D. Patients can absolutely hurt themselves while restrained. Often that harm comes from a patient's confusion, the use of the restraints themselves, or trying to extricate themselves from the restraints. A Posey vest can, as a last resort, be used to restrain a patient such as this related to dementia or their risk for falling. There are a number of interventions we can try before we use restraints. It would also require an order by a licensed provider before implementing. Therefore, choice D is correct.

Nitroglycerin (choice A) is indicated for hypertension; there is nothing wrong with this administration. Insulin followed by dextrose (choice B) is indicated for hyperkalemia; there is nothing wrong with this administration.

While we commonly place post-stroke patients as nothing by mouth (*nil per os,* or NPO) due to aspiration risk, an ice chip here or there is generally allowed as long as the nurse has performed a bedside swallow evaluation, choice C. A swallow study is performed in radiology using barium-infused liquids (thick to thinner textures) using small amounts of liquids and solids to assess for phases of swallowing, noting any aspiration events. Once the patient is cleared, the team will begin to advance the diet.

Prioritization

What patient do you see first? This is the dreaded all-too-common question on the NCLEX. There is a strategy to prioritization, but one must understand a fair amount of the content and signs and symptoms of the patient before being able to correctly rank importance. So much of the English on the NCLEX makes things seem small, when in fact they are a big deal and vice versa. This chapter will run through all of these considerations when dealing with priority questions.

What Can Kill Your Patient the Quickest?

The answers to priority questions tend to revolve around people who are in immediate danger. Whenever you see a question that contains one of these words—**immediate, priority, highest,** or **first**—approach the question by asking, "What can kill my patient the quickest?" And make sure you know the following:

- ABC priorities: airway, breathing, circulation
- Medical emergency priorities: loss of life, loss of limb, loss of sensory organ
- Maslow's hierarchy of needs: physiological needs, safety needs, psychological needs

Loss of Life
- ABC issues
- Airway trumps breathing trumps circulation
- More important than all other medical emergencies

Loss of Limb
- Distal blood flow loss (no distal pulse)
- Compartment syndrome
- Priapism

Loss of Sensory Organ
- Vision changes (loss)
- Hearing/balance changes (loss)
- Retinal detachment
- Ototoxicity

Medical Emergencies

The below list of medical emergencies is not all-inclusive to the NCLEX. When thinking about emergencies, put them in the context of signs and symptoms and nursing process. The entire book is written from a pathophysiology, signs and symptoms, and interventions approach. Take the same mentality when approaching these emergencies. Treat the emergency as a checklist. Once you are closer to being prepared for the NCLEX, come back to this list and ask yourself: "Am I familiar with the pathophysiology, signs and symptoms, and interventions for this disease or problem?"

Signs and symptoms can be crucial in ruling out a true emergency versus something else. A good example is a patient with a laceration. It is not a bleeding laceration unless the question says so. Do not make that assumption. Alternate realities have to be avoided on the NCLEX. Take each question at face value and move forward.

The vast majority of these emergencies are included in the respective med-surg chapters in this book. Remember to follow nursing process and work through the list.

Airway

- Angioedema
- Myxedema coma
- Epiglottitis
- Asthma crisis
- Drowning/choking
- Smoke inhalation

Nx Tip: Remember to learn signs and symptoms for these airway emergencies. It is rare the NCLEX would give the name of the emergency verbatim; that would be too easy. For example, hoarseness of voice or noisy lung sounds could easily be a sign of an airway loss. Stridor is a red flag for airway loss as well.

Breathing

- Air embolism
- Pulmonary embolism
- Pneumothorax
- Flail chest (rib cage fracture)
- Severe croup
- Acute respiratory distress syndrome (ARDS)
- Severe pneumonia (desaturating)
- Respiratory failure
- Myasthenia gravis crisis
- Guillain-Barre syndrome
- Amyotrophic lateral sclerosis (ALS; Lou Gehrig's disease) crisis

Nx Tip: As with airway emergencies, understanding the signs and symptoms of breathing emergencies is crucial. One of the largest red flags is when a patient desaturates below 93% (unless they are a COPD patient). Other issues with breathing might be a gas exchange problem, also called ventilation.

Circulation

- Rupture of organs
- Heart rhythms (V. Tach, V. Fib, asystole)
- Acute coronary syndrome
- Myocardial infarction (MI)
- Aortic aneurysm rupture
- Aortic dissection
- Hypertensive crisis
- Cardiac tamponade
- Sickle cell crisis
- Cerebral vascular accident
- Addisonian crisis (acute adrenal crisis)
- Placental abruption
- Hypovolemia
  - Shock (all types)
  - Burns (30% BSA or more)
  - Heat stroke
  - Hemorrhage
  - Severe dehydration (excessive vomiting/diarrhea)

Body Homeostasis

- Traumatic brain injury (TBI)
- Malignant hyperthermia
- Serotonin syndrome
- Hypothermia
- Eclampsia/HELLP syndrome
- Spinal cord injury (SCI)
- Autonomic dysreflexia
- Neuroleptic malignant syndrome (NMS)
- Acid-base imbalances (ABGs)
- Emaciation
- Suicidal ideation
- Homicidal ideation
- Toxicities/overdoses/poisonings
- Alcohol withdrawal
- Benzodiazepine withdrawal
- Hypoglycemic coma
- Diabetic ketoacidosis
- Severe electrolyte imbalances
  - Natremia; brain can swell or shrivel
  - Kalemia; rhythm issues
  - Hypercalcemic crisis
- Rhabdomyolysis
- Severe glaucoma
- Priapism
- Testicular torsion
- Thyroid storm/thyrotoxicosis
- Cholangitis
- Bowel obstruction/toxic megacolon
- Bacterial meningitis (meningococcal)

Changes in Patient Presentation

When to Call the MD/HCP

- Any decompensation in the patient
- No longer controlled in scope of RN
- Examples:

Potassium	Excessive New Bleeding	Level of Consciousness	Pain Management
3.5 → 6	100 mL/hr or more Saturated blue pad (OB) in 30 minutes	Awake → stuporous	No response or improvement to pain meds

New Onset Changes

- Where is this coming from?
- Is there a diagnosis in the patient?
- Do these signs and symptoms have a cause?
- Can this be fixed inside an RN scope of practice?
  - Yes → least invasive to most
  - No → reach out for help (refer to other practices)

When NOT to Call the MD/HCP – Improvement

- 8 → 10 (hemoglobin)
- Patient responds to pain medication.

Time Proximity

Past . . . Present . . . Future

- Focus on the present in prioritization.
- 2 hours post-op, 2 days post-op, pre-op, etc.
- Age of patient, age of child
- Gestation of mother, weeks, postpartum

Nx Tip: The nature of a question can quickly change the perspective of how to read a question. Focus on the present. If someone was having a medical emergency 4 hours ago, then we would have been worried about it 4 hours ago, not right now. Anything that may be a problem in the future would fall under a "risk" for a problem. Therefore, the priority is almost always living in the present: Who is going to die or be at risk of harm right now?

Maslow's Hierarchy of Needs

Maslow's hierarchy of needs can help you with prioritization questions. Physiological needs are the highest priority, followed by safety needs, and, lastly, psychological needs.

Physiological

- Most important
- ABCs: airway, breathing, circulation
- Medical emergencies (see lists earlier in this chapter)

Safety

- Fall risk
- Isolation risk
  - Contact, droplet, airborne
- Disaster scenarios (radiation, biochemical)
  - 1st: Quarantine.
  - 2nd: Protect yourself (PPE).
  - 3rd: Treat the patient.

Psychological

- Rarely the correct answer
- Feelings ("I feel sad"; "I feel bad"): Difficult to interpret subjective feelings.
- Pain: not the priority unless associated with a medical emergency (MI, compartment syndrome, sickle cell crisis)

Nx Tip: Maslow's hierarchy technically has more components, but for the sake of the NCLEX, separating into these three needs makes it much easier to approach priority questions. Nobody dies from a lack of self-actualization, which is at the top of the pyramid, technically. How you feel about yourself on this planet is something to talk about another time, not with someone who is bleeding out in the emergency room.

How to Prioritize

Expected versus unexpected

Normal versus abnormal

Chronic versus acute

Active ABC/Medical Emergency

- Present/acute problems
- Happening NOW!

Risk for Problems

- Risk for ABCs and medical emergencies come first.
  - Example: post-op neck dissection laryngectomy (airway risk)
  - Example: post-op lobectomy (breathing risk)
  - Example: post-op carotid endarterectomy (circulatory risk)
- Risk for other problems are secondary.
  - Example: falls
  - Example: malnourishment
  - Example: pain (least important unless associated with medical emergency)

Non-Priority Issues

- ADL issues (activities of daily living: urination, eating, etc.) should be delegated to unlicensed assistive personnel (UAP).
- Discharging patients
- Scheduled patient procedures or tests (diagnostic, surgery, etc.)

Nx Tip: Keep in mind everyone is sick in a hospital. Just because someone has a diagnosis does not mean that person is having an active ABC issue, even if the diagnosis is associated with one of those risks. Do not make anything up on the NCLEX. Alternate realities occurring in your mind are not what test-makers were thinking when the question was written.

Triaging in the Field

Red tags take priority. You must move past people who likely will not survive or who are deceased.

Black Tag (Dead)

- Injuries are extensive; expected not to survive
- High cervical injury with lack of breathing
- Fixed and dilated pupils

Red Tag (Emergent)

- Most important: require immediate treatment to survive
- ABC issues
- Medical emergencies

Yellow Tag (Urgent)

- Mild issues: require observation; condition stable for the moment
- Stable vital signs

Green Tag (Non-Urgent)

- Can walk and talk: will need medical care at some point but can wait
- Minor bleeding or fractures

White Tag (Dismiss)

- Minor injuries: Care is not required.

Delegation

An easy way to think about delegation is as reverse prioritization. When delegating, it is typically best to assign the patient who is the most stable. That means do not assign patients who are having ABC issues or medical emergencies. Appropriate delegation provides new nursing personnel a safe learning environment and ensures patient safety until individual competencies are met. Delegation can also free the experienced nurse to attend to more complex patient issues. Delegation allows for skills development of nursing assistive personnel, and, in turn, strengthens your team and promotes more cost-effective care in your organization. Mastering the skills of delegation is a critical step on the path to effective nursing leadership.

Below is a quick run-through of basic delegation skills to help you make delegation decisions for the NCLEX.

Nursing Hierarchy

HCP/MD

- Do not dictate to higher licenses. Nurses may request or recommend, but not dictate.

RN

- See the "Scope of Practice – RN" chapter.
- Pay close attention to the type of unit the nurse may be coming from:
  o Med-surg
  o Labor and delivery
  o Intensive care unit/stepdown
  o Pediatrics/NICU
  o Rehab
  o Emergency room
  o Psych

LPN

- No IV skills without special certification
- No NG tube placement without special certification
- May perform sterile dressing changes, but not central line dressings
- Oral/PO/non-IV parenteral therapies

UAP

- May implement RN care plan when orders already exist
  - Starting oxygen (when order exists)
- Assist with ADLs: bathing/shower, feeding, changing clothes.
- CPR
- Documenting amount (I/O's) and color (urine, chest tube blood, NG drainage)
- Finger-stick glucose checks
- Suctioning and care of chronic tracheostomy
- Perform 12 lead EKGs (if documented competent and per institutional policy)
- Sterile specimen collection such as blood, urine, and wound drainage
- Oral/throat suctioning
- Vital signs, weight/height
- Turning, positioning, remind to cough/deep breaths (initial education by RN)
  - Except in cases of spinal cord injury
- Ambulation
- Skin care
  - Except in cases of non-intact skin
- Gather equipment.

Nx Tip: UAPs can also *remind* a patient about how to do something, but teaching is done by the RN or other licensed provider. Remember, UAPs will assist, NOT teach. The main word above is "remind."

How to Delegate

- Begin by delegating the most stable patient.
  - Uncomplicated procedures
  - Common and stable diseases
    - Avoid ABC issues
    - Post-op day 1 or greater
- Lower licenses cannot
  - Assess (admissions)
  - Teach
  - Educate (discharges)

Pressure Ulcers (Decubitus)

Stage I

- Non-blanchable redness (erythema)
- Superficial (intact skin)
- Epidermis tissue showing

Stage II

- Red or pink (erythema) ulcer
- Dermis tissue showing
- Partial thickness (damage of epidermis and dermis)
- Risk for infection
  o Hydrocolloid dressing needed for autolytic debridement; should be left on for several days at a time to be effective

Stage III

- Yellowish ulcer
- Adipose tissue showing
- Full thickness (damage of epidermis, dermis, and deeper tissues)
- Wet-to-dry dressing until debrided to establish granular tissue
- Consult wound care; debridement needed

Stage IV

- Bone or muscle showing
- Wet-to-dry dressing until debrided to establish granular tissue
- Consult wound care; debridement needed

Unstageable

- Black
- Unable to assess underlying tissues; wound base is obscured by slough or eschar

Nx Tip: A wet-to-dry dressing consists of gauze moistened with normal saline and placed in the wound bed, then covered with dry gauze. When the dressing is removed, a mechanical debridement occurs. This is a very basic method of wound care, and can cause discomfort when the dressing is removed. It can be used initially for open wounds until an appropriate dressing or wound vac can be applied. Wound-care teams will be consulted on wound management and will generally assume the care/treatment of acute and chronic wounds until healed inpatient and outpatient follow-up.

Prophylaxis for Pressure Ulcers

Basic Care and Comfort

- Turn patient every 2 hours (minimum) to off-load any pressure areas.
- Never massage bony prominences, as it can cause more tissue damage.
- Use specialty rotation beds for Stage III and Stage IV pressure ulcers.
- Do range-of-motion (ROM) exercises.
- Use heel cushions designed to off-load pressure from heels to protect from injury.

Braden Scale Risk Assessment

The six variables evaluated on this scale are listed below and are scored on a scale of 1 to 4. The resultant risk levels are as follows:

Severe Risk:	High Risk:	Moderate Risk:	Mild Risk:
Total Score ≤ 9	Total Score 10–12	Total Score 13–14	Total Score 15–18

- Sensory perception
- Moisture
- Activity
- Mobility
- Nutrition
- Friction and shear

Nx Tip: Do not worry about memorizing every component of the Braden Scale. Understand the six variables and how they are ranked. If the NCLEX would want a Braden calculated, it would provide the scale in the question. For other questions, however, it is important to simply know what is included versus what is not. Important: Total Score of 12 or less represents a high risk.

Taking Care of Skin

Intact Skin

For intact skin:

- Soap and water

Broken/Infected Skin

For skin that is broken and at risk for infection or already has an infection:

- Alcohol, diluted hydrogen peroxide, chlorhexidine, neomycin
- Betadine, povidone (surgical use) decreases superficial bioburden
- Use normal saline (NS) for flushing wounds; avoid cytotoxic agents.

Falls

Prophylaxis for Falls

- Frequent rounding
- Room close to nurses' station
- Bed/chair alarms

Morse Fall Risk Assessment

The six variables evaluated on this scale are as follows:

- History of falls
- Secondary diagnosis
- Ambulatory aid
- IV therapy/heparin lock
- Gait
- Mental status

Infections

Horizontal transmission: Person to person

Vertical transmission: Mother to child

PRIORITY: Wash hands! Always! Handwashing is the best way to prevent the spread of infection. Wash when entering the room and again when leaving the room.

Standard/Universal Precautions

- Wear gloves to reduce risk of bodily fluid exposure.
- Blood-borne infectious diseases: Ebola, Hep B, Hep C, HIV
- Anthrax
  - Inhaled as a white powder
  - Not communicable

Contact Precautions

Wear gloves and gown as a precaution for the following:

- C. Diff
  - Handwashing with soap and water
  - Often caused by overuse of antibiotics
  - Severe and foul-smelling diarrhea
- VRE/MRSA (including infected open wounds)
- Gastroenteritis (viral)
  - Often called the stomach flu
  - May be caused by rotavirus
  - May be caused by norovirus (also called Norwalk virus)
  - Vomiting and diarrhea
- Croup (also called laryngotracheal bronchitis)
  - Caused by diphtheria virus
  - Barking cough and stridor
  - Minor: Treat with anti-inflammatories.
  - Major: Treat with epinephrine.
- Rabies
  - Leads to meningitis
- Hepatitis A
  - Enteric precautions (similar to contact)
- Impetigo
  - Common in pediatric population
  - Honey-crusted lesions on mucous membranes (sometimes on back)
- Lice/scabies
- Respiratory syncytial virus (RSV)
  - Contact precautions unless productive cough exists, then droplet precautions
- Conjunctivitis (pink eye)

Droplet Precautions

Wear gloves, gown, mask, and goggles as a precaution for the following:

- Epiglottitis
  - Often caused by H. influenzae (Hib vaccine to prevent)
  - Also caused by bacterium
- Influenza type b (Hib)
  - Vaccinate to prevent.
- Meningococcal meningitis
- Mumps
  - Vaccinate to prevent (MMR).
  - Swollen salivary glands
  - Fever and headache
- Rubella (German measles)
  - Vaccinate to prevent (MMR).

- Streptococcus
  - Most commonly respiratory
  - Pharyngitis
  - Pneumonia
  - Pertussis
- Parvovirus
  - Causes fifth disease (common in children)
  - Appears as rash on face (looks like redness from a slap to the face)
- Sepsis
- Pertussis (whooping cough)
  - Common in children

Airborne Precautions

Wear an N95 mask or a surgical mask and use a negative airflow room as a precaution for the following:

- Herpes zoster (shingles)
  - Only possible if chickenpox infection occurred in past
  - Begins with pain; rash forms after
- Measles (rubeola)
  - Vaccinate to prevent (MMR).
  - Fever, irritability

- Varicella zoster (chickenpox)
  - 7-day incubation period
  - Oatmeal baths
  - Tzanck test
  - Pain when chewing
- Sudden acute respiratory syndrome (SARS)
- Tuberculosis

Other Infection Routes

- Yersinia pestis
  - Transmitted by rats and fleas
  - Cause of bubonic plague
- Shigella
  - Similar to salmonella
  - Contracted by consuming undercooked food
  - Causes diarrhea
- Yellow fever
  - Transmitted by mosquitoes
  - Causes headache and vomiting
- West Nile virus
  - Transmitted by mosquitoes
  - May lead to meningitis

- Lyme disease
  - Transmitted by ticks
  - Bullseye rash
  - Causes flu-like symptoms
- Brucellosis
  - Contracted by consuming uncooked meat or unpasteurized milk
- Typhoid fever
  - Contracted by consuming contaminated food or water
  - Causes diarrhea

- Pinworm
  - Transmitted via ingestion
  - Fecal-oral route
  - More common in children
  - Place tape on anus during sleep to diagnose.

- Legionnaires' disease
  - Contracted by inhaling droplets of contaminated water
  - Found in fountains and ponds with stagnant water

Cohorting of Patients

- Post-operative patients
  - No cohorting with risk for infection (immunosuppressed, chronic kidney disease, HIV)
  - No cohorting with actual infections (anything that ends in "itis")
- Do not cohort airborne-infection patients.
- Contact and droplet infections
  - Cohort same infection, such as VRE with VRE or flu with flu.
- 4-foot rule
  - Distance to the infected
  - Patients apart from each other
  - Visitor may sit by the door without a mask.

Transporting of Patients

- Contact infection: Patient wears gown.
- Droplet or airborne infection: Patient wears mask.

Neutropenic Precautions

- Suppressed immune system
  - AIDS, major burns, lupus
  - Cryptosporidium (common in AIDS patients; causes diarrhea)
- Do not cohort.
- Similar to contact precautions
- No fresh fruit, no fresh veggies, no fresh flowers, no pets, no kids

Open Wounds

- Cover the wound (in room or in transport).
- Follow contact precautions.

Removing Personal Protective Equipment (PPE)

- Hands are most contaminated body part; remove gloves first.
- Gloves → Goggles → Gown → Mask → Wash hands

Preventions

Primary Prevention

- Prevent problem from ever existing (Examples: vaccinations, condoms, exercise, diet).

Secondary Prevention

- Screenings (Examples: mammogram, colonoscopy, PSA blood levels, pap smear)

Tertiary Prevention

- Prevent the progression of disease/illness (Example: post–heart attack aspirin regimen).

The 5 W's of Post-Op Fever

The 5 W's is a mnemonic that is often utilized in medicine; however, it also has its uses for nursing—we simply do not have to take it to as high of a degree. Use the 5 W's not so much as a tool, like doctors do, but as a guideline for distinguishing general post-operative complications that nurses have to look out for. The information below presents those risks and how, as nurses, we prevent them.

Wind

- Atelectasis/pneumonia
- Post-op days (POD): 1–2
- Normal prevention
  - Deep breathing
  - Incentive spirometry (10 times an hour)
  - Splint chest with pillow and manage pain (post–open-heart surgery)
- Ventilator-associated pneumonia
  - Elevate head of bed.
  - Frequent oral care (every 4 hours)
  - Administer PPI (pantoprazole).

Water

- UTI/CAUTI
- Post-op days (POD): 3–5
- Prevention
  - Switch catheter out every 72 hours.
  - Perineal care
  - Push fluids.

Wound

- Surgical site infection
- Post-op days (POD): 4 and greater
- Prevention
  - Surgical staff performs the first dressing change.
  - After 24 hours, nursing staff changes dressing.
  - Sterile technique when needed
  - Use cleaning agents (alcohol, chlorhexidine, etc.).

Walking

- DVT/PE
- Prevention
  - Early ambulation
  - Sequential compression devices (SCDs)
  - TED stockings
  - SubQ heparin/enoxaparin

Wonder Drugs

- Not on NCLEX

It is incredibly important to understand the nursing scope of practice. It is also important to understand the scope of practice of other positions, including those holding higher licenses. It would be hard to delegate or refer to other positions without the knowledge of what can legally be done by that position. This is scope of practice. "Delegation" is another chapter in this book. In this chapter, you will learn exactly how to follow the nursing scope of practice, in addition to some information about other jobs in a hospital.

It is important to reach out for help when a problem arises. The trickier question is then to assess whether a problem is within a nursing scope of practice or if other help is needed. Throughout this book, there is information about independent diseases and problems. Within that information, you'll find key points on interventions the healthcare team may execute.

Utilize the information that follows to study all of the different types of people in a hospital and how they may help the interdisciplinary team in the care of a patient. When taking the NCLEX, be very careful when clicking on answer choices that are interventions. Make sure interventions are within your scope of practice and follow nursing process (ADPIE).

How to Follow Orders

Nurses may be completely aware of how to treat a problem they encounter; however, many issues require a higher license to prescribe orders to proceed. It is generally accepted that you should not click on answer choices on the NCLEX that are outside of the nursing scope of practice UNLESS one of the following three circumstances occurs:

1. **"As ordered," "anticipate giving," "recommend giving"**
   - Do not click on interventions unless the answer choice says "as ordered," "anticipate giving," or "recommend giving."
   - Example:
     - Administer vasopressin as ordered **(CORRECT)**
     - Administer vasopressin (INCORRECT)

2. **Medical emergencies**
   - For medical emergencies, interventions may be performed without **rule #1** above.
   - When practicing for NCLEX questions, it is easier to assume a physician is next to the RN providing verbal orders.

3. **Nurse-managed orders**
   - For nurse-managed orders, interventions may be performed without **rule #1** above.
   - A nurse-managed order is one that already exists in the chart, so the nurse can proceed with following the order.
   - Example:
     - Sliding scale (insulin, heparin, warfarin)
     - PRN anything (oxycodone, etc.)

How to Utilize Scope of Practice

Ask yourself:

1. Is this within my scope of practice, and can I do this legally?
   - If yes, follow ADPIE.
   - If no, refer to other practices.
2. Do I have time to do this?
   - There are other patients on the floor, and time management is an important consideration to achieve care goals for your shift. It is unrealistic to think an RN can be on the phone for 30 minutes with an insurance company trying to work out a problem. The same rule applies to many situations and questions posed by a patient or by a patient's family. Refer questions and concerns to specialty and support services within your organization: Spiritual Care, PT, OT, Patient Services, Continuity of Care before discharge for insurance concerns, support services at home, long-term care placement, Respiratory Care, Wound Care, Nutrition, or Speech Therapy, to name a few.
   - Remember, the job of an RN is to act as the hub of care for all other services to filter through during the 8 or 12 hours you are working with your patients.
     - The RN is **NOT** a bouncer; get security if patient or patient family behavioral issues occur.
     - The RN is **NOT** Dr. Phil; refer big problems to specialty and patient care services for support.

Hospital Personnel

Below are other positions that work together within the hospital to achieve patient care goals. They are important to understand for the NCLEX. Nurses may "refer" to other practices in the hospital, but nurses do not "consult." Physicians in the various med-surg specialties are requested to provide consults.

HCP/MD/NP/PA

- Prescribes orders and medications
  - Refer to for change in orders
  - Refer to for change in medication dose or change in route of administration
- Performs larger procedures (surgeries, scopes, etc.)
- Multiple specialties
- Follow SBAR when communicating with these providers:
  - Situation
  - Background
  - Assessment
  - Recommendation

Nurse Hierarchy

- Charge nurse/nurse manager
- Follow RN hierarchy, even regarding a problem with another department. Do not go to that department head. Go to your nurse manager.

LPN/UAP

- Licensed practical nurses and unlicensed assistive personnel assist RNs in daily care.
- Covered in more detail in the "Delegation" chapter

Respiratory Therapist

- Administers postural drainage (chest physiotherapy)
- Oversees function of mechanical ventilator
- Administers nebulizer treatments

Social Worker

- Assists in social issues (financial concerns, housing, food, transportation, etc.)
- Assists in money-related problems (medications, wound-care supplies, etc.)

Case Manager

- Coordinates outpatient medical care (assistive devices, home health care, etc.)
- Note: The RN manages inpatient care.

Pharmacist

- Call for information regarding liquid versus tablet formats.
- Call with questions about administration (onset and duration of action, side effects, etc.).

Physical Therapist/Occupational Therapist

- Examines patients and develops plan of care to promote movement, reduce pain, restore function, and prevent disability; restores passive and active range of motion

IT

- Provides computer charting access
- Maintains a 24-hour service line for password issues or computer access problems
- Provides training during orientation

Chaplain

- Provides religious and spiritual services
- Acts as sounding board for patients and stressed family members who need someone to talk to

Housekeeping

- Cleans rooms between patients, cleans spills, cleans and maintains public areas

Security

- Provides safe environment
- Holds patients' valuables
- Assigns access to staff in the organization

Facilities/Maintenance

- Utilizes a work order system for repair requests
- Maintains grounds and all hospital buildings

Radiology

- Administers all imaging: x-ray, MRI, CT, nuclear medicine, interventional radiology, etc.

Labs

- Includes chemistry, microbiology, serology, hematology, etc.

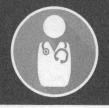

The similarities between the NCLEX-PN and the NCLEX-RN are numerous. The style of questioning is similar, as is the content. This chapter is for those who are planning on testing for the NCLEX-PN. If you are testing for the NCLEX-RN, ignore this chapter.

The PN scope of practice has limitations. For example, an LPN is allowed to perform focused assessments, such as listening to lung sounds or bowel sounds. The LPN would do this when the patient may be experiencing a problem, but should be very careful. Few assessments are allowed to be performed by an LPN. When in doubt, refer to the RN. A good rule of thumb is that if you find yourself not knowing what the underlying cause of the patient problem may be, ask the RN. Any acute change or emergency requires a higher license, such as an RN.

Another thing to keep in mind is that an LPN cannot do anything invasive. The only exception to this rule is if an LPN has special certification to perform an NG tube or IV placement. LPNs can perform sterile procedures such as an indwelling catheter placement or changing a sterile dressing, but only when it is uncomplicated. It can be tricky to be able to tell if such a procedure will be uncomplicated, so it is recommended that you study your specific scope of practice so nothing is missed.

As you read this book chapter by chapter, you'll find information regarding diseases and the important assessments and interventions revolving around those diseases. As someone testing for the LPN, understand that not all of the assessments and interventions fall under the purview of an LPN. While the LPN may not be the one performing that action, the NCLEX can still ask about what is likely or what may be performed in general by the interdisciplinary team. Being a well-rounded LPN in a hospital and on the NCLEX revolves around the general understanding of roles and responsibilities of all those on the patient care team.

Moving forward, be very careful when clicking on answer choices that are interventions. They should be within your scope of practice and follow nursing process (ADPIE) to be correct. The "Delegation" chapter will provide an overview of these things and aid in the ability to tell the difference between what you can legally do and not do.

Nursing Ethics

There are six key ethical principles of nursing that should be followed in all nursing situations. On the NCLEX, you may be presented with a scenario and be required to distinguish which answer choice applies to which ethical principle. For example, if the nurse does not relay patient desires to the appropriate people, you are effectively burying patient autonomy and their right to self-determination of care.

Autonomy	Justice	Fidelity	Beneficence	Nonmaleficence	Veracity
Freedom of choice, self-determination	Fairness, equal treatment	Faithfulness to commitments, following through	Doing good	Doing no harm	Truthfulness

IVs and Central Lines

IV Gauge/Length

- 0.5 inch needle subcutaneous for child or adult
- 0.5 inch needle intramuscular (IM) for young child
- 1–2 inch needle intramuscular for older child/adult
- 1 mL maximum administration per IM shot
  - If order says 2 mL, two shots must be given.
- The higher the gauge, the smaller the needle:
  - 28 gauge: subQ
  - 24 gauge: IM
  - 20 gauge (or larger): blood administration

The Three IV Problems

- Infiltration
  - Catheter falls out of the vein (third spacing of fluid)
  - Coolness, redness, swelling, discomfort
  - Stop the IV infusion, discontinue the IV, apply a warm compress, elevate extremity.
- Thrombophlebitis
  - Formation of a clot/inflammation at the catheter site
  - Warmth, redness, swelling, pain, discoloration of vein
  - Stop the IV infusion, discontinue the IV, apply a warm compress, elevate extremity.
- Extravasation
  - Infiltration of third space with a vesicant medication (chemotherapy, dopamine)
  - Destruction of cells and pain at the site

- o Stop the IV infusion, aspirate out as much fluid as possible, call the HCP.
- o A medication may be ordered to soak up vesicant.

Central Line Types

- PICC/Midline
  - o Placed by specialist RN
  - o Long-term antibiotics
- Broviac/Hickman/Groshong
  - o Commonly used for therapy for leukemia and bone marrow or stem cell transplant
  - o Some types are used for apheresis or dialysis.
- Vas Cath/Port-a-cath/Perm-a-cath
  - o Commonly used for chemotherapy

Troubleshooting Central Lines

- Small clot on the end of line: Do not force flush.
- Kink: Change patient position.
- Sitting on side of vessel: Attempt to flush.
- Infiltrates: more common in peripheral

Disaster Scenarios

Code Red (Fire)

- RACE mnemonic:
  - o Rescue
  - o Alarm
  - o Contain
  - o Extinguish
- PASS mnemonic:
  - o Pull
  - o Aim
  - o Squeeze
  - o Sweep

Code Black/Pink/White

- Bomb threat, infant abduction, aggression—every hospital has these as overhead pages to alert staff.
- Focus on the role of the RN in that moment.
- Do not respond as a manager unless the question specifically says "nurse manager."
- Stay in current location and assess area needs.

Culture and Religion

In nursing, you'll interact with patients (and families) with various religious, spiritual, and cultural backgrounds. If a question specifically identifies a culture, it is a safe bet that the question writer included the culture information for a reason. Frame your mind in a culturally sensitive manner. Many NCLEX test-takers may be Anglo-Saxon in background, but an easier way to think about it is simply "American." For example, most Americans would be comfortable with physical touch. This is NOT the case with many other cultures. Be familiar with the following common practices regarding culture and religion.

Religious Beliefs

- Christianity
  - Anointing of the oil upon death
- Judaism
  - 2–3 hour gap between eating dairy and meat
- Islam
  - Face east toward Mecca to pray
  - Genuflect (kneel) upon praying; assist a patient to the floor if able.
  - Do not touch deceased Muslim if not Muslim yourself.
  - Direct eye contact considered sexually advancing

- Buddhism
  - Commonly practiced in China
  - Karma (consequences come from actions)
- Hinduism
  - Reincarnation
- Jehovah's Witness
  - No blood products

Nx Tip: Religion does not allow parents to refuse lifesaving medical treatment for a child. It is considered illegal. They do not have the right to leave without care. Example: meningitis in child.

Spirituality

Not necessarily needing of religion to follow. Religion is a collection of beliefs that people follow together, often in a congregation format. Many spiritual people do so on their own. All religion is spiritual, but not the other way around. Think more Golden Rule.

Culture

- Anglo Saxon
  - Caucasian
  - Eye contact considered respectful
  - May sit closer
- Mexican
  - Hot milk concept
- Asian
  - Stoic in relation to pain
  - Hot-cold concept (cold food given for a sickness of heat, and vice versa)

- Native American
  - Higher prevalence of diabetes mellitus
- Muslim
  - Do not sit too close; considered rude
  - No caring for patient of opposite sex
  - Men often are the decision makers.

Nx Tip: If a client turns away with no eye contact during teaching, continue the teaching and assess for understanding afterward. At times, avoiding eye contact is cultural and not to be taken as a lack of attention. Do not immediately assume the patient needs a different form of teaching.

Nx Tip: The same thought above needs to be taken into account if a patient of a different culture simply smiles and nods when asked questions. It's possible that smiling and nodding is a cultural sign of respect rather than an actual sign of understanding. Continue the teaching and assess for understanding afterward.

Legal Issues

Assault

- Verbal
  - Telling a patient if he or she does not do something, a bad consequence will occur

Battery

- Physical
  - Injecting a medication when a patient refuses
  - Unlawful restraint of a patient

Good Samaritan Law

- Cannot be sued for trying to help someone within your scope of practice

False Imprisonment

- Hospital, nursing home, etc.
- Holding someone against their will
  - Exceptions: Patient at risk to self or others, patient under influence of a substance
- People have the right to refuse.

Informed Consent

- Must be obtained by physicians
- Nurse may witness.

Advance Directive/Living Will

- May include a do not resuscitate (DNR) order
- Specifies healthcare decision making (healthcare power of attorney)
- Specifies healthcare decisions
  - No tube feedings
  - No intubation past 20 days

DNR

- No extraordinary measures, such as CPR, intubation, vasopressors, defibrillation

Post-Mortem Care

- Allow the family to help if they desire.
- Leave dentures in.
- Keep head of bed elevated (semi-Fowler's).
- Non-Muslim cannot touch deceased Muslim.

Gerontological Considerations

Normal Changes in Aging

- Skin loses collagen and elasticity.
- Decreased kidney/liver function
- Decreased thirst mechanism
- Decreased peripheral sensation
- Decreased hair on scalp
- Solar lentigo (sun spots)
- Xerostomia (dry mouth)

Elder Abuse

- RN mandatory reporting (call authorities)
- Physical, psychological, sexual
  - Untreated bedsores, withdrawing from activities
- Financial abuse
  - Stolen checks, money
- Neglect
  - Soiled sheets, build-up of trash
  - Poor grooming

Nurse-Client Relationship

- 1st: Address client anxiety.
- 2nd: Assess learning needs.
- 3rd: Assess knowledge level.
- 4th: Acknowledge specifics.

NPO Rules for Medical Procedures

The rule of thumb here is that if the procedure does not qualify as one of the three things listed below, do not place the patient on NPO (nothing by mouth) status unless there is a good reason. There are many medical reasons why a patient may be NPO; the following list is a very specific showcase of why this order would be given for a procedure. It is not as vast as many people believe.

General Anesthesia	Upper/Lower GI Series	Upper/Lower GI Scopes
- NPO to prevent aspiration - Typically 8–12 hours before	- X-ray/fluoroscopy - Barium swallow/barium enema - Typically 8 hours before	- Esophagogastroduodenoscopy (EGD) - Colonoscopy (includes bowel prep) - Typically 8 hours before

Routes of Administration

This list of routes is presented in order of the fastest route of administration to the slowest as well as a most invasive to least invasive mentality. It is important to pay attention to route on the NCLEX. If a patient is having an emergency, it is the goal of healthcare workers to fix the problem as soon as humanly possible; that often removes oral medications since they take time to digest and work. Think about how to fix the emergency right now.

Intrathecal

- Administration into central nervous system (CNS)
- Performed by certified registered nurse anesthetist (CRNA) or anesthesiologist
- Types: subdural catheter, epidural catheter
- Risks
  - Meningitis
  - Shift of cerebrospinal fluid (CSF)

Inhaled

- Administration via lungs
- Performed by respiratory therapist or RN
- Types: nebulizers, inhalers

Intraosseous

- Administration via bones
- Performed by RN (with training)
- Used when veins are not good to use
- Used mostly in trauma scenarios

Intravenous

- Administration via veins
- IV cannulation (starts) performed by RN
- Administration may be done by RN or LPN with specialized certification. (An NCLEX question must specifically state that the LPN has certification; otherwise, assume the LPN does not.)
- IV line may be discontinued by unlicensed assistant personnel (apply pressure for 5 minutes; no peeking).

Intramuscular

- Administration via muscles
- Performed by RN or certified LPN

Subcutaneous

- Administration via adipose (fat) tissue
- Insulin, heparin
- Performed by RN or certified LPN

Oral/Sublingual

- Administration via mouth and under tongue
- Performed by RN or certified LPN

Transdermal

- Administration via skin (patch or topical)
- Performed by RN or certified LPN
- Remove old patch before new applied.
- Rotate patch sites.
- Always wear gloves.

Intradermal

- Administration via dermis
- Performed by RN or certified LPN
- Allergy testing
- Mantoux TB skin test/PPD

Patients Unable to Leave: Against Medical Advice (AMA)

- Under influence of substances (alcohol, drugs)
- Parents with minor (child) requiring life-saving treatment (meningitis)
- Homicidal or suicidal
- Psychotic, delusional, or demented

ADPIE (Nursing Process)

When reading and analyzing a question, it is of utmost importance to follow nursing process. The healthcare team, including the RN, do not perform actions without having a specific reason for doing so. Ask yourself, "Do I have the assessment that warrants this intervention?" Correct answers will not be interventions that do not have clear reasoning in the question itself. Do not click on answer choices just because they sound good; there must be a reason.

ADPIE (Assess, Diagnose, Plan, Implement/Intervene, and Evaluate) can be applied to numerous questions found on the NCLEX. ADPIE can be used to answer questions that ask what the nurse should do **first.** Such questions are testing if the nurse understands how to apply the scope of practice to a patient situation. It is important to use ADPIE while also applying scope of practice and prioritization. Reading questions and answer choices very carefully, thinking critically, and applying these thought processes will aid you in eliminating incorrect answer choices. Process of elimination is incredibly helpful on the NCLEX.

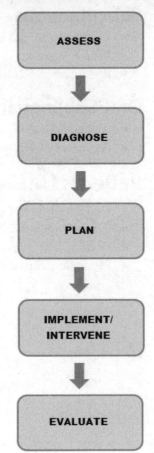

Assess

- Process is chronological: inspection, palpation, percussion, auscultation.
- Do not go backward. Repetition or redundancies are not correct on the NCLEX.
- Example: While assessing a patient post cardiac catheterization, the nurse is unable to palpate the dorsalis pedis pulse. What action should the nurse do **first?**
  - Doppler the extremity **(CORRECT)**
  - Inspect the leg (INCORRECT)

  If the nurse is palpating for a pulse, it is implied that an inspection has already been performed. Do not go back and redo work that is done.
- For abdominal/renal assessment, follow this order: inspection, auscultation, percussion, palpation.

Diagnose

- The nursing diagnosis provides the basis for selecting nursing interventions to achieve optimal patient outcomes.

Plan

- Develop a plan and establish SMART goals (specific, measurable, attainable, realistic/relevant, and time restricted).

Implement/Intervene

- Follow less invasive measures first.
  - Non-pharmacological over pharmacological
  - Elevating the head of bed over oxygen
- Follow scope of practice.

Evaluate

- Focus on good and positive answers.
- Do not "expect" bad outcomes; healthcare providers who perform actions without any clear goal to achieve are committing malpractice.
- Look for factual, specific answers.
  - Weight gain for anorexics
  - Weight loss for fluid overload
- Objective over subjective
  - Weight gain or loss over "feelings"

What to Do When People Are Doing Something Wrong!

Questions may come up on the NCLEX that ask how a nurse should respond in a given situation. Many times they are worded "most appropriate" or "best response." There are many ways such questions could be phrased, but the key point of the question and what should be felt upon reading it is "this does not sound good!"

Someone may be doing something improper or, as the nurse, something may be worrisome to you about the safety of the patient. Working in a hospital requires a high level of professionalism that we are all expected to follow. People are responsible for doing their jobs. There are a series of questions that fall back on this key point. Safety of the patient, basic respect, and safety of the patient again, because it bears repeating.

The vast majority of the time, the best answer is to simply go directly to the source of the problem and address it. I like to call this "acting like an adult." It really is the best way to go in a variety of situations.

Case Study

A nurse is working on a unit when a fellow employee says something sexually inappropriate. What is the **most appropriate** action by that nurse?

A. Contact human resources.
B. Speak with the nurse manager about the unwanted advances.
C. Take the fellow employee to a private area and tell him or her it is inappropriate.
D. Ignore the advances, as it is part of the job.

Answer: C

In this situation, what the person is doing is absolutely inappropriate for a hospital setting. What he or she is doing is not going to cause harm to a patient, nor is it worthy of taking it to someone higher as if it were illegal (at least not yet). If a problem happened repeatedly, then it would be more appropriate to reach out to a superior. Harassment is still a problem in many careers and is no different for nurses. Oftentimes it may be a patient who is being sexually inappropriate with a nurse. The same intervention would apply. If a patient is acting inappropriately and is cognitively aware of what he or she is doing, then the patient needs to be told the behavior is not appropriate. It is completely legal for the nurse to do this.

See the directions below for how to apply this strategy in other situations.

Minor Problem

Go directly to the person and solve. Examples:

- Witnessing an RN do a procedure incorrectly (never interrupt; inform after)
- Witnessing an MD not wash his or her hands before entering a room
- Interacting with a UAP (unlicensed assistive personnel) who does not do a finger-stick check
- Witnessing an RN giving incorrect discharge instructions

Legal Problem

Go directly to a superior (charge nurse, nurse manager). Examples:

- Witnessing an RN pocket narcotics
- Witnessing an intoxicated RN
- Witnessing an RN verbally threaten or abuse a patient

Patient Harm Problem

1. Fix the problem.
2. Assess the problem (the patient).
3. Call the HCP.
4. Fill out an incident report (does not go in chart).

Examples:
- Walking into a room and noticing an infusion running faster than ordered
- Witnessing a patient fall or other sentinel event

Myocardial Infarction (Heart Attack)

Pathophysiology
- Ischemia of heart muscle

Causes
- Clotting (embolism)
- Atherosclerotic (narrowed coronary)
- Vasospastic (Prinzmetal's angina)
  - Caused by stimulants (cocaine)

Signs and Symptoms
- Common in men
  - Chest pain radiating down the left arm
  - Shortness of breath
  - Chest pressure
  - Tachycardia
  - Jaw pain
- Common in women
  - Nausea/vomiting
  - Malaise
  - Cold sweats
  - Jaw pain

> Nx Tip: The elderly's signs and symptoms are similar to those in women.

Interventions
MONA Protocol (1st treatment):

- <u>M</u>orphine: treats pain; also aids in vasodilation
- <u>O</u>xygen: delivery to the point of infarct
- <u>N</u>itroglycerin: vasodilator
- <u>A</u>spirin/clopidogrel: prevents growth or further exacerbation

> Nx Tip: Oxygen and nitroglycerin can be given by paramedics and RNs without an order.

Morphine, oxygen, nitrates, and aspirin, known as MONA, are no longer collectively considered the preferred interventions for chest pain. Oxygen can actually cause harm if used inappropriately, so remember, only provide oxygen if the patient truly needs it. A dyspneic patient does not necessarily need oxygen; assess the pulse ox.

Case Study

For questions on "what action does the nurse perform first," follow the sequence given below.

A 43-year-old male comes in with chest pain, dizziness, and shortness of breath.

1. Assess vitals/ask patient to describe pain.
2. Do EKG/ECG.
   o Check ST elevation.
   o Note STEMI versus NSTEMI.
3. Check troponin and creatine kinase levels.
4. Take chest x-ray.
   o Rule out other causes (GERD, PE, pneumothorax).

Cardiac Catheterization/Percutaneous Coronary Intervention (PCI)

- Remember: Time is muscle.
- Types:
  o Angiogram (x-ray and/or visualization)
  o Angioplasty (surgical, stent, etc.)
  o Alteplase (clot buster, thrombolytic)
- Procedure:
  o Arterial sheath in radial or femoral artery
    - Risk for bleeding (PRIORITY)
    - Risk for infection
- Post-cath:
  o Neurovascular exams
    - Capillary refill
    - Pulses (dorsalis pedis, posterior tibialis)
      • Doppler if cannot be palpated
    - Sensation/strength (bilateral)
  o Hourly (q1) assessments of the sheath site (always RN)
    - Compression devices/dressings used to prevent bleeding
    - Is the patient complaining of feeling wet or damp? (not good . . . it might be blood)
  o Patient positioning
    - Femoral entry sheath: Patient must lie supine for **4 hours.**
    - Radial entry sheath: Patient may be semi-Fowler's (affected extremity must remain immobilized for **4 hours**).
- Coronary artery bypass graft (CABG)
  o Graft harvested from the greater saphenous vein (thigh)
    - Swelling (edema) and bruising expected on the thigh after surgery
  o 100 mL/hr or more of drainage into the chest tube is considered **hemorrhage** (PRIORITY).

Heart Failure/Cardiomyopathy

Pathophysiology

- Preload: pressure of blood filling into relaxed ventricles
- Afterload: pressure ventricles overcome to push blood out of the heart

Nx Tip: Both preload and afterload may increase in heart failure (right- or left-sided).

- Cardiac output (HR × SV): decreases in heart failure
  - Diagnosed via echocardiogram
    - External
    - Transesophageal echocardiogram (TEE): sedation and oxygen required
  - Men and pregnant women have higher cardiac outputs.
- Ejection fraction (percentage showing function of heart)

Causes

- R-sided
  - Pulmonary hypertension (pulmonary vasculature)
  - Myocardial infarction
- L-sided
  - Systemic hypertension
  - Myocardial infarction

Signs and Symptoms

- R-sided
  - Edema: peripheral, dependent (gravity), generalized, legs, ankles, abdominal ascites
  - Jugular venous distention (JVD)
    - Assess at 30–45 degrees
  - Hypertrophy
- L-sided
  - Fatigue and shortness of breath
  - Decreased cardiac output and ejection fraction leading to hypotension
  - Pulmonary edema
    - Fine crackles (auscultate)
    - May increase a pulmonary pressure
  - Hypertrophy

Interventions

- Low-salt diet (less than 2,000 mg per day)
  - o No canned foods, no Chinese food, no processed foods
  - o Fluid restriction
- Pharmacology
  - o Diuretics, ACE inhibitors, digoxin
- Intra-aortic balloon pump (IABP)
- AICD Defibrillator placement
- Surgery/transplant

Nx Tip: Remember, interventions are LEAST invasive to MOST.

Endocarditis/Pericarditis/Valvulitis

Pathophysiology

- Inflammation of the layers of the heart
- Common in those with a history of grafts, IV drug users, and previous heart surgery patients

Nx Tip: Any abnormalities in heart structure (anatomy) increase the risk of these infections.

Signs and Symptoms

- Elevated WBC, fever, pain
- May decrease cardiac output, causing hypotension
- Pericardial friction rub

Interventions

- IV antibiotics

Cardiac Tamponade

Pathophysiology

- Medical emergency
- Pericardial effusion (fluid build-up)
  - o May be blood (trauma)

Signs and Symptoms

- Shortness of breath
- Tachycardia
- Narrowing pulse pressure
  - o Systolic minus diastolic
  - o 120/80: Pulse pressure equals 40.
  - o 110/90: Pulse pressure equals 20 (narrowed).
- Muffled heart sounds
- Pulsus paradoxus
  - o BP drops more than 10 mmHg during inhalation.

Interventions

- Pericardiocentesis
  - Patient supine
  - May cause a pneumothorax (RN to assess)

Aortic Aneurysm/Aortic Dissection

Pathophysiology

- Bulging of the aorta (aneurysm)
- Tearing away of the aortic lining (dissection)

Signs and Symptoms

- Thoracic
  - Back pain indicates emergent rupture (PRIORITY).
- Abdominal (AAA)
  - Palpable pulsating mass
    - Never palpate it again.

Interventions

- BP management (beta blockers)
- Interventional radiology
- Surgical graft repair
  - Assess for post-op pre-renal acute kidney injury (oliguria).

Marfan Syndrome

Pathophysiology

- Genetic
- Abnormal weakening of the vessel lining (affects the connective tissue)

Signs and Symptoms

- Frequent aneurysms
- Tall body with thin and long fingers

Interventions

- Screening and preventions to treat the various complications

Heart Sounds

S1/S2: normal "lub dub"

S3: extra heart sound after S2

S4: fluid overload (normal in pregnant women)

Murmurs

- Expected when blood moves in an abnormal direction
- Grades 1–6
  - Grade 1 (softer than heart sounds)
  - Grade 6 (very loud)

APE 2 MAN Strategy

This strategy and the figure that accompanies it work as a pictorial mnemonic. Beginning with the "a" for the aortic valve, you begin by assessing on the right-hand side of the body at the 2nd intercostal space. From there, the "p" for pulmonic, "e" for Erb's Point, "2" as a stand-in for the letter "t" for "tricuspid," and "m" for "mitral." When auscultated, you create a wave. Try practicing on your own body with your stethoscope.

Nx Tip: On NCLEX assessment questions, it may help to close your eyes and imagine the movement.

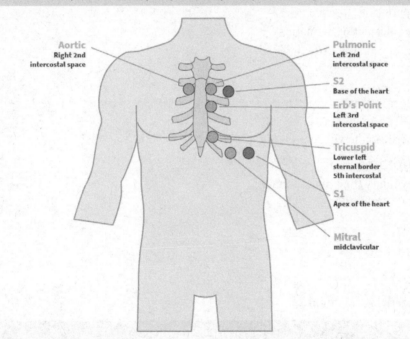

Aortic
Right 2nd
intercostal space

Pulmonic
Left 2nd
intercostal space

S2
Base of the heart

Erb's Point
Left 3rd
intercostal space

Tricuspid
Lower left
sternal border
5th intercostal

S1
Apex of the heart

Mitral
midclavicular

Arterial Versus Venous

Arterial

- Has a blood pressure/pulse
- Dangle the arteries.
- Intermittent claudication
  - Pain in the calves
  - Light ambulation helps with increased blood flow.
  - Pentoxifylline may help.

- Peripheral arterial disease (PAD)/arterial insufficiency
  - Diabetes mellitus
  - Decreased peripheral sensation

| Inspect the feet daily | Wear cotton socks | Snug-fitting shoes (not loose) |
| Lotion prevents cracking | Cotton between toes prevents friction | Take care cutting toenails |

Venous

- Elevate the veins.
- Ambulate (venous valves prevent blood from pooling).
  - Varicose veins if valves fail
- DVT prophylaxis
  - Anti-embolism stockings (delegate to UAP)
  - Sequential compression devices (delegate to UAP)
  - SubQ heparin
- Venous stasis ulcer/stasis dermatitis
  - Painful ulcer on lower extremities

Shock

Pathophysiology

- Decreased perfusion to vital organs and tissues

Signs and Symptoms

- Acute kidney injury (first organ to fail)
  - Decreased urine output
- Elevated lactate

Interventions

- Fluids
- Vasopressors
- Treat the underlying condition.

Types of Shock		
Anaphylactic • Allergic response • Vasodilation • EpiPen, antihistamines, diphenhydramine	Cardiogenic • Decreased cardiac output • MI, HF, cardiomyopathy • Dobutamine, dopamine, epinephrine	Hemorrhagic/Hypovolemic • Loss of blood volume • Hypovolemia • Stop the bleeding or loss of fluids (burns).
Neurogenic • CNS damage • Loss of vessel tone (smooth muscle) • Vasodilation	Septic • Caused by sepsis • Vasodilation • May lead to acute respiratory distress syndrome (ARDS) • Antibiotics	

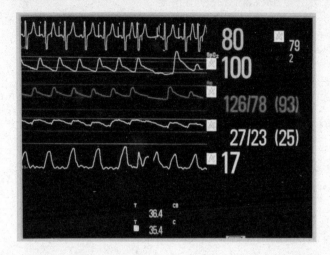

Hemodynamic Monitoring

Arterial Line (Red)

- Catheter typically radial or femoral artery
- Continuous blood pressure
- ABG blood draws (must be an RN)

Central Venous Pressure (Blue—Not Seen on Image)

- Sensor via central line catheter
  - Sits in a venae cavae
- Good indicator of preload and pressure from the right side of the heart
- Often used in heart failure
- Normal CVP is 2 to 6.
  - Elevated (worsening heart failure)
  - Decreased (hypovolemia)

Pulmonary Pressure/Pulmonary Wedge Pressure (Yellow)

- Sensor via Swan-Ganz catheter
  - Sits in the pulmonary artery
- Good indicator of pulmonary hypertension
- Can inflate balloon for pulmonary wedge pressure
  - Never inflate for prolonged periods of time.
  - Never remove specialized syringe to inflate.

Vital Signs

Use the below numbers as benchmarks for NCLEX vitals of concern. Individual patients may vary, but these numbers are general benchmarks for the board exam. Pediatric vital signs can be found in the "Pediatrics" chapter; this section does not apply to peds.

Blood Pressure (BP)

- 89 mmHg or lower: shock
- 180 mmHg or higher: hypertensive crisis
- Anything in between is not a priority unless the patient exhibits signs and symptoms of compromise.

Mean Arterial Pressure (MAP)

- 60 mmHg or higher: indicates adequate perfusion to organs
- NCLEX does not require knowledge on how to calculate MAP.

Temperature

- <95° (hypothermia)
- 98.6°–100.5°: rarely of concern
- 100.5°–101.5°: minor infection
- 101.5°–103°: serious infection (peritonitis, meningitis)
- 103° or higher: likely a medical emergency
  - Neuroleptic malignant syndrome (NMS), malignant hyperthermia, autonomic dysreflexia, thyrotoxicosis, serotonin syndrome

Nx Tip: Slowly warm or cool down the body; never instigate rapid changes (no heat, no ice). For hypothermia, a patient should not be pronounced as deceased until they are re-warmed.

Heart Rate (HR)

- 60 to 100 beats per minute: normal
- Rebound tachycardia is a typical compensation by the body.
- Tachycardia is much more common than bradycardia.

Respiratory Rate (RR)

- 12 to 20 breaths per minute
- Tachypnea (typical compensation)

Pulse Ox (SpO$_2$)

- 93% or higher: normal
- 88% to 92%: COPD normal
- May be lower for cyanotic heart defects

Nx Tip: When prioritizing, do not let HR or RR determine priority. They are often compensation for an underlying problem. For example, a patient with an infection often is tachycardic; this is expected. Remember to focus on the unexpected, not the expected.

To interpret an EKG, take the following steps:

1. Count the beats (BPM).
   - Multiply by 10.
   - Count the QRS complexes.
2. Look at the P.
   - If there is a P, then the patient is in sinus.
   - If there is no P, then go to Step 3.
3. Look at the QRS wave.
   - Narrow → junctional rhythm
   - Wide → ventricular rhythm
4. Look for consistency in the rhythm. Do the components look the same for every beat? What about the spacing between beats?
   - Consistencies help you identify dysrhythmias.

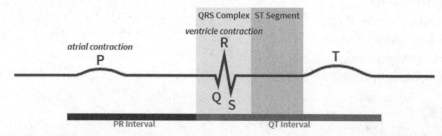

Nx Tip: EKG strips on the board exam are 6 seconds in length. Multiplying the total QRS count by 10 brings the count to 1 minute. Simply understanding if a rhythm is bradycardic or tachycardic can oftentimes eliminate two of the answer choices.

Atrial Arrhythmias

Sinus Tachycardia
- Assess for underlying causes.
  - Substances (caffeine, stimulants)
  - Medical (infection, anemia)

Sinus Bradycardia
- May affect blood pressure
- May be expected due to medications (beta blockers, digoxin)
- Symptomatic bradycardia (hypotension leading to dizziness)
  - Atropine

Supraventricular Tachycardia (SVT)

- Assess for underlying causes.
  - Electrolyte imbalances
- Vagal/Valsalva maneuver (bear down)
  - Baroreceptors cause lowering of the heart rate.
  - Do not perform in patients with underlying heart conditions.
- Adenosine
  - Push rapid: half-life <10 seconds
  - Central line push preferred
  - Chemical cardioversion
  - Expect ventricular asystole for a few seconds.
- Cardioversion (synchronized shock)
  - Do not confuse with defibrillation.
  - Sedate the patient.
- Cardiac ablation
  - Destroys tissue causing electrical activity

Atrial Fibrillation

- No discernable/multiple P waves
- Risk for clotting/clotting events
  - Prevention (aspirin, warfarin, clopidogrel)
  - Risk for pulmonary embolism, stroke, heart attack

Atrial Flutter

- Sawtooth pattern
- Same risks as with atrial fibrillation: clots/clotting events

Ventricular Arrhythmias

Preventricular Contractions (PVCs)

- Wide QRS complex
- May be caused by stimulants
- Six or more per minute requires a call to the HCP.
- Prevent or treat with amiodarone.
- Assess for hyperkalemia.

Ventricular Tachycardia (V. Tach)

- Code Blue
- Pulse or pulseless
  - Assess carotid.

- Torsades
  - Type of V. Tach
  - Assess for hypomagnesemia.
  - Assess for long QT syndrome.
- No pulse
  - CPR first
  - Defibrillation (shock) second (defib is priority if CPR is not an answer choice)

Ventricular Fibrillation (V. Fib)

- Code Blue
- Always pulseless
- CPR first
- Defibrillation second (defib is priority if CPR is not an answer choice)

Asystole

- Code Blue
- Flatline
- CPR first

Code Blue

- V. Tach, V. Fib, asystole
- CPR
  - 2 inches for an adult
  - 1 inch with the palm of the hand for children
  - 1 inch with two fingers for infants
  - Avoid any pauses in compressions.
- Defibrillation
  - Biphasic: 200 joules
  - Monophasic: 360 joules
- Medications
  - Epinephrine, amiodarone

Additional Considerations

ST Elevation/T Wave Inversion

- ST elevations indicate injury to myocardial tissue.
- T wave inversions indicate ischemia to myocardial tissue.
  - Inversion would be a precursor to a full-blown STEMI.

Third-Degree Heart Block

- Heart block rhythm analysis not needed for this rhythm on the board exam
- Dangerous rhythm, may revert to something more fatal

- Pacemaker is required.
  - Transcutaneous pacing (performed via defibrillator machine, but do not confuse with actual defibrillation)
  - Permanent pacemaker/ICD

> **Nx Tip:** First- and second-degree heart block rhythms are not important for the board exam. Simply understand that heart block is not good. Focus on the atrial and ventricular arrhythmias listed above.

Pacemakers/Implantable Cardioverter Defibrillator (ICD)

- Made of metal (no MRIs)
- Avoid direct stress, including exercise, to the ICD site.
- Avoid blunt trauma to the ICD site (steering wheels, rifles, anything that could kick back on the ICD).

Choking

- Conscious: Perform Heimlich maneuver.
  - Adult: right below the xiphoid process
  - Child: abdominal thrusts
  - Infant: back thrusts
- Unconscious: Begin CPR.

EKG Lead Placement

Various mnemonics help ensure correct lead placement. "Whitey Righty" means the white lead is generally the first placed—always negative polarity of the Einthoven's triangle.

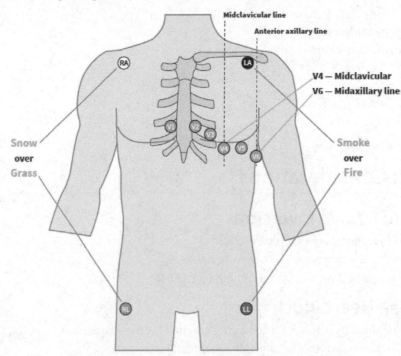

Common Upper Respiratory Tract Infections (URTIs)

Rhinitis	**Pharyngitis/Laryngitis**
■ Common cold	■ Sore throat, cough
■ Viral	■ Bacterial
■ Rhinorrhea (runny nose)	
Sinusitis	**Influenza**
■ Frontal sinus: forehead	■ Fever, muscle aches, malaise
■ Maxillary sinus: zygomatic bone (cheek)	■ Viral

Strep Throat

Pathophysiology
- Caused by the streptococcus bacterium through droplet transmission
- Diagnosed via throat culture

Signs and Symptoms
- Fever, sore throat, enlarged lymph nodes
- Tonsillar exudate (whitish tonsils)

Interventions
- Early treatment with antibiotics; prevent progression to rheumatic fever or post-strep glomerulonephritis
- Antibiotics may be given even with a negative culture (protect the patient).

Rheumatic Fever

Pathophysiology
- Complication secondary to streptococcus infection
- May progress to rheumatic heart disease (a permanent condition)
- Heart damage increases risk for subsequent infections (endocarditis).
- Prophylactic antibiotics common for procedures (dental)

Signs and Symptoms
- Systemic inflammation
- Muscles, joints, and the brain

Interventions
- Treat strep throat early.
- Monitor and treat inflammation.

Epiglottitis

Pathophysiology

- Most common in pediatric clients
- Inflammation of the epiglottis
- Potential airway loss (medical emergency; prioritization)

Signs and Symptoms

- Difficulty swallowing and stridor (early signs)
- Drooling, loss of consciousness (LOC) (late signs)
- Quieting stridor (late sign); red flag

Interventions

- Assess and treat inflammation early.
- Emergency intubation may be needed if it progresses to an airway obstruction.
- Keep tracheostomy kit bedside.

Cystic Fibrosis

Pathophysiology

- Genetic disorder with no cure
- Diagnosed via sweat test (measures chloride in the sweat)
- Abnormally thick mucus secretions lead to lung disease.
- May affect multiple organs (lungs, liver, kidneys, intestines, pancreas)

Signs and Symptoms

- Cough with or without blood/phlegm
- Frequent lung infections
- Pancreatitis
- Difficulty gaining weight (GI/endocrine related)
- Steatorrhea (fatty stools)

Interventions

- Vaccinations (pneumococcal, flu)
- Chest physiotherapy (helps break up mucus); often performed by the respiratory therapist
  - Postural drainage (vibrations on the back)
  - Flutter valve (blow out; expiratory effort)
- Lung transplant (last resort)

Nx Tip: Genetic disorders and terminology are important for the NCLEX. Remember, you do not need to memorize which disorder is which type of genetic issue (recessive or dominant); however, you do need to know what "recessive" and "dominant" mean so you can appropriately measure risk through a Punnett square.

Asthma

Pathophysiology
- Commonly diagnosed in childhood
- Often triggered by environmental factors (pollution, pollen, etc.)
- Chronic inflammation and/or constriction of the airway leading to airway obstruction

Signs and Symptoms
- Coughing and shortness of breath (dyspnea)
- Three or more ED visits in past year
- Wheezing (auscultate)
  o If diminishing, sign of worsening condition
- Loss of airway (status asthmaticus): medical emergency

Interventions
- Reduce triggers (environmental, lifestyle, etc.).
- Pharmacological (bronchodilators, anti-inflammatory agents)
- Emergency intubation (status asthmaticus)

Chronic Obstructive Pulmonary Disease (COPD)

Pathophysiology
- Chronic inflammatory disease (bronchitis)
- Emphysema (ballooning out of the alveoli, dysfunctional)
- Risk with smoking

Signs and Symptoms
- Dyspnea, especially upon exhalation (pursed lips)
- Barrel chest (larger diameter anterior-posterior)
- Chronic respiratory acidosis
- Chronic hypoxia (88%–92% SpO_2 normal for COPD)

Interventions
- Low oxygen supplementation
- Bronchodilators/inhaled glucocorticoids

Nx Tip: In a healthy person, the trigger to breathe is caused by an increase in carbon dioxide (CO_2) in the blood. In a COPD patient, the trigger to breathe is regulated by oxygen levels in the blood. It is crucial that oxygen is not increased too much, otherwise the respiratory rate will decrease because the body believes it does not need to breathe. Oxygen is typically required, however, so if your patient is on room air, do not hesitate to start 2 L nasal cannula; be careful going above that.

Atelectasis

Pathophysiology

- Partial collapse of the lung (alveoli)
- Risk with post-op patients
- May lead to pneumonia if not treated or prevented

Signs and Symptoms

- Soft or absent lung sounds at the base
- Desaturation via pulse ox (SpO_2) and/or serum oxygen (PaO_2)

Interventions

- Deep breathing and incentive spirometry (sustained inhalation over a period of seconds)
- Splint the chest with a pillow during coughing or painful breathing.

Pneumonia

Pathophysiology

- Caused by the pneumococcal bacterium
- Droplet transmission
- May lead to fluid accumulation (lung consolidation)

Signs and Symptoms

- Fever, chills, dyspnea, cough, increased WBC
- Chest pain (pleuritic); pain upon breathing
- Hemoptysis (blood in cough, green- or rust-colored sputum)

Interventions

- Acute stabilization (bed rest, elevate HOB, oxygen, breathing treatments)
- Antibiotics
- Chest x-ray to confirm
- May require intubation if worsening

Pleural Effusion

Pathophysiology

- Fluid build-up in the pleural space
- May be any type of fluid (water, blood, pus)

Signs and Symptoms

- Difficulty breathing (dyspnea)
- May lead to a tension pneumothorax

Interventions

- Pleurocentesis/thoracentesis
  - o Patient positioned leaning forward as if leaning over a desk
  - o Risk for pneumothorax

Pneumothorax

Pathophysiology

- Collapsed lung
- Build-up of air in the pleural space
- Loss of partial vacuum in the pleural space/the lung collapses
- One-way valve movement of air causes rare tension pneumothorax.

Signs and Symptoms

- Dyspnea/desaturation/displaced PMI
- Diminished/absent breath sounds
- Deviation of trachea opposite side of collapse
- Possible hypoxemia (PaO_2 on ABG)

Interventions

- Pleurocentesis/thoracentesis
- Chest tube placement to suction out the air

Chest Tubes

You should have an understanding of both wet and dry chest tube systems.

Purpose

- Removal of air or fluid from the pleural cavity
- Suction out blood (chest cavity/mediastinum) post-cardiac surgery.
- Oscillating water-seal chamber: normal

Complications

- Continuous bubbling in water-seal chamber: not normal (air leak)
- No output may be a sign of a clogged tube: risk for blood build-up
- Tube accidentally removed from patient: Apply petrolatum (Vaseline) gauze.
- Tube accidentally removed from the chest tube: Place tube in sterile water.
- Do not strip a chest tube; you may cause a clot to break.
- Do not clamp the chest tube; you may cause a tension pneumothorax.

Nx Tip: Do not confuse the difference between the water-seal chamber and the suction chamber if the chest tube has both. Bubbling in the suction chamber simply shows that it is indeed working and connected to suction on the wall.

Mechanical Ventilation

Purpose

- Assisted ventilation of oxygen and carbon dioxide
- Endotracheal or tracheostomy
- Commonly used in acute respiratory distress syndrome (ARDS)

Nx Tip: ARDS is a potential complication of septic or hypovolemic shock. It is one of the few times a patient may be placed prone.

Settings

- Can regulate four different settings:

Respiratory rate (RR)	FiO_2 (oxygen)—up to 100%
Tidal volume (volume in a normal breath)	PEEP (post-expiratory end pressure) Keeps alveoli open

- Can ventilate on three basic modes:

Assist Control	Synchronized Intermittent Mechanical Ventilation (SIMV)	Pressure Support
<ul><li>Complete control of all four settings</li><li>Used for critically ill patients and those in the operating room (OR)</li></ul>	<ul><li>A demand/backup setting (Example: The ventilator is set at 14 breaths per minute; if the patient breaths are below 14, the machine will kick in.)</li></ul>	<ul><li>Also called a CPAP setting</li><li>Provides inward pressure to aid breathing, but does not trigger a rate or tidal volume</li><li>Used before extubation to test for readiness to wean</li></ul>

Nx Tip: There are a number of different modes that a ventilator may be used for. The list above is not all-inclusive, but it is what you'll need to know for the NCLEX.

Complications

- High-pressure alarm (obstruction, biting tube, mucous plug, kinking tube)
- Low-pressure alarm (air leak, disconnection)
- Ventilator-associated pneumonia (VAP)

Ventilator-Associated Pneumonia (VAP)

- Elevate head of bed.
- Administer proton-pump inhibitors.
- Oral care q4 hours
- Monitor residuals/distention, and do not overfeed.
- Maintain endotracheal cuff pressure.

Non-Invasive Pressure Support Ventilation (NIPPV)

BiPAP

- Pressure support during inhalation and exhalation
- Commonly the last resort before intubation is necessary
- May deliver added oxygen if needed
- Improvement of oxygenation is the goal (even if the patient is in restraints, do not think safety; physiology is the priority).

CPAP

- Continuous pressure support
- Used for sleep apnea

Oxygen Support

Rebreather Mask

- Reservoir bag holds patient's carbon dioxide (CO_2).
- Patient breathes back some CO_2.
- Use in respiratory alkalosis (similar to using a brown paper bag).

Non-Rebreather Mask

- Carbon dioxide escapes the mask during exhalation.
- Patient breathes higher concentration of oxygen.

Simple Mask/Venturi

- Venturi masks utilize color-coded jets that deliver set amounts of oxygen.
- Regulate oxygen liter flow via the wall oxygen piping.
- RN may start without an order; LPN may initiate if the order exists.

Nasal Cannula

- Use humidification to reduce irritation.
- RN may start without an order; LPN may initiate if the order exists.

Nx Tip: If oxygen is initiated by the RN without an order, obtain the order after initiation. Reach out to the healthcare provider using SBAR communication.

Nx Tip: Oxygen is highly flammable. Avoid flames, wool, petroleum products (Vaseline), and anything that may cause a spark or open flame.

Ventilation/Perfusion Problems

Early Hypoxia

- Anxiety
- Pallor (whitish skin)
- Discoloration of mucous membranes (dark-skinned patients)

Late Hypoxia

- Delirium
- Mottled skin appearance
- Clubbing of fingers (chronic hypoxia)

Anoxia

- Complete lack of oxygen supply to cellular tissue
- After 5 minutes, permanent damage is likely (myocardial infarction, anoxic brain injury).

Carbon Monoxide (CO) Poisoning

- CO competes with oxygen in hemoglobin (carboxyhemoglobin).
- Leads to oxygen deprivation of tissues
- Early sign: a dull headache
- Treat with oxygen supplementation.

Nx Tip: Supplemental oxygen is not always good for the patient's health! O_2 is a drug, and new research indicates that it can cause harm if it's administered without good reason. In the absence of low saturations (<93%), oxygen will not help patients with shortness of breath, and it may actually hurt them. The same holds true for neonates and virtually any patient with ongoing tissue injury from stroke, MI, or trauma.

Lung Sounds

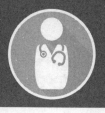

Normal Lung Sounds

Tracheal
- High pitch
- Heard over the trachea

Bronchial
- Medium pitch
- Heard over the upper lobes

Bronchovesicular
- Medium to low pitch
- Heard over the middle lobes/center of the lungs

Vesicular
- Low pitch
- Heard over the lower lobes

Adventitious (Abnormal) Lung Sounds

Crackles (Rales)
- Popping sound (bubble wrap)
- Consolidation in the lungs
- Fine crackles: pulmonary edema
- Coarse crackles: pneumonia

Wheezing (Rhonchi)
- Musical in quality
- Continuous
- Typically louder during expiration
- Common in asthma and COPD patients

Stridor
- High-pitched sound during inspiration
- A sign of obstruction (airway compromise)
- Common symptom in laryngotracheobronchitis (croup)

Pleural Friction Rubs
- Crunching sound
- Common symptom in inflammatory diseases of the lungs, especially the pleural lining

Nx Tip: An audio question is not unheard of on the NCLEX. Listen to adventitious lung sounds utilizing online resources to help you prepare for such questions.

Arterial Blood Gases (ABGs)

Diagnostics

Allen Test

- Tests for collateral blood flow (radial and ulnar arteries)
- Occlude both arteries, pump fist causing pallor, then open one of the arteries.
- The hand should pink up when one of the arteries is opened.
- Failed Allen test denotes no radial arterial line in that hand.

ABG Blood Draw

- RNs may draw blood from an A-line.
- Commonly performed in an intensive care unit (ICU)

Lab Values

- pH: 7.35–7.45
- CO_2: 35–45
- HCO_3 (bicarb): 22–26
- PaO_2: 80–100

Basics

- CO_2 is an acid. More acid means a drop in pH (acidosis).
- HCO_3 (bicarb) is a base. More base means an increase in pH (alkalosis).
- ROME acronym: respiratory opposite, metabolic equal

> Nx Tip: You do not need to know the difference between a partially compensated ABG and a fully compensated ABG. It is most important that you learn how to identify the primary problems listed below, such as respiratory acidosis.

Steps of ABG Analysis

1. Is the pH out of range?
2. Is the pCO_2 normal?
3. Is the HCO_3 out of range?
4. Match the abnormal result with the pH.

Respiratory Acidosis

Pathophysiology

- Retention of CO_2 (acid)
- Patient is not breathing enough.
- Obstruction (COPD, emphysema)
- Respiratory distress/ARDS
- Brainstem trauma

Signs and Symptoms

- Hypercapnia (increase in carbon dioxide)
- Respiratory depression/bradypnea (slow breathing)
- High CO_2, low pH

Interventions

- Treat the underlying problem.
- CPAP, BiPAP
- Intubation (last resort)

Nx Tip: The priority outcome for a patient with respiratory distress will be proper oxygenation. Remember Maslow's hierarchy: physiology over psychology. Often, patients may be put in restraints because they try to take off their O_2 supplementation. The priority is still oxygenation, even over something such as "patient safety." The patient is already safe; you are keeping them safe by using restraints.

Respiratory Alkalosis

Pathophysiology

- Loss of CO_2 (acid)
- Patient is breathing too often.
- Anxiety, fear, pain

Signs and Symptoms

- Hypocapnia (decrease in carbon dioxide)
- Hyperventilation (tachypnea)
- Paresthesias, dizziness

Interventions

- Rebreather mask/brown bag
- Treat the underlying condition (pain meds, anxiolytics).

Metabolic Acidosis

Pathophysiology

- Decrease in bicarb (HCO_3)
- Production of too much acid (lactic acidosis, ketoacidosis)
- Kidneys not producing enough bicarb (chronic renal failure)
- Long-term diarrhea may cause

Signs and Symptoms

- Kussmaul breathing (ketoacidosis)
- Arrhythmias
- Coma, death (if left untreated)

Interventions

- Correct the underlying problem (provide oxygen if needed).
- Intravenous bicarbonate

Metabolic Alkalosis

Pathophysiology

- Increase in bicarb (HCO_3)
- Long-term vomiting may cause (also chronic NG tube suctioning)
- Conn's syndrome (hyperaldosteronism)
- Excessive intake of antacids

Signs and symptoms

- Confusion
- Muscle twitching
- Paresthesias

Interventions

- Treat the underlying problem.
- Condition is secondary to a broader problem.

Nx Tip: The body can only compensate pH in one of two ways: respiratory or metabolic. It is much quicker for the body to regulate pH through breathing (respiratory). Metabolic issues oftentimes take days to build up. This is also why it is common to see quick changes in the breathing before anything else. The patient may be breathing fast or slow, depending on the direction of pH.

Oxygenation

Hypoxemia

- Low oxygenation in the blood
- Early signs: pallor, mucous membrane discoloration, anxiety, irritability
- Late signs: delirium, begins to affect organs

Hypoxia

- Low oxygenation to the tissues
- Pulse Ox (SpO_2): Infrared technology reads hemoglobin concentration. Falsely elevated in carbon monoxide poisoning; carboxyhemoglobin
- Early signs: shortness of breath, tachypnea, anxiety
- Late signs: delirium, clubbing of fingers (chronic)

Fluid and Electrolytes

Osmosis: Water moves into higher solute concentrations (water follows salt).

Diffusion: Movement of molecules from low to high concentration

Hyperosmolar: Higher concentration than blood

Iso-osmolar: Same concentration as blood

Hypo-osmolar: Lower concentration than blood (diluted)

Crystalloids

3% and 7% NaCl

- Hypertonic solution (higher concentration than blood)
- Used in severe hyponatremia and increased intracranial pressure (ICP)
- Causes water to shift into the vasculature
- Risks to dehydrate the surrounding cells
- Do not use in hypertension (remember, low salt).

0.9% NaCl (Normal Saline)

- Isotonic solution (same concentration as blood)
- Used in dehydration and hypovolemia ("fill up the tank")

0.45% NaCl (Half-Normal Saline)

- Hypotonic solution (lower concentration than blood)
- Often combined with dextrose to maintain iso-osmolality

Lactated Ringer's (LR)

- Isotonic solution
- Contains potassium, chloride, sodium, and calcium
- Used in trauma, volume loss, and especially burns
- Alkalizing agent used to counteract acidosis (contains bicarb)

Dextrose 5% and 10%

- Glucose-containing solution
- Becomes hypotonic once the dextrose is metabolized out
- Typically combined with other salines
- Used in hypoglycemia (often severe infection)
- Contained in vials such as D5 (50%), pushed IV for hypoglycemic protocol

Colloids

Albumin

- Responsible for 60% of blood osmolality (maintaining blood concentration)
- Serum protein created by the liver
- Also given via IV like crystalloids
- Commonly used in liver failure, burn victims, and general hypoalbuminemia

Blood Products

Platelets

- Given for thrombocytopenia (cancer, infection, sepsis, liver failure, heparin-induced thrombocytopenia, disseminated intravascular coagulation)

Fresh Frozen Plasma (FFP)

- Contains everything but red blood cells
- Patient has normal hemoglobin, does not require RBCs

Packed Red Blood Cells (PRBCs)

- Given for anemia (low hemoglobin)
- Hemorrhage

Whole Blood

- Entire composition of blood (plasma and RBCs)

Nx Tip: An autologous blood donation (to oneself) may be performed for elective surgery. The patient would receive his or her own blood back if needed. This donation is typically done weeks in advance of surgery, as it takes time for the body to make new RBCs. However, this time frame is not an absolute; the patient may donate 3–5 days before surgery.

RN Considerations for Blood Products

Chronological Order of Completion

- Confirm the transfusion order.
- Confirm type and cross (redraw every 72 hours).
- Two RNs must sign off.
- Obtain Y blood tubing, 20-gauge needle or larger, and an infusion pump.
- Must be administered with only normal saline
- Hang blood within 30 minutes of receiving it from blood bank or it must be sent back.
- Initiate the infusion and perform the first 15-minute assessment (remember, baseline vitals before you start).
- Most severe reactions occur in the first 15 minutes.
- Milder reactions occur later, but before the end of the transfusion.
- Subsequent vitals may be delegated to an LPN.
- RN to assess any potential negative changes to the patient
- Administer the whole unit within 4 hours.
- 250 mL per unit (on average)

Transfusion Reactions

Allergic Reaction

- Minor: localized rash (individual area), pruritus
  - Slow the drip rate and notify the HCP for an antihistamine (diphenhydramine).
- Major: diffuse or generalized rash (all over), difficulty breathing, sweating, complaints of feeling hot
  - Stop the drip, flush normal saline through alternate tubing, and call the HCP.
  - Epinephrine may be needed.
  - Send remaining blood to blood bank for analysis.

Nx Tip: There are very few times when it would be safe to say the RN can simply slow a drip rate. It is often much safer to simply stop the drip altogether. A minor reaction is one of the few times (especially on the NCLEX) where it is okay to simply slow the drip. Other situations where slowing the drip would be acceptable would be if it is a titratable medication, like oxytocin, but even that med needs to be stopped if it is causing an emergency.

Hemolytic/Cytotoxic Reaction

- Incompatible blood (ABO mismatch)
- Flank/back pain (costovertebral)
- Fever
- Dark-colored urine (cola-colored)
- Stop the drip, flush normal saline through alternate tubing, and call the HCP.
- Send remaining blood to blood bank for analysis.

Lab Values

The lab value numbers detailed in this chapter are benchmarks for the NCLEX. Do not get hung up on questions or answer choices that are slightly off of what you may consider normal. You must assess your patient for symptoms based off of those numbers. Critical thinking is important here. Do not marry yourself to a number. If a number is omitted from a specific lab, you do not need to know it for the NCLEX. Conserve your neurons for the important information.

Complete Blood Count

White Blood Cells (WBCs)

- 5,000–10,000
- If high: leukocytosis
  o Active infection
- If low: neutropenia/leukopenia
  o Risk for infection

Nx Tip: Neutrophils make up 80% of the body's WBCs.

Red Blood Cells (RBCs)

- 4.2–5.5
- Reticulocytes (baby RBCs)
- If high: polycythemia vera
  o Risk for clotting events (MI, PE, CVA)/poor circulation
- If low: anemia

Nx Tip: Refer to the "Hematology" chapter for an in-depth analysis of anemias.

Hemoglobin (HgB)

- 12–16
- Oxygen-carrying component of blood
- Transfusion likely under 8 (especially 7)

Hematocrit (HcT)

- Percentage of RBCs to total blood volume
- 37–50
- If high: dehydration, polycythemia, hypovolemia
- If low: fluid overload, anemia, hypervolemia

Nx Tip: Hematocrit typically correlates with RBC and HgB numbers. This is not always the case, however, especially in cases of fluid volume shifts (for example, someone who has been vomiting for days or someone who has diabetes insipidus).

Platelets (Plt)

- 150,000–300,000
- If low: thrombocytopenia
  o May be caused by numerous factors (heparin-induced, chemotherapy, bone marrow suppression)
  o Bleeding risk (no razors, no hard edges, no rectal temps, no enemas, no suppositories, no hard-bristle toothbrushes, etc.)

Chemistry Panel/Basic Metabolic Panel

Sodium (Na)

- 135–145
- Water follows salt (osmosis).
- If high: hypernatremia
  - Dehydration
  - Follow a low-sodium diet.
- If low: hyponatremia
  - Fluid retention
  - Very low sodium (water intoxication) is a potential medical emergency leading to seizures.
  - Replete with sodium chloride.

Potassium (K)

- 3.5–5
- If high: hyperkalemia
  - Cardiac dysrhythmias (PVCs)
- If low: hypokalemia
  - May be caused by vomiting, diarrhea, and GI suctioning *N G Tube*
  - Muscle weakness, malaise, dysrhythmias
  - May lead to digoxin toxicity
  - Replete with potassium chloride "K-rider" (10 mEq/hr).

Nx Tip: Potassium chloride may burn going in. If the patient complains of pain at the infusion site, slow down the drip. Recommended administration rates should not exceed 10 mEq/hr.

Calcium (Ca)

- 8–10
- If high: hypercalcemia
  - CNS-related issues (irritability, paresthesias)
  - May lead to hypercalcemic crisis and death (typically secondary to bone cancer)
- If low: hypocalcemia
  - Chvostek's sign/Trousseau's sign
  - Muscle tetany
  - Replete with calcium chloride/gluconate (reversal agent for hypermagnesemia as well).

Magnesium (Mg)

- If high: hypermagnesemia
  - Decrease in deep tendon reflexes
  - Potential adverse effect of magnesium sulfate for preeclampsia
- If low: hypomagnesemia
  - Muscle weakness or tetany

Phosphorus (Phos)

- Inverted relationship to calcium; one goes up, the other goes down
- If high: hyperphosphatemia
  - May lead to osteopenia/osteoporosis
  - Carbonated beverages are high in phosphorus (colas).
- If low: hypophosphatemia
  - May be due to alcoholism
  - Replete with IV phosphorus.

Glucose

- 70–100 (adult)
- If high: hyperglycemia
  - The 3 P's (polydipsia, polyuria, polyphagia)
- If low: hypoglycemia
  - Diaphoresis, tachycardia, clammy skin, confusion, death

Albumin

- 3.5–5
- If high: hyperalbuminemia
  - Dehydration
- If low: hypoalbuminemia
  - Malnutrition, liver failure
  - Replete with IV albumin.

Cardiac Markers

Troponin

- By-product of dead heart muscle
- If high: myocardial injury/infarction

Creatine Kinase

- Inflammation of muscles (MI, rhabdomyolysis, autoimmunity)

Creatinine

- 0.1–1.5
- If high: azotemia
  - Acute kidney injury (formerly called acute renal failure)
  - Chronic renal failure (CKD)

BUN (Blood, Urea, Nitrogen)

- 8–20
- If high: azotemia
  - Acute kidney injury/chronic renal failure
  - Heart failure/dehydration

Liver Enzymes (ALT, AST)

- If high: liver injury

Brain Natriuretic Peptide (BNP)

- Hormone released by ventricles when stretched
- If high: heart failure

Lipid Panel

Total Cholesterol: Less than 200

- If high: hypercholesterolemia
- Risk for cardiovascular disease (CVD)

LDL: Less than 150

- Bad cholesterol
- If high: hyperlipidemia
- Risk for CVD

HDL: More than 40–60

- Good cholesterol (carries away LDL)
- Diet and exercise encourage high HDL.

Additional Labs

D-Dimer

- Indicates abnormal clotting (thrombus, coagulation, active clotting)
- Elevation may indicate DVT/PE/DIC.

C-Reactive Protein

- Indicates inflammation in the body (acute)

Erythrocyte Sedimentation Rate (ESR)

- Indicates inflammation in the body (chronic)

Coagulation Studies (Coags)

Normal/Subtherapeutic	Therapeutic	Elevated	Dangerous
aPTT: 20–40 seconds (heparin) PT/INR: 0.5–1.5 seconds (warfarin) **Increase the dose.**	aPTT: 40–80 seconds PT/INR: 2–3 seconds **Give/maintain the dose.**	3 times baseline **Decrease the dose.**	Signs of bleeding (petechiae) **Hold the dose; call the HCP.**

Toxic Medications

Normal/Subtherapeutic	Therapeutic	Elevated	Dangerous
digoxin: 0 lithium: 0 theophylline: 0 phenytoin: 0 **Increase the dose.**	digoxin: 0.5–1.5 lithium: 0.6–1.4 theophylline: 10–20 phenytoin: 10–20 **Give/maintain the dose.**	Early signs and symptoms of toxicity **Decrease the dose.**	Signs of severe toxicity **Hold the dose; call the HCP.**

Adrenal Glands (Corticosteroids, Catecholamines)

Addison's Disease

Pathophysiology

- Adrenal insufficiency
- Hypocortisolism/ hypoadrenalism

Signs and Symptoms

- Fatigue, weakness
- Weight loss, anorexia
- Increased pigmentation of skin
- Painful muscles/joints
- Inability to cope with stress, intolerance to cold
- Hyponatremia (salt cravings), hyperkalemia

Interventions

- Lifelong cortisol replacement

Addisonian Crisis

Pathophysiology

- Medical emergency
- Cortisol levels dangerously low
- Often triggered by infection or stress

Signs and Symptoms

- Hypotension
- Nausea, vomiting
- Fever, chills
- Skin rash

Interventions

- Immediate cortisol administration

Cushing's Syndrome

Pathophysiology

- Elevated cortisol levels
- Hypercortisolism/ hyperadrenalism

Signs and Symptoms

- Weight gain, central obesity (abdominal)
- Moon face
- Thinning skin, easily bruised
- Fatigue, muscle weakness
- Depression, anxiety
- Hypertension
- Hypernatremia (polydipsia), hypokalemia

Interventions

- Stop steroid medications.
- Removal of the adrenal glands (adrenalectomy)

Parathyroid Gland

Hyperparathyroidism

Pathophysiology

- Excessive release of parathyroid hormone
- Hypercalcemia caused by the body pulling calcium from the bones

Signs and Symptoms

- CNS issues (irritability, fatigue, confusion)
- Kidney stones
- Osteopenia/osteoporosis: may lead to fractures

Interventions

- Pharmacological (calcitonin, bisphosphonates)
- Resection of the parathyroid

Hypoparathyroidism

Pathophysiology

- Decreased production of parathyroid hormone
- Leads to hypocalcemia
- Common complication post-thyroidectomy

Signs and Symptoms

- Muscle tetany, cramping
- Paresthesias
- Chvostek's sign/Trousseau's sign

Interventions

- Pharmacological (calcitriol, vitamin D, calcium gluconate)
- Decrease intake of phosphorus.

Thyroid Gland (T3, T4)

Hyperthyroidism

Pathophysiology

- Decreased thyroid-stimulating hormone (TSH) from the brain
- Excessive release of thyroid hormones
- Radioactive iodine uptake test (diagnostic)

Signs and Symptoms

- Body function sped up (metabolism)
- Weight loss
- Heat intolerance
- Thyroid storm (thyrotoxicosis): medical emergency

Interventions

- Pharmacological (methimazole, propylthiouracil, iodine)
- Radioactive iodine: results in ablation of thyroid function
- Thyroidectomy

Hypothyroidism

Pathophysiology

- Increased TSH
- Decreased production of thyroid hormones

Signs and Symptoms

- Fatigue
- Cold intolerance
- Weight gain
- Muscle weakness
- Myxedema coma (throat tightness): medical emergency

Interventions

- Lifelong hormone replacement

Graves' Disease

Pathophysiology

- Autoimmune disorder leading to overactivity of the thyroid gland
- Mimics hyperthyroidism
- More common in women over 20

Signs and Symptoms

- Similar to hyperthyroidism
- Exophthalmos (bulging eyeballs)

Interventions

- Similar to hyperthyroidism
- Immunomodulators

Hashimoto's Thyroiditis

Pathophysiology

- Autoimmune disorder leading to underactivity of the thyroid gland
- Mimics hypothyroidism
- More common in women
- May be caused by high intake of selenium or iodine

Signs and Symptoms

- Similar to hypothyroidism

Interventions

- Similar to hypothyroidism

Goiter

Pathophysiology

- Enlarged thyroid
- Lack of iodine in the diet
- Tumor or nodules on thyroid

Signs and Symptoms

- Visible enlargement of the neck
- May be benign
- Dizziness when raising arms above head
- Dysphagia
- Respiratory distress: medical emergency

Interventions

- Monitoring
- Surgical

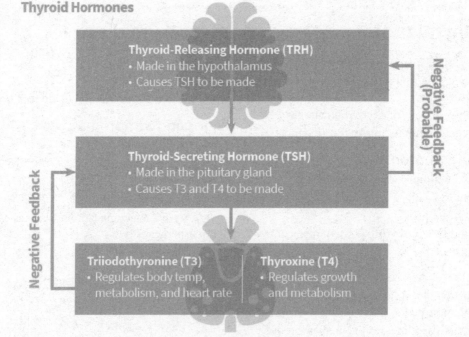

Thyroid Hormones

Thyroid-Releasing Hormone (TRH)
- Made in the hypothalamus
- Causes TSH to be made

Thyroid-Secreting Hormone (TSH)
- Made in the pituitary gland
- Causes T3 and T4 to be made

Triiodothyronine (T3)
- Regulates body temp, metabolism, and heart rate

Thyroxine (T4)
- Regulates growth and metabolism

Negative Feedback (Probable)

Negative Feedback

Pancreas (Insulin)

Hypoglycemia

Pathophysiology

- Not enough glucose
- Using ginseng while on insulin
- Beta blockers with insulin
- Diabetes mellitus (DM) patient exercising more than normal
- Too much insulin

Signs and Symptoms

- Hypotension, tachycardia
- Anxiety, diaphoresis
- Cold, clammy
- CNS issues (irritability, fatigue)

Interventions

- 15/15 rule
  - Intervention for slight hypoglycemia
  - 15g of carbs followed by a 15-minute assessment
- Simple carbs (juice)
- D5/dextrose (IV infusion or push)
- Glucagon (severe hypoglycemia)

Hyperglycemia

Pathophysiology

- Diabetes mellitus (DM)
- Total parenteral nutrition (TPN)
- Long-term steroid use

Signs and Symptoms

- 3 P's (polydipsia, polyuria, polyphagia)

Interventions

- Diet and exercise
- Oral antidiabetic agents
- Insulin

> Nx Tip: Hyperglycemia is NOT a medical emergency unless the signs of diabetic ketoacidosis (DKA) are beginning to show. Do not confuse this on priority questions. Even a person with a glucose of 450 is NOT dying. Simply administer sliding scale insulin and call the HCP regarding the high number.

Diabetes Type 1

- Insulin dependent
- Possibly caused by coxsackievirus
- Typically presents in children (juvenile)
- No production of insulin from pancreas

Diabetes Type 2

- Insulin resistant
- Obesity (poor cellular response to insulin)
- Lack of exercise (sedentary)
- Poor diet

Diabetic Complications

Dawn Phenomenon

- Higher glucose level in the morning

Somogyi Effect

- Rebound hyperglycemia due to hypoglycemic event overnight
- Encourage checking glucose at night and bedtime snack.

Comorbidity with Cardiovascular Disease (CVD)

- May lead to CVD, increasing risk of myocardial infarction

Diabetic Nephropathy

- May lead to chronic kidney disease

Diabetic Retinopathy

- Begins with blurred vision
- Patient may lose vision.

Foot Ulcers/Infection

- Decreased sensation due to arterial insufficiency
- Wet-to-dry dressings for open wounds
- Prevention is key (refer to pp. 61–62).

Diabetic Ketoacidosis (DKA)

Pathophysiology
- Glucose cannot get into cells for energy.
- Body switches to fat for energy (breakdown of ketones).
- Uncontrolled type 1 DM

Signs and Symptoms
- 3 P's
- Fruit-scented breath
- Nausea, vomiting, weakness
- Kussmaul breathing (fast and deep)
  - Compensatory for metabolic acidosis

Diagnostic Testing
- Glucose level >600
- Ketones in urine

Interventions
- Fluid (priority) and electrolyte replacement
- Insulin

Hyperosmolar Hyperglycemic Nonketotic Syndrome

Pathophysiology
- Kidneys excrete too much water in attempt to rid glucose.
- Dehydration
- Prevalent in type 2 DM
- Prevalent in elderly (decreased thirst mechanism)

Signs and Symptoms
- Glucose level >600
- 3 P's
- Hot and dry (may see fever)
- Sleepy and confused
- May lead to seizures, coma, and death

Interventions
- Fluids (priority)
- Insulin
- Potassium may be needed.

Diabetes Management/ Interventions

Glycosylated Hemoglobin (A1C)
- Gives a 3-month outlook on glucose management
- Displays adherence of meds, diet, and exercise
- Higher A1C indicates unregulated diabetes.

Bedside Glucose Checks
- Device monitors glucose typically between 40–600.
- May be delegated to an unlicensed assistive personnel (UAP)
- If the result is strange, double-check.

Basal Dose/Scheduled Dose
- Outside the scope of a nurse to change scheduled medications
- Doses meant to stabilize the patient long term

Prandial Dose
- Extra dose of insulin at mealtime
- 15g of carbs equals 1 carbohydrate exchange.
- Typically 1 unit per exchange

Mixing Insulins
- First: Inject air into long-acting insulin (NPH).
- Second: Inject air into short-acting insulin (Regular – R).
- Third: Draw up short-acting insulin (R).
- Fourth: Draw up long-acting insulin (NPH).

Nx Tip: R before N. Clear before cloudy. Never shake insulin. Keep insulin refrigerated.

SICK Day Rules
- S – Sugar: Check more often (q4hr).
- I – Insulin: May need more.
- C – Carbs: Pay attention to diet.
- K – Ketones: Watch for signs of DKA.

Insulin Infusion Pump

- Do not confuse with subQ.
- Needle change every 3 days
- Sterile technique
- Cleanse insertion site with alcohol.

Pituitary Gland (Antidiuretic Hormone)

Diabetes Insipidus

Pathophysiology

- Lack of antidiuretic hormone (ADH)

Signs and Symptoms

- Frequent urination
- Dehydration leading to hypovolemia
- May lead to hypotension (dizziness)
- Rebound tachycardia
- Hyperosmolar blood: concentrated lab values

Interventions

- Pharmacological (vasopressin, desmopressin)

Syndrome of Inappropriate Antidiuretic Hormone (SIADH)

Pathophysiology

- Excessive release of ADH

Signs and Symptoms

- Decreased urine output (oliguria)
- Fluid retention leading to hypervolemia
- May lead to hypertension
- Hypo-osmolar blood: diluted lab values

Interventions

- Water restriction (ice chips)
- Diuretics
- Vasopressin antagonist

Hepatology/Liver

Anatomy

- Blood through portal vein rich in nutrients from GI tract
- Portal vein and hepatic artery deliver blood to Kupffer cells for filtration

Physiology

- Glucose metabolism
- Ammonia conversion
- Protein metabolism
- Fat metabolism
- Vitamin and iron storage
- Bile formation
- Medication metabolism

Interventions

- Lifelong cortisol replacement

Nx Tip: The NCLEX assumes test-takers know enough about anatomy and physiology already. The liver can be complicated; make sure to study if needed.

Hepatitis

Pathophysiology

- Caused by a virus (HAV, HBV, HCV)
- Hep A (HAV): transmitted by food (contact, uncooked food, fecal-oral)
- Hep B (HBV): transmitted via bodily fluids (blood)
- Hep C (HCV): transmitted via bodily fluids (blood)
- Subsequent hepatitis infections (Hep D and Hep E) are secondary to HBV or HCV

Signs and Symptoms

- Fatigue
- Nausea/vomiting
- Hep C may lead to liver damage and liver cancer.

Interventions

- Vaccination (Hep A and Hep B)
- Treat the symptoms and ride it out.

Liver Failure/Cirrhosis

Pathophysiology

- Late stages of scarring (fibrosis) of the liver
- Hardening and thickening
- Chronic alcohol (ETOH) use
- Hepatitis
- Fatty liver disease

Signs and Symptoms

- Easy bruising and bleeding
- Jaundice (icterus) of skin and sclera
- Ascites and swelling of the legs
- Muscle wasting
- Decrease in chest/axillary hair
- Late stage cirrhosis; fetor hepaticus (musty breath smell) identifies increased blood ammonia

Diagnostics

- Liver panel (ALT, AST)
- Bilirubin levels (elevated)
- Clotting factors (elevated)

Interventions

- Avoid alcohol.
- Weight loss
- Liver transplant

Liver Complications

Hepatic Encephalopathy

- Build-up of toxins normally cleaned by the liver (ammonia)
- Leads to confusion, drowsiness, slurred speech, and delirium

Portal Hypertension

- Cirrhosis slows flow of blood through portal vein.
- Leads to splenomegaly, esophageal varices, gastric varices
- May require a transjugular intrahepatic portosystemic shunt (TIPS) surgery

Nx Tip: If a patient known to abuse alcohol begins vomiting blood, you should worry. A rupture of a varices is a medical emergency. A good rule of thumb is that a rupture of ANYTHING is a medical emergency. A Sengstaken-Blakemore tube is used to tamponade the bleeding. It is a specialized type of NG tube that inflates. Keep scissors bedside; if the patient begins to exhibit respiratory distress, cut the tube to release the air.

Pancreatitis

Pathophysiology

- Pancreatic enzymes become activated while inside the organ, causing damage.
- Alcoholism, smoking
- Cholelithiasis (gallstones) most common cause of acute pancreatitis in adults
- Cystic fibrosis

Signs and Symptoms

- Upper abdominal pain radiating to the back, worse after eating
- Nausea and vomiting
- Fever
- Cullen's sign (superficial edema and bruising at the umbilicus)
- Grey-Turner's sign (bruising on the flank, sign of bleeding)

Diagnostic Testing

- Elevated amylase and lipase
- CT/MRI
- Endoscopic retrograde cholangiopancreatography (ERCP)
  - May include fluoroscopy

Interventions

- Bowel rest for the pancreas (NPO)
- High-carb diet with no fatty acids when diet is restored
- Pain meds
- IV fluids
- Antibiotics
- Whipple procedure (pancreaticoduodenectomy)

Cholangitis

Pathophysiology

- Infection of the common bile duct
- Medical emergency
- Secondary to cholelithiasis/cholecystitis

Signs and Symptoms

- Charcot's triad:
  - Jaundice (rapid onset)
  - Abdominal pain
  - Fever

Interventions

- ERCP with lithotripsy

Gallbladder

Cholelithiasis (Gallstones)

- Stones are usually made of bile.
- Risk factors: female, fertile, 40, overweight
- Diagnosed by ultrasound
- Lithotripsy may be effective in breaking up stones.
- Ursodiol used to break up stones
- May lead to infection

Cholecystitis

- Right upper quadrant (RUQ) rebound tenderness (Murphy's sign)

Cholecystectomy

- Typically laparoscopically
- Low-fat diet post-surgery

Oral/Mouth

Stomatitis

- Inflamed sore in the mouth
- Avoid spicy food.
- Avoid hot and cold.

Stomach/Peptic/Gastrology

Gastroesophageal Reflux Disease (GERD)

- Do not lie supine after meals; sit up 3–4 hours after eating.
- Small frequent meals
- No spicy food, no caffeine, no alcohol, no smoking

Fundoplication

- Surgical wrap of the fundus of the stomach around the esophagus
- Treats advanced GERD or hiatal hernias

Gastrectomy (Subtotal or Total)

- Loss of intrinsic factor (needed for B12 absorption)
- Patients require B12 (cobalamin) injections for life; can lead to pernicious anemia if B12 not administered.

Dumping Syndrome

- Ingest fluids between meals, not with
- Risk after gastric bypass (gastrectomy)

Pyloric Stenosis

- Narrowing of pylorus (bottom of the stomach)
- Infants: projectile vomiting after feeding
- Corrected surgically

Achalasia

- Abnormal narrowing of the lower part of the esophagus
- Dysphagia is common.
- Dilation of the esophagus on the top
- Barium swallow to diagnose

Gastrointestinal Tubes

Nasogastric (NG) Tube

- Measure from the nose to the back of the throat to the xiphoid process
- Placed by RNs or LPNs with specialized certification
- OG tube passed through mouth instead of nose
- Cannot use without x-ray confirmation

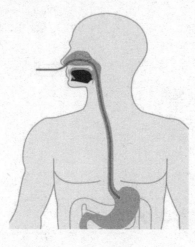

Sengstaken-Blakemore Tube

- Used in ruptured esophageal or gastric varices

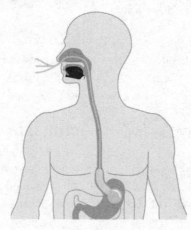

PEG Tube

- Typically placed when patients cannot feed orally
- Common in post-stroke or comatose patients

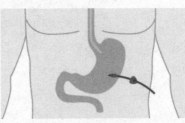

Nx Tip: Check equipment for kinks and malfunction when the patient complains of fullness, nausea, or bloating. If kinking is suspected, first push a small amount of fluid. The RN may also tug very gently on the tube in attempt to remove it from the mucosal wall (contraindicated in post-GI surgical patients).

Stomach Decompression

- Suction to the wall for decompression.
- Initiated for GI bleeding, pancreatitis, etc. (stop bowel movement)
- Document color and amount as output (UAP may perform).
- Chronic suctioning may lead to hypokalemia.

Tube Feedings

- Feedings have 24-hour shelf life.
- Monitor for signs of intolerance (nausea, bloating, fullness).
- Keep head of bed (HOB) elevated at all times during feedings.
- Assessing residual and effectiveness of feedings:
  - 50% or more residual being aspirated: discard, halve the rate on pump
  - 50% or less residual being aspirated: push back in, keep the rate on pump
- Confirmation
  - Aspiration of contents for pH
  - Gold standard is x-ray.
- Feedings cannot begin until x-ray confirmation.

Total Parenteral Nutrition (TPN)

- Used when oral and NG tube intake are not possible
- Intravenous nutrition
- Risk for hyperglycemia, infection, and fluid overload

Appendicitis

Pathophysiology

- Inflammation and infection
- May lead to rupture

Signs and Symptoms

- Right lower quadrant (RLQ) pain – McBurney's point
- Nausea and vomiting
- Fever

Interventions

- Appendectomy
- Easy delegation to LPN or new RN

Peritonitis

Pathophysiology

- Risk of peritoneal dialysis
- Sign of rupture of organs (medical emergency)
- Sign of internal bleeding (medical emergency)

Signs and Symptoms

- Abdominal pain and distention
- Rigid/board-like abdomen
- Cloudy output (peritoneal dialysis)
- May lead to sepsis/septic shock

Interventions

- Surgical abdominal washout
- Antibiotics

Nx Tip: Peritonitis is oftentimes a sign of a ruptured organ. Remember: On the NCLEX, a rupture of anything is a medical emergency.

Inflammatory Bowel Disease

Pathophysiology

- Colitis, ulcerative colitis, gastroenteritis, diverticulitis, Crohn's disease
- Bacterial, viral, fungal, autoimmune

Signs and Symptoms

- Abdominal cramping, diarrhea
- Blood in stool (fecal occult)
- Change in bowel habits

Interventions

- Avoid tobacco, caffeine, alcohol, and tea (GI stimulants).
- Avoid popcorn, nuts, and gas-producing foods.
- Low-residue diet while in hospital (no need at discharge)
  - Less frequent and looser stool
- No gluten (celiac disease)

GI Bleeding

Pathophysiology
- Common cause is helicobacter pylori.
- Peptic ulcers, duodenal ulcers

Signs and Symptoms
- Upper GI: black, tarry stool (melena)
- Lower GI: bright red stool
- Esophagogastroduodenoscopy (EGD) to diagnose upper GI
- Colonoscopy to diagnose lower GI

Interventions
- NPO until bleeding is controlled

Bowel Obstructions

Pathophysiology
- Fecal obstruction
- Intussusception (common in pediatric patients)
- Volvulus (twisting of the bowel)

Signs and Symptoms
- Sudden onset of abdominal cramps and vomiting
- Drawing of legs up to chest (intussusception)
- Watery discharge with no stool
- Can lead to infection or perforation if left untreated

Interventions
- Push fluids (2–3 L per day is recommended for any human being).
- Increase fiber for constipation.
- Laxatives and enemas
- Air enema (intussusception)

Additional Organ Problems

Dehiscence

- Montgomery strap used to prevent
- Opening of a surgical wound
- Intestines may protrude from opening.
- Apply gentle pressure and call HCP.

Hemochromatosis

- Abnormal collection of iron in organs

Wilson's Disease

- Abnormal collection of copper in organs

Colostomy/Ileostomy

Indications

- Inflammatory bowel diseases (providing bowel rest)
- Colorectal cancer (bypass resected bowel)

Stoma Care

- Swelling and slight bleeding are normal after placement.
- Prevent excoriation post-op.
- Red or pink is normal color for stoma.
- Purple, maroon, or black is sign of cyanosis.
- Refer to stoma nurse for body image issues.

Diet

- Formed stool: colostomy
- Loose stool: ileostomy
- Roughage may obstruct the stoma (caution).
- Ileostomies require increased water intake.

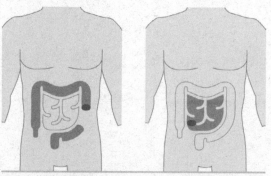

Colostomy   Ileostomy

Colonoscopy

Indications

- Age 50 or older
- Every 5 years (more frequently if problems present)
- Secondary prevention (screening)
- Early identification of colorectal cancer (polyps)

Procedure Care

- Bowel prep (polyethylene glycol)
- NPO (8–12 hours prior)
- Strong benzodiazepine (midazolam) with fentanyl (moderate sedation)
  - Anterograde amnesia is the goal (forget the procedure).
- RN monitors vital signs, especially the respiratory rate and O_2 saturation.

Post-Procedure Care

- Same-day procedure (patient must urinate before discharge).
- Slowly advance diet after procedure.

Nx Tip: Similar considerations are taken into account for an esophagogastroduodenoscopy (EGD). An EGD is not, however, used as a screening tool for cancer. It is more commonly used to diagnose upper GI bleeding, ulcers, gastritis, esophageal problems, etc.

Hematology

Blood Typing

O, A, B

- A and B: dominant alleles
- O neg: universal donor
- AB pos: universal recipient
- Rh factor: dominant allele

Nx Tip: See the "Genetics" chapter. It is important to understand the basics of genetics for blood typing and certain diseases.

Blood Component Changes

- Leukocytosis: increase in WBC
- Erythrocytosis: increase in RBC
- Thrombocytosis: increase in platelets
- Pancytopenia: universal decrease of blood components

Blood Dyscrasias

- Changes in the complete blood count (CBC)
- Typically an adverse effect of a medication

Disseminated Intravascular Coagulation (DIC)

Pathophysiology

- Minor trauma causing platelets to be used up
- Complication of sepsis

Signs and Symptoms

- Abnormal bleeding: oozing from IV sites (patient complaining of wetness on arm or dried blood)
- Bleeding can be external and internal.
- Prolonged aPTT and PT/INR

Interventions

- Treat the underlying problem (stop the bleed).
- Platelets and FFP

Thallasemia

Pathophysiology
- Genetic blood disorder
- Abnormal RBCs

Signs and Symptoms
- Anemia
- Bone deformities, dark urine, jaundice

Interventions
- Pharmacological
- Blood transfusions
- Bone marrow transplant

Hemophilia

Pathophysiology
- Genetic bleeding disorder caused by a lack of factor VIII
- Hemophiliacs do not bleed any faster than normal, but they clot slower.
- X-linked recessive disorder (affects men more than women)

Signs and Symptoms
- Spontaneous bleeding
- Prolonged coags
- Long-term joint destruction

Interventions
- Inpatient: bleeding precautions with factor VIII infusions
- Avoid activities with a high risk of trauma (contact sports).
- Peripheral injuries do not warrant an ER visit.
- Central injury (organs) or head injury warrants an ER visit.

Anemias

Aplastic Anemia
- Production issue: bone marrow not producing
- Renal failure: lack of erythropoietin
- High-dose radiation or chemotherapy: destruction of bone marrow
- Chloramphenicol and gold components used for RA treatment
- Treat with epoetin alfa, transfusions.
- Look for increase in reticulocyte count (baby RBCs).

Hemolytic Anemia
- Destruction issue: RBCs being lysed/sliced
- Bilirubin is released when hemoglobin is destroyed.
- Elevated bilirubin leads to hemolytic jaundice.

Sickle Cell Anemia
- RBCs coagulate: Cells become rigid and crescent shaped when not oxygenated.
- Leads to capillary obstruction: pain
- Most common in African American women
- Sickle cell crisis (medical emergency)
- First nursing intervention is fluids, then treat pain.

Pernicious Anemia
- Deficiency of B12 (cobalamin) and lack of stomach cell intrinsic factor
- Sore red tongue, easy bruising
- B12 injections needed in postgastrectomy patients

Iron Deficiency Anemia
- Common in intestinal disorders
- Supplements (take with vitamin C for absorption)
- Take iron on empty stomach and never with milk.
- May supplement with foods high in iron (leafy greens, meats)

Immunology

Humoral immunity: Antibodies or immunoglobulins (gained by colostrum and breast milk at birth)

Acquired immunity: Learned by infection or vaccination

Cell-mediated immunity: B and T cells (problem in HIV/AIDS)

Herd immunity: Indirect protection when the majority of a population is vaccinated

Allergies

Pathophysiology
- Histamine response to a harmless trigger
- Triggered by food, environment, animals, etc.

Signs and Symptoms
- Seasonal allergies (allergic rhinitis)
- Atopic dermatitis
- Anaphylaxis (airway risk)
- Allergy testing (intradermal, patient must stay at the clinic immediately after injection; every visit)

Interventions
- Antihistamines (diphenhydramine, fexofenadine)
- EpiPen (IM injection may be given through clothes)

Vaccinations

The NCLEX removed vaccination scheduling years ago, so luckily you are no longer required to memorize when (at what age) each vaccination is due. Focus on what type of person the vaccinations are administered to and why.

Hepatitis A
- Two rounds

Hepatitis B
- Three rounds

Varicella (Chickenpox)/Herpes Zoster (Shingles)

- Typically given in older age
- Live vaccine (cannot be given to immunocompromised)
- In shingles, the virus reactivates in the ganglia (nerves), leading to pain first, then a rash forms.
- If a patient comes in saying they never had chickenpox, no matter the age, do not think shingles; think actual chickenpox (isolation room).

Tdap (Tetanus, Diphtheria, and Pertussis)

- Every 5 years
- Booster tetanus shots given for patients at risk (dirty open injury)
- DTaP vaccine given up to age 7; Tdap is a booster for adolescents and adults.

Hib (Haemophilus influenzae Type B)

- Every year
- Attenuated virus
- Can be given IM to immunocompromised, but not nasally
- Also helps prevent upper respiratory issue in children (epiglottitis)
- Allergy alert (eggs)
- Injection reaction normal (small fever, pain at the injection site)

Human Papillomavirus (HPV)

- Boys and girls (during adolescence)
- Prevents cervical, oropharyngeal, and anal cancers

Pneumococcal

- Every 5 years
- High risk populations (immunocompromised, elderly)

Meningococcal

- Every 3–5 years
- High risk populations (immunocompromised, elderly)
- People living in tight quarters
- Dorms (college)
- Service members (military)
- MSM population (men who have sex with men)

Measles, Mumps, Rubella (MMR)

- Live vaccine (cannot be given to immunocompromised)
- Cannot be given to pregnant women (administer after delivery)

Autoimmune Disorders

Autoimmune diseases are characterized as the body attacking itself.

Systemic Lupus Erythematosus

Pathophysiology
- Commonly affects African Americans and women
- Systemic disease affecting multiple organs (heart, lungs, skin, liver, kidneys, nervous system)

Signs and Symptoms
- Systemic inflammation
- Pericarditis
- Butterfly rash, photosensitivity, fatigue
- Sjogren's syndrome (dry mouth, dry eyes)

Interventions
- Steroids, immunomodulators

Additional Autoimmune Disorders

Rheumatoid Arthritis
- See the "Musculoskeletal" chapter.

Myasthenia Gravis
- See the "Neurosensory" chapter.

Guillain-Barre Syndrome
- See the "Neurosensory" chapter.

Graves' Disease
- See the "Endocrinology" chapter.

Hashimoto's Thyroiditis
- See the "Endocrinology" chapter.

Crohn's Disease
- See the "Gastrointestinal" chapter.

Kawasaki's Disease
- See the "Pediatrics" chapter.

Immune Disorders

Graft-Versus-Host Disease
- Potential complication from stem cell or bone marrow transplantation
- Occurs when the transplanted cells attack the host's body tissues
- Do not confuse with transplant rejection.

Transplant Rejection

- Occurs when the host attacks the transplanted cells
- Early sign of rejection is fever and elevated WBC (pay close attention).
- Rejection will manifest with signs and symptoms of organ dysfunction.

Nx Tip: An example of an organ beginning to fail is oliguria in a post-kidney transplant patient. The most important thing that you can be on the lookout for is a fever.

Human Immunodeficiency Virus (HIV) and Acquired Immunodeficiency Syndrome (AIDS)

Pathophysiology

- Retrovirus: integrates into the DNA of the host CD4 cell (T cell)

Signs and Symptoms

- Flu-like (early signs of seroconversion)
- Elevated viral load (undetectable is the goal)
- Decreased CD4 count (less than 200 means AIDS)
- Monitor for signs of comorbidities due to the medications (liver and kidneys).
- Opportunistic infections in AIDS (pneumocystis jirovecii, Kaposi's sarcoma—purple, black lesions)

Interventions

- Pre-exposure prophylaxis (PrEP) given to high risk individuals at risk for infection
- PrEP also given to newborns birthed by an HIV-positive mother
- Post-exposure prophylaxis (PeP) given to healthcare workers who get stuck by a needle (administered within 48 hours)
- Antiretroviral medication
- Vaccinations (pneumonia, flu, meningitis)

Nx Tip: A pregnant woman can give birth to an HIV-negative baby. As a precaution, the baby will be bathed immediately, before the Vitamin K injection, and will also receive a few weeks of antiretroviral medication.

Urinary Incontinence

Pathophysiology

- Stress incontinence
  - Poor closure of sphincter muscles
  - Common during laughing or coughing
- Urge incontinence
  - Overactive bladder causing loss of function
- Nocturnal enuresis (bed-wetting)

Signs and Symptoms

- Dribbling
- Urgency/frequency
- Poor control

Interventions

- No caffeine, no alcohol (stress incontinence)
- Kegel exercises (pelvic muscle)
- Urination schedule (urinate every 2 hours)
- Pharmacological (tolterodine)

Nx Tip: Never restrict things from your patients without an order; an answer choice indicating to restrict without an order will never be the right answer on the NCLEX. Do not have the patient use a bedpan if they are perfectly capable of walking to a bedside commode or a bathroom with assistance. Do not restrict water or food without an order. Facilitate the best outcome of ADLs for your patient within the realm of their diagnosis. Critically think, "What can I do for my patient here?"

Male Considerations

Balanitis

- Inflammation of the glans (head) of the penis

Epididymitis

- Inflammation of epididymis within the scrotal sac
- Scrotal pain (do not confuse with testicular pain)

Epispadias/Hypospadias

- Congenital at birth
- Epispadias: abnormal urethral opening on top (dorsal) of penis
- Hypospadias: abnormal urethral opening on bottom (ventral) of penis
- Tissue from a circumcision is saved and used to create the new urethra.
- Catheter will hold urethra open after surgery.

Testicular Torsion
- Scrotal twisting causing obstruction of spermatic cord
- Medical emergency: lack of blood flow

Hydrocele/Varicocele
- Hydrocele: painless fluid around testicle
- Varicocele: enlarged vein in scrotum

Cryptorchidism
- Undescended testicles
- Ensure the room is warm during assessment.
- Not of large concern at birth
- Increased risk for testicular cancer later in life

Phimosis
- Foreskin of uncircumcised penis too tight to retract and expose glans
- Prevented by circumcision

Inguinal Hernia
- Bowel bulges through inguinal canal into groin.

Nx Tip: Female considerations are covered in the "Obstetrics/Gynecology" chapter.

Benign Prostatic Hyperplasia (BPH)

Pathophysiology
- Enlargement of the prostate
- Normal as a male ages
- May squeeze the urethra

Signs and Symptoms
- Difficulty with urination

Interventions
- Monitor for worsening symptoms.
- Saw palmetto (an herbal supplement)
- Transurethral resection of the prostate (TURP)
  - Continuous bladder irrigation (CBI)
  - Pink output normal and good; red output bad
  - Normal for fluid to leak around the catheter
  - Monitor for no output; may lead to medical emergency rupture of the bladder.
  - Retention of urine or semen increases risk for cystitis.

Nx Tip: Prostate cancer is covered in the "Oncology" chapter.

Urinary Tract Infection (UTI)

Pathophysiology
- Bacteria leading to urethritis, cystitis, nephritis
- Urinary stasis may cause a UTI.
- More common in women
  - Shorter urethra
  - Urethra closer to anus
- Indwelling catheters may cause a UTI (CAUTI).

Signs and Symptoms
- Dysuria/polyuria
- Bacteriuria
- Cloudy urine (color may be charted by UAP)
- Possible level of consciousness (LOC) changes in the elderly

Interventions
- Antibiotics
- Push fluids (2–3 L/day).
- Cranberry juice
- Education for girls (wipe from front to back)

Pyelonephritis

Acute
- UTI has worked up to kidneys.
- Flank/costovertebral (lower back) pain, fever

Chronic
- Due to repeated UTIs

Urine Testing

Urinalysis/Dipstick Test
- Normal specific gravity (SG) range: 1.005–1.035
  - Higher SG: more concentrated (dehydrated)
  - Lower SG: more dilute (well hydrated)
- Color
  - Straw: acute kidney injury
  - Amber: dehydrated
  - Clear: well hydrated
  - Red: hematuria

- Bacteriuria
- Calciuria
- Proteinuria
  - Nephrotic/nephritic syndrome
  - Preeclampsia
- Ketonuria
- Hematuria
- Glucose

Creatinine Clearance Test

- Not sterile
- Discard the first void, collect after.
- 24-hour collection
- Goes in jug on ice

Urine Culture

- Sterile collection (may be delegated to LPN even if through catheter)
- Always culture before giving antibiotics.
- Draw urine from the port of a catheter if indwelling in place (do not collect from bag).

Post-Streptococcal Glomerulonephritis

Pathophysiology

- Occurs after a strep infection
- Inflammation of the kidneys

Signs and Symptoms

- Edema
- Proteinuria
- Hypertension

Interventions

- Supportive treatment (antihypertensives, diuretics, ACE inhibitors)
- Steroids (sometimes immunosuppressants)

Nx Tip: Post-streptococcal glomerulonephritis is similar to nephritic/nephrotic syndrome, which is covered in the "Pediatrics" chapter, as it is more common in that patient population.

Sexually Transmitted Infections

Chlamydia

- Bacterial
- Discharge/dysuria
- In men: may lead to sperm damage, scarring, permanent infertility
- In women: may lead to pelvic inflammatory disease
- Pelvic inflammatory disease (PID)
  - May lead to infertility
  - Lower abdominal pain

Herpes

- Viral
- Painful clustered lesions (vesicular sores)
- Herpes simplex (cold sores)

Genital Warts

- Caused by the HPV virus
- May have cryotherapy or be surgically removed

Human Papillomavirus (HPV)

- Technically a sexually transmitted infection (STI)
- Vaccine for boys and girls prevents STI/cancer.
- Does not need to be reported to the state department

HIV

- See the "Immunology" chapter.

Syphilis

- Bacterial
- Primary, secondary, tertiary (infects the brain, leading to dementia)
- Painless sore (chancre)

Trichomoniasis

- Parasitic infection of the vagina
- Foul-smelling discharge
- No symptoms typically in men, but males can spread the infection.

Kidneys

Anatomy/Physiology

- Kidneys maintain body homeostasis of water, sodium, potassium, and other minerals.
- Renin-angiotensin-aldosterone system (RAAS) regulates blood pressure.
- Production of erythropoietin stimulates RBC production in the bone marrow.

Polycystic Kidney Disease

- Inherited disease
- May spread throughout the body
- May lead to need for transplantation

Acute Kidney Injury

Pathophysiology

- Sometimes called Acute Renal Failure (ARF)

Signs and Symptoms

- Decreased urine output
- Elevated creatinine/BUN (azotemia)

Interventions

- Four phases:
  1. Onset phase
  2. Oliguric phase
  3. Diuretic phase
  4. Recovery phase

Causes of Acute Kidney Injury		
Prerenal	**Intrarenal**	**Postrenal**
■ Perfusion to the kidneys interrupted ■ Low BP, shock, hypovolemia ■ Obstruction ■ Abdominal aortic aneurysm (Triple A) repair graft failure	■ Nephritis ■ Tumor ■ Contrast (CT/MRI) ■ Medications (toxicities)	■ Obstruction issues (urine cannot get out) ■ Kidney swells ■ Nephrolithiasis ■ Benign prostatic hypertrophy (BPH)

End-Stage Renal Disease (ESRD)/Chronic Kidney Disease

Pathophysiology

- Worsening kidney function over time
- Leading causes: hypertension and diabetes

Signs and Symptoms

- Decrease in glomerular filtration rate (GFR%)
- Oliguria or anuria (normal) in ESRD
- Uremic frost (scalp)
- Azotemia
- Anemia
- Fluid volume overload
- Electrolyte imbalances (hyperkalemia, hypocalcemia)

Interventions

- Pharmacological
- Peritoneal dialysis
  - Continuous ambulatory
  - May cause peritonitis (pink or bloody discharge)
  - Dialysate is clear (goes in clear, should come out clear).
- Hemodialysis
  - Fistula takes months to mature (for use).
  - No BP cuff on the extremity
  - Auscultate for a bruit.
  - Palpate for a thrill.
  - Disequilibrium (too much fluid removed too fast) – hypotension
  - Contraindicated in hemodynamically unstable patients
- Transplant

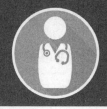

Osteomyelitis

Pathophysiology

- May be an acute or chronic infection
- Severity often depends on skeletal location.
- Bones with extensive vasculature at higher risk (femur, tibia)
- Common in diabetics

Signs and Symptoms

- Elevated WBC, fever, pain
- CT/MRI
- Bone malformation (tissues destroyed around infection)
- Poor wound healing

Interventions

- Long-term antibiotic therapy
- PICC line or central line catheter commonly used
- Amputation may be necessary.

Nx Tip: Central lines are covered in more detail in the "Basic Care and Comfort" chapter.

Musculoskeletal Inflammations

Tendonitis

- Swelling of the tendons due to repeated motion

Epicondylitis

- Tennis elbow

Ankylosing Spondylitis

- Vertebral inflammation

Bursitis

- Bursae within synovial joints

Lyme Disease

- Mimics arthritis
- Caused by ticks
- Bullseye rash

Gout

Pathophysiology

- Uric acid build-up in the blood
- Leads to formation of crystals
- Crystals deposited in certain joints
- A form of arthritis

Signs and Symptoms

- Redness and swelling
- Joint pain (big toe [podagral] and knee)
- Arthrocentesis (tophi visualized in synovial fluid)

Interventions

- Low purine diet (no seafood, no meats)
- Weight loss
- NSAIDs
- Pharmacological (colchicine, allopurinol)

Osteoarthritis (OA)

Pathophysiology

- Degenerative loss of cartilage
- Often unilateral, depending on physical use and stress
- Risk factors: age, obesity, occupation, and genetics

Signs and Symptoms

- Joint pain upon movement and pressure
- Joint stiffness (give patient time to warm up, especially in the morning)
- Joint grating upon movement (crepitus)
- Bouchard's nodes, Heberden's nodes
- X-ray confirmation

Interventions

- Swimming and other low-impact exercises
- Heat/cold therapy
  - Heat for comfort
  - Cold for pain or swelling
- Weight loss
- Pharmacological (NSAIDs, acetaminophen)
- Joint replacement surgery

Rheumatoid Arthritis (RA)

Pathophysiology

- Autoimmune disorder
- Typically bilateral

Signs and Symptoms

- Redness and swelling
- Joint pain upon movement
- Joint stiffness (give patient time to warm up, especially in the morning)
- Most common in hands and wrists (deformity)
- Rheumatoid nodules (hard bumps under skin)
- May lead to inflammation around the lungs and heart
- May lead to osteoporosis and carpal tunnel syndrome
- Positive rheumatoid factor in blood
- X-ray confirmation

Interventions

- Pharmacological (immunomodulators, steroids, NSAIDs)
- Heat/cold therapy

Osteopenia/Osteoporosis

Pathophysiology

- Decrease in bone density
- Osteoclasts break down bone faster than osteoblasts form.
- Risk factors:
  - White, Asian, postmenopausal women
  - Long-term steroid use
  - Alcohol, smoking, sedentary lifestyle
  - Hyperthyroidism
  - Excessive intake of carbonated beverages
  - Aging

Signs and Symptoms

- Abnormal fracturing of bones
- Kyphosis (stooped posture)
- Losing height during aging
- DEX/DEXA scan showing bone loss (specific type of x-ray)

Interventions

- Reduce fall risk.
- Pharmacological (estrogen, bisphosphonates, calcium with vitamin D)
- Weight-bearing exercises

Fractures

Pathophysiology

- Simple (closed) – does not penetrate the skin
- Compound (open) – penetrates the skin
  - Risk for fat embolism syndrome
  - Risk for infection
  - Risk for compartment syndrome (if in long bone such as femur)
- Spiral
  - Often the result of child abuse
  - Confirm the story matches the injury.
- Comminuted
  - Crush injury
  - Multiple small pieces of bone
  - Surgery with rod placement may be needed.
- Spinal
  - Airway and neck protection first
  - Put on a neck brace.
  - Only do a jaw-thrust maneuver to open the airway.
  - May move the patient once C-spine is cleared

Signs and Symptoms

- Pain and swelling
- Possible cramping
- X-ray confirmation

Interventions

- Bone may need to be re-aligned (reduction or fixation).
- Cast immobilization
- Surgery (titanium rods and screws)
- RICE protocol:
  - Rest (reduce swelling)
  - Ice (vasoconstriction, reduce swelling)
  - Compress (reduce venous pooling)
  - Elevate (reduce venous pooling)

Nx Tip: Although the RICE protocol is an intervention for musculoskeletal injuries, it is good behavior for anyone after injury or trauma.

Bone Deformities

Rickets

- Vitamin D deficiency
- Genu varum (bowing of the legs)

Paget's Disease

- Malformation of bone
- Typically isolated in a few bones

Scoliosis

- Curvature at the middle of the spine
- Risk in preteen and teenage girls
- Assess by forward bend test.
- Thoracolumbosacral orthosis (TLSO) brace
  - Must be worn the entire day, except while in the shower
  - Do not use lotion underneath; wear a cotton t-shirt under brace.

Kyphosis

- Curvature at the top of the spine (thoracic)
- More common in elderly

Lordosis

- Curvature at the bottom of the spine (lumbar)
- Risk in pregnant women

Traction

Indications for Use

- Corrects broken bone or spinal pressure issues
- Skeletal traction (on bone)
- Skin traction (Buck's traction)
- Bryant's traction (pediatrics for hip or femur)

RN Considerations

- Assess skin and pin sites for skin breakdown, infection.
- Neurovascular checks (distal pulses, sensation, movement, color)
- DO NOT touch any piece of traction (this cannot be delegated either)
- Turn the patient per physician orders
  - Q2hr specific orders required
  - Logroll if needed (do not delegate; however, LPN or UAP may assist if RN is present)
- Isometric exercises to prevent muscle atrophy
  - Flexion and relaxation of the muscle without movement

Halo Vest

Indications for Use

- Cervical spine (neck) injuries
- Must be worn continuously
- Skin and pin site assessment by RN
- Lined with sheepskin to prevent skin breakdown
- Prioritize safety.
- Sponge baths needed
- Lie on the back during sleep.

Rhabdomyolysis

Pathophysiology

- Rapid breakdown of muscle (skeletal muscle)
- Crush injury
- Medications (statins)
- Medical emergency

Signs and Symptoms

- Extreme quick onset of pain
- Kidney failure (myoglobinuria – urine is brownish color)
- Elevated creatine kinase, D-dimer, hyperkalemia
- Urinalysis

Interventions

- IV fluids
- Treat the signs and symptoms.

Compartment Syndrome

Pathophysiology

- Build-up of pressure in the third-space around the artery
- Pressure eventually occludes blood flow.
- Crush injury, orthopaedic casts, burns
- Loss of limb (medical emergency)

Signs and Symptoms

- Loss of distal pulses
- Extreme pain
- Swelling of the extremity

Interventions

- Fasciotomy (incision into the muscle to relieve pressure)
- Remove the cast (bivalve cast removal performed by HCP, not RN).

Rehabilitation

Physical Therapy

It is proven the sooner a patient ambulates after a surgery, the better the outcome. Decrease post-op risks like atelectasis/pneumonia, DVT, and UTI by engaging physical therapy consultations.

- Gross motor movement
- Range of motion (ROM) to prevent atrophy
- Post-ortho surgery

Occupational Therapy

- Fine motor skills/dexterity
- Ability to write
- Using silverware
- Common post-CVA

Speech Therapy

- Speech post-CVA
- Swallowing exams (dysphagia)

Surgeries/Procedures

Arthroscopy/Arthroplasty

- Joint visualization/joint replacement
- Destruction of the joint
- Trauma, tumor, infection
- Post-op considerations
  - Physical therapy
  - Monitoring for signs of infection

Hip Replacement

- Hip fractures and/or pain
- Post-op considerations
  - Head of bed (HOB) max at 45 degrees
  - No adduction (inward) movement
  - Utilize abduction pillow to prevent this.
  - Call surgeon if joint dislocated

Amputation

- Trauma, compartment syndrome, tumors
- Frostbite, diabetic ulcers, chronic pain
- Post-op considerations
  - Elevate the stump (immediately after surgery).
  - Prone position after 24 hours (prevent contractures)
  - RICE protocol
  - Do not use heat (bleeding risk).
  - Transplant/prosthesis (protect the stump)

Burn Trauma

Pathophysiology

- 1st degree (sunburn, radiation burn, superficial)
- 2nd degree (blistering, partial thickness)
- 3rd degree (through dermis, potential nerve damage, full thickness)
- 30% or more is a medical emergency.
- Third-spacing of fluid
- Destruction of cells leads to hyperkalemia.

Signs and Symptoms

- Hypovolemia → hypotension
- Shock (circulatory collapse)
- Hyperkalemia (PVCs)

Interventions

- Monitor vitals and heart rhythm.
- Fluid resuscitation (most important)
  - Parkland formula: 4 × patient's weight in kg × % burned = number of mL
- Lactated Ringer's infusion
- Albumin infusion
- Look for adequate urine output (sign of improvement).

The Rule of Nines

If an NCLEX question displays any type of patient burn, think of the rule of nines as detailed in the following graphic. Ask yourself, "Is this a medical emergency?" To find the answer to that question, do the math using this graphic.

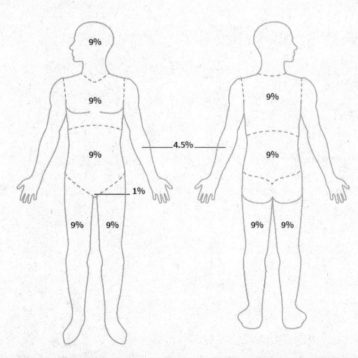

Nx Tip: Do not get confused by the rule of nines. If an NCLEX question says the left arm, that means 9%. If a question says the anterior aspect of the right arm, that means 4.5%. Read very carefully.

Assistive Devices

Crutches

- Stairs: up with the good leg, down with the bad leg
- Crutches in same hand when sitting to standing position
- Save a little room below the armpit to prevent axillary nerve damage.
- Patient must have upper body strength (issue in elderly).
- Patient must have ability to make fists (clench the hand).

Canes

- Cane goes in the opposite hand from the affected extremity.
- If left leg is the injured limb, then cane is in right hand.

Walkers

- Trauma, compartment syndrome, tumors
- Do not place tennis balls on legs.

Lobes of the Brain

Temporal Lobe	Occipital Lobe	Parietal Lobe
▪ Auditory, language (Broca's area), memory	▪ Vision	▪ Motor cortex, depth perception
Frontal Lobe	**Brain Stem**	**Cerebellum**
▪ Personality, emotions	▪ Breathing, heart rate	▪ Balance, coordination

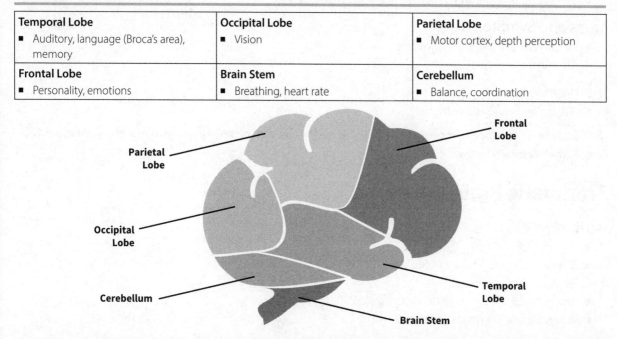

Nx Tip: Broca's area is found on the left side of the brain. If damaged, it often leads to aphasia (difficulty articulating words).

Cranial Nerves

It would be rare for the NCLEX to specifically call out how to assess for each of the twelve cranial nerves; however, it is a good idea to memorize the names of them at minimum. By simply recognizing the name, you can oftentimes understand what it does. Utilizing mnemonics is an easy way to memorize.

- Olfactory (I)
- Optic (II)
- Oculomotor (III)
- Trochlear (IV)
- Trigeminal (V)
  - Trigeminal neuralgia (tic douloureux)
  - Facial pain (avoid hot and cold)
- Abducens (VI)
- Facial (VII)

- Vestibulocochlear (VIII)
- Glossopharyngeal (IX)
  - Important in swallowing (dysphagia risk)
- Vagus (X)
- Accessory (XI)
- Hypoglossal (XII)
  - Important in swallowing (dysphagia risk)

Encephalopathy

Pathophysiology

- Overarching term for disorders or dysfunction of the brain
- Wernicke-Korsakoff syndrome
- Depletion of vitamin B1, oftentimes upon drinking alcohol

Signs and Symptoms

- Abnormal eye and body movements
- Confusion, delirium

Interventions

- Treat the underlying condition.

Nx Tip: Many encephalopathy disorders are discussed in other sections of the book, such as *hepatic encephalopathy* in the "Gastrointestinal" chapter.

Traumatic Brain Injury

Pathophysiology

- Concussion
- Coup-contrecoup injury (whiplash)
- Shaken baby syndrome
- Intracranial hemorrhage (leads to stroke)
- Brain herniation (leads to brain death)

Signs and Symptoms

- Intracranial pressure (ICP)
  - Normal (5–15 mmHg)
- Pupillary dilation
  - PERRLA (pupils equal, round, and reactive to light and accommodation)
  - Blown pupils (unilateral or bilateral)
  - Fixed and dilated pupils (patient has expired)
- Headache, nausea, vomiting
- Cushing's triad (medical emergency)
  - Apnea
  - Bradycardia
  - Widening pulse pressure (systolic minus diastolic)
- Glasgow Coma Scale (LOC)

Eye Opening	Motor Response	Verbal Response
- Spontaneous opening	- Follows commands	- Oriented
- No eye movement	- Decorticate/decerebrate posture	- No verbal response
	- No movement (flaccid limbs)	

- States of alertness (LOC):
  - 15 (awake)
  - 8 (coma)
  - 3 (brain death)
- Noxious stimuli (LOC testing)
  - Vocal stimulation
  - Tactile stimulation (good for infants)
  - Sternal friction rub
  - Lunula pressure (fingernail or toenail)

Nx Tip: Do not confuse the Glasgow Coma Scale with mental status. The patient may be alert and delirious at the same time.

Interventions

- Concussion/contrecoup
  - Do not let the patient sleep.
  - Acute memory loss is common.
  - Mental rest
  - Avoid physical activity.
- ICP
  - Semi-Fowler's position
  - No suctioning
  - Prevent agitation, coughing, sneezing, pain.
  - Hyperventilation (alkalosis shrinks the brain)
  - Pharmacology (mannitol)
  - Induced hypothermia (often performed after a patient survives a Code Blue)
  - Sedation (induced coma)
  - Surgical evacuation (craniotomy)

Basilar Skull Fracture

Pathophysiology

- Blow to the head resulting in posterior skull break
- May cause a leak of cerebrospinal fluid (CSF)
  - Nose (rhinorrhea)
  - Ears (otorrhea)
- Risk for meningitis

Signs and Symptoms

- Battle's sign (bruising behind the ear)
- Raccoon eyes (bruising around the eyes)

Interventions

- Management of bleeding and CSF leakage
- Typically resolves on its own

Cerebrovascular Accident (CVA) and Transient Ischemic Attack (TIA)

Pathophysiology

- CVA (stroke) is a medical emergency.
- TIA (mini-stroke) is not a medical emergency.
- Hemorrhagic stroke (bleeding)
- Ischemic stroke (lack of oxygen or blood flow)
- Leads to anoxic brain injury
- Risk factors:
  - Atrial fibrillation
  - Hypertension
  - Obesity
  - Hyperlipidemia
  - Diabetes mellitus
  - Smoking

Signs and Symptoms

- Headache ("worst of their life")
- Permissible hypertension (high BP expected in this case)
- Hemi issues (loss of sensation and motor function on one side)
- Loss of vision on one side (hemianopia)
- Speaking problems (aphasia)
- Signs and symptoms may reflect the lobe affected.

Interventions

- Immediate CT or MRI
- Prevention (blood thinners, carotid endarterectomy)
  - Risk for stroke or bleeding post-endarterectomy
- Tissue plasminogen activator (tPA)
  - Only for ischemic stroke
  - Must be given within the golden window (3–4 hours)
  - Risk for bleeding
- Craniotomy (evacuation of bleeding or clot)

Stroke Rehabilitation

- Heightened care during immediate recovery (continuous monitoring, help with ADLs, etc.)
- Place usable objects in the dominant hand.
- Speak slow and clear (no reason to yell).
- Do not lift the patient by the weak shoulder (it can dislocate).
- Physical therapy, occupational therapy, speech therapy

Cerebral Palsy and Bell's Palsy

Pathophysiology

- Caused by trauma to a developing brain

Signs and Symptoms

- Cerebral palsy
  - Movement disorder
  - Spasticity, rigid muscles
  - Scissor or pigeon-toed gait
  - Potential sensory problems
- Bell's palsy
  - Facial paralysis (typically one-sided)
  - Caused by dysfunction of the facial nerve (VII)
  - Do not confuse with stroke; Bell's is only the face.

Interventions

- Cerebral palsy
  - Pharmacological (baclofen pump)
  - Therapy and orthotic devices (crutches)
  - Surgery (rhizotomy – spinal surgery severing causative nerves)
- Bell's palsy
  - Steroids
  - Patients typically recover within weeks.

Meningitis/Encephalitis

Pathophysiology

- Trauma to the cranium or abnormal exposure to the CNS
- Inflammation of the meninges (dura, arachnoid, pia) and/or brain
- Viral (West Nile, rabies)
- Bacterial (much more serious)
  - Neisseria meningitis (meningococcal)
  - Vaccination exists.

Diagnostics

- Lumbar puncture
  - Patient lying on side with the knees up to the chest, chin in neutral position
  - Manometer (pressure measurements)
  - Supine for 4 hours after to prevent spinal headache
- Blood tests
  - Cultures (always culture before antibiotics)
  - Inflammatory markers (C-reactive protein)

Signs and Symptoms

- Fever and headache
- Nuchal rigidity (neck)
- Petechial rash (meningococcal)
- Brudzinski's sign/Kernig's sign
- Level of consciousness changes
- Opisthotonic posturing (arched back) → call the HCP

Interventions

- Droplet precautions
- Antibiotics
- Antivirals
- Reduce stimuli.
- Seizure precautions (if warranted)

Spinal Cord Injuries (SCI)

Pathophysiology

- Partial or complete distal loss of function below the point of injury
  - Sensory
  - Autonomic

Nx Tip: Refresh yourself on the autonomic nervous system and the fight-or-flight response. It is important to recognize the signs and symptoms, along with potential complications, such as hyperglycemia.

- Brown-Séquard syndrome
  - Incomplete SCI (hemi)
  - More common in stab wounds

Signs and Symptoms

- Cervical
  - High cervical (breathing issues, death)
  - Low cervical (quadriplegia)
- Thoracic
  - Strength of upper limbs (brachial-plexus)
  - Reduced cough reflex and strength
  - Paraplegia (may affect abdominal muscles)
- Lumbar
  - Weakness of lower limbs
  - Bladder retention/bowel incontinence
  - Sexual dysfunction
  - Cauda equina syndrome (disk herniation causing severe back pain, immediate decompression of nerves necessary – medical emergency)
- Sacral
  - Bladder retention/bowel incontinence
  - Sexual dysfunction

Interventions

- Immediate immobilization
  - Clear the C-spine (may move the patient after).
  - Logroll for q2hr turning (do not delegate).
- Pharmacological (steroids)
- Traction (covered in more detail in the "Musculoskeletal" chapter)
- Surgery

Complications

- Spinal shock
  - Temporary loss of function
  - Not a medical emergency (no BP involvement)
  - Function will return over time (purposeful, not twitching).
- Neurogenic shock
  - Medical emergency
  - Hypotensive and bradycardic
  - Body cannot compensate as usual.
- Autonomic dysreflexia
  - Medical emergency
  - Hypertensive crisis, hyperthermia (diaphoresis)
  - Headaches, bradycardia, anxiety
  - Triggered by bowel impaction and bladder retention
  - Perform a straight cath, enema, laxatives, digital removal of fecal matter.

Spinal Stenosis

Pathophysiology
- Narrowing of the spinal cord
- More common in elderly

Signs and Symptoms
- Pain
- Paresis
- Paresthesias

Interventions
- Physical therapy
- Laminectomy
  - Surgical decompression
  - Bone graft from the iliac crest

Nx Tip: Be able to count the lumbar spine. On the NCLEX, you may be asked to "hot spot" where the fusion is occurring in a laminectomy procedure. You do not need to memorize the count of all the vertebrae of the spine, but the lumbar are important. The first lumbar vertebra begins directly after the last floating rib.

Seizure Disorders

Pathophysiology
- Causes
  - Epileptic – no trigger
  - Febrile – fever
  - Infections of the brain (meningitis)
  - Severe "natremic" changes
  - Anoxic brain injury (also called cerebral hypoxia or hypoxic-anoxic injury or HAI)
  - Traumatic brain injury (TBI)
  - Phenylketonuria (PKU)
  - Eclampsia
  - Pharmacological
  - Delirium tremens (alcohol withdrawal)
  - Benzodiazepine withdrawal

Signs and Symptoms
- Partial seizures (singular part of the brain)
- Generalized seizures (both hemispheres)
- Absence seizures
  - Loss of consciousness
  - Person appears awake.
  - Seconds to minutes
- Tonic-clonic (grand mal) seizures: convulsions, muscle spasms, relaxing (clonic)
- Status epilepticus
  - Seizure followed by another seizure (repeated)
  - Medication necessary to break cycle

Diagnostics
- Electroencephalogram (EEG)
  - Shampoo hair in the morning.
  - Non-painful (no discomfort)
  - No caffeine, no stimulants before procedure
  - No sedation needed

Interventions
- Monitor the seizure
  - Start time
  - Duration
  - Severity
  - Stage/phase
- Seizure precautions
  - Pad the side rails.
  - Protect the head.
  - Put nothing in the mouth.
  - Do not hold the patient down.
  - Turn sideways only if patient aspirating.
- Pharmacological (benzodiazepines, anticonvulsants)

Neuromuscular Disorders

Multiple Sclerosis

Pathophysiology

- Autoimmune disorder destroying the myelin sheath
- Relapsing-remitting (comes and goes)
- Progressive
- No cure

Signs and Symptoms

- Fatigue, weakness, vision changes

Interventions

- Pharmacological (disease-modifying)

Amyotrophic Lateral Sclerosis (ALS)

Pathophysiology

- Lou Gehrig's disease
- Begins in adulthood
- No cure

Signs and Symptoms

- Upper and lower motor dysfunction
- Sensory and cognitive function intact (locked-in syndrome)
- Progressive motor weakness and atrophy
- Dysarthria, dysphagia (red flag – prioritization)
- Respiratory compromise
- Death

Interventions

- Early: pharmacological (treat symptoms)
- Late: ventilator support

Huntington's Disease

Pathophysiology

- Genetic (autosomal)
- More common in women
- No cure

Signs and Symptoms

- Choreiform movements (rapid)
- Progresses similar to ALS
- Cognitive changes (mood swings, dementia)

Interventions

- Pharmacological (treat symptoms)

Parkinson's Disease

Pathophysiology

- Decreased dopamine levels in the brain
- Degenerative/progressive
- No cure

Signs and Symptoms

- Tremors
  - Typically worse at rest
  - Purposeful movements improve tremors.
- Bradykinesia/dyskinesia
  - Parkinsonian gait (shifting gait)
  - March-in-place and then begin to walk
- Facial weakness
  - Smiling, blinking
- Dysphagia
- Cognitive changes (dementia, depression)

Interventions

- Physical and occupational therapy
- Pharmacological
- Deep brain stimulation

Myasthenia Gravis

Pathophysiology

- Autoimmune neuromuscular disease
- Attacks nerves blocking acetylcholine (motor function)
- More common in women
- Often triggered by infection and/or medications

Nx Tip: Refer to the "Motor Neurons and Glands" chapter for an overview of acetylcholine and what it is responsible for.

Signs and Symptoms

- Facial weakness
  - Ptosis (eyelid droop)
  - Diplopia (double vision)
  - Dysphagia
- Muscle weakness that improves with rest
- Diaphragmatic weakness
  - May lead to myasthenic crisis (medical emergency)
  - Intubation may be necessary.

Diagnostics

- Tensilon (edrophonium) test
  - Used to distinguish between myasthenic crisis and cholinergic crisis
- Blood test for antibodies attacking acetylcholine

Interventions

- Pharmacological
- Surgical (thymectomy – may cure)

Guillain-Barre Syndrome

Pathophysiology

- Autoimmune disorder destroying myelin sheath
- Acute and reversible
- Quick onset
- May be triggered by infection

Signs and Symptoms

- Peripheral loss of sensation and function
- Moves centrally, eventually affecting the diaphragm
  - Breathing problems
  - Medical emergency (intubation)

Interventions

- Plasmapheresis to remove antibodies destroying the nerves
- Protect the breathing and wait it out (time heals).
- Physical therapy (rehab)

Nervous System Syndromes

Raynaud's Syndrome

Pathophysiology

- Rapid vasospasms of the arterioles (fingers and toes)
- Often caused by stress and cold
- Typically benign

Signs and Symptoms

- Discolorations
  o Pallor (white)
  o Cyanosis (blue)
  o Rubra (red)
- Paresthesias (tingling, pain, numbness)

Interventions

- Reduce stress (physical and mental).
- Stop smoking.
- Wear mittens/gloves when outdoors in cold.
- Sympathectomy (removal of causative nerves)

Carpal Tunnel Syndrome

Pathophysiology

- Median nerve compression of the wrist
- May be caused by repetitive motion (occupational hazard)

Signs and Symptoms

- Paresthesias (numbness and tingling)
- Pain
- Phalen's maneuver
  o Flexing the wrist to elicit symptoms
- Tinel's sign
  o Percuss over the median nerve (wrist)

Interventions

- Rest and splinting
- Steroids
- Surgery

Sensory Organs

Eyes

Aqueous humor: fluid in the eye

Cone cells: for color vision

Rods: for black-and-white vision

Eye Drop Administration

- Do not directly drop on the cornea (may cause damage).
- Do not place the applicator on the eye.
- Administer in the lower conjunctival sac.
- Have the patient look up.
- Absorption occurs at tear ducts.
  o Inner canthus palpation may be used.

Snellen Chart

- Measures visual acuity
- 20/20: perfect vision
- 20/40: sees at 20 feet what a normal person can see at 40 feet

Ophthalmological Problems

- Nystagmus: abnormal movements of the eyes (twitching)
- Diplopia: double vision
- Strabismus: crossed eyes
- Amblyopia: lazy eye (place patch over good eye to strengthen the weaker one)
- Myopia: nearsighted
- Hyperopia: farsighted

Glaucoma

Pathophysiology

- Increased intraocular pressure (IOC)
- May lead to permanent vision loss (optic nerve damage)

Signs and Symptoms

- Loss of peripheral vision
- Tonometry: pressure above 20

Interventions

- Pharmacological: Avoid antihistamines.
- Reduce pressure causative factors.

Macular Degeneration

Pathophysiology

- More common in elderly

Signs and Symptoms

- Loss of central vision field
- Scotomas (vision field loss)

Interventions

- Sweep head when walking (to avoid running into things).
- Pharmacological
- Laser therapy
- Surgery

Nx Tip: Avoid hydroxychloroquine; it may lead to macular or corneal toxicity.

Cataracts

Pathophysiology

- Blurring (cloudy) lens
- Common in aging
- Common in diabetes mellitus

Signs and Symptoms

- Decreased visual acuity
- Loss of vision in certain fields

Interventions

- Surgical removal (outpatient)
  - No anesthesia
  - Patch placed for 24 hours
  - Protect the eye from trauma.
  - Nausea expected post-op

Retinal Detachment

Pathophysiology

- Medical emergency (loss of sensory organ)

Signs and Symptoms

- Flash of light
- Veil or "curtains" pulled over visual field

Interventions

- Surgery (vitrectomy, retinopexy)
  - Place patient on side of detachment post-op.
  - Continue to monitor for signs of complications.

Ears

- Tympanic membrane (ear drum)
  - Normally pinkish/pearly gray
  - Barotrauma can lead to rupture (infection risk).
- Middle ear bones
  - Malleus (hammer), incus (anvil), stapes (stirrups): amplify/conduct sound to the inner ear
  - Oval window

Ear Drop Administration

- Must be an external ear issue
- Tilt the head to the side, administer in ear, and place cotton to hold.

Assessment

- Pull auricle down for children.
- Pull auricle up for adults.
- Conductive hearing loss (middle ear)
- Sensorineural hearing loss (inner ear)
- Weber test (vibrating tuning fork on forehead)
- Rinne test (vibrating tuning fork behind ear)

Ear Infections

Otitis Interna/Labyrinthitis/Vestibular Neuritis

- Vertigo, tinnitus, nausea, vomiting

Otitis Media

- Common in children
- Crying, pulling at ear, poor sleep
- Do not feed infants sideways.

Otitis Externa (Swimmer's Ear)

- Ear pain (tragus), pulling at ear
- Ear drops needed

Meniere's Disease

Pathophysiology

- Disorder of the inner ear

Signs and Symptoms

- Sensation of fullness of the ear
- Vertigo, tinnitus, hearing loss

Interventions

- Decrease salt intake (avoid Chinese food)
- Motion sickness meds (scopolamine, Dramamine)

Neurological Pain Disorders

Pain Assessment

- Pain assessment before pain med administration (ADPIE)
- Pain is subjective (it is what the patient says it is).

- Types of pain
  - Nociceptive (tissue damage)
  - Neuropathic (pain by nerve damage)
- PQRST (pain assessment method)

Nx Tip: *Pain* is not the answer to a priority question unless the pain is associated with a medical emergency. Remember Maslow's hierarchy.

Chronic Pain Conditions

Migraine Headaches

Pathophysiology

- Often caused by triggers
- Typically affects one side of the head

Signs and Symptoms

- Phases
  - Prodromal
  - Aura (changes in vision)
  - Headache (photophobia, blurred vision, nausea, vomiting, pain)
  - Post-headache (fatigue)

Interventions

- Pharmacological (beta blockers, pain meds)
- Reduce triggers.

Fibromyalgia

- Affects women more than men
- Heightened level of sensation (pain and pressure)
- Sufferers often experience anxiety, depression, and/or PTSD.

Chronic Back Pain

- Common result of spinal diseases

Anesthesia

Levels of Anesthesia

- General
  - Managed by an anesthesiologist or certified registered nurse anesthetist (CRNA)
  - Total unconsciousness
  - Patient NPO before
  - Paralytic ileus common after use (absent bowel sounds)
  - Complete paralysis of the patient
- Moderate (conscious sedation)
  - Inhibits anxiety and pain
  - Anterograde amnesia (inability to form new long-term memory)
  - Managed by registered nurses
- Local
  - Blocks nerve impulses to specific areas (nerve block, spinal block, epidural)
  - Performed by anesthesiologist or CRNA

Nx Tip: Barbiturates are occasionally used for moderate sedation to inhibit anxiety and pain. However, they are highly addictive. The prototype is phenobarbital.

NPO Rules for Surgeries and Procedures (8 or 12 hours)

There are multiple reasons a patient may be NPO medically. The following list is only for procedures.

- General anesthesia
- Upper or lower GI series (CT, x-ray, barium swallow, barium enema)
- Upper or lower GI scopes (EGD, colonoscopy)

Malignant Hyperthermia

Pathophysiology

- Medical emergency
- Caused by general anesthesia and other medications
- Overactive stress on skeletal muscle

Signs and Symptoms

- Hyperthermia (103° or higher)
- Tachycardia
- Tachypnea

Interventions

- Pharmacological (dantrolene)

Post-Anesthesia Care Unit (PACU)

- Priority assessment (ABCs, vitals)
- Risk for self-extubation (restraints may be needed)

Oncology

Cancer/Tumor/Neoplasm Assessment

Generally speaking, cancer presents with the bold hallmarks listed below. This is not a surefire rule, but for the NCLEX, it is a solid benchmark. For example, if you are palpating a swollen painful lymph node, it is a sign of infection rather than cancer.

Asymmetrical versus symmetrical

Immobile versus mobile

Non-painful versus painful

Hard versus soft

Undifferentiated versus differentiated

Staging

TNM System

T - Primary tumor (Tis = Carcinoma in situ)

N - Nodal involvement

M - Metastasis

Size	Origin	Benign/Metastatic

- The higher the stage, the poorer the prognosis.
- Stages I, II, III: fairly isolated cancer with possible neighboring growth
- Stage IV: metastasis to organs and tissues far from the origin

Family history is always a risk factor for cancer, but also be aware of environmental or demographic information such as smoking or occupation. Some cancers are simply rare for the age of the patient, such as an 85-year-old female who is worried about breast cancer; it is unlikely, but not impossible.

Leukemias

Types of Leukemia	
Acute lymphocytic leukemia: Children: ages 4–12	**Acute myelogenous leukemia:** Adults
Chronic lymphocytic leukemia: Adults	**Chronic myelogenous leukemia:** Adults

Pathophysiology

- Bone marrow proliferation
- Elevated number of WBCs (100,000)

Signs and Symptoms

- Infections
- Lymphadenopathy (swollen lymph nodes)
- Fever
- Blood dyscrasias (thrombocytopenia)

Diagnostics

- CBC
- Lymph node biopsy
- CT/MRI (check for metastasis)

Interventions

- Chemo, radiation
- Pharmacological
- Bone marrow transplant
  - Hospital stay (weeks), neutropenic precautions

Lymphomas

Pathophysiology

- Lymphatic cell proliferations
- Commonly spreads if not caught early

Signs and Symptoms

- Lymphadenopathy
- Night sweats
- Fatigue

Diagnostics

- CBC
- Lymph node biopsy
- CT/MRI (check for metastasis)

Interventions

- Chemo, radiation
- Pharmacological
- Surgery

Nursing Consideration

Radiation Burns

- Superficial; think sunburn
- Wear loose-fitting cotton.
- No ice to treat
- Nothing too hot on skin; avoid sunlight (protect skin)
- Warm water and soap (no lotions or powders)
- Steroid cream may be needed (call HCP).

Brain Tumors

Pathophysiology

- Commonly secondary to a tumor in other locations (usually lungs)

Signs and Symptoms

- Tumor location important (lobe symptoms)
- Headache, seizures, behavioral changes, etc.

Diagnostics

- CT/MRI

Interventions

- Chemo, radiation
- Surgery

Pituitary Tumors	Transsphenoidal Hypophysectomy
- Understand hormones - Hormonal imbalances (thyroid, ADH, etc.) - Surgical cure (hypophysectomy)	- Tumor is pulled out through nose - Nose is packed post-op - No blowing of the nose - Potential risk for CSF drainage (monitor nasal drip for halo or glucose)

Osteosarcoma (Bone Cancer)

Pathophysiology

- Commonly a metastasis

Signs and Symptoms

- Pain
- Unexpected fractures
- Hypercalcemia (may become a medical emergency: hypercalcemic crisis)

Diagnostics

- Biopsy
- CT/MRI

Interventions

- Chemo, radiation
- Pharmacological (methotrexate)
- Surgery

Skin Cancer

Pathophysiology

- Burning as a child dramatically increases risk.
- UV light (sun, tanning beds)
- Strong familial component
- Melanoma is often confused with seborrheic keratosis, a benign skin condition.

Signs and Symptoms

- Melanoma: dark irregular edges (spreads fast)
- Squamous cell carcinoma: relatively benign (common in older age)
- Basal cell carcinoma: relatively benign (common in older age)

Diagnostics

- Biopsy
- CT/MRI (check for metastasis)

Interventions

- Chemo, radiation
- Immunotherapy
- Surgery

Nx Tip: Do not confuse skin cancer with sun spots (solar lentigo) in older adults, which are a normal sign of aging.

Lung Cancer

Pathophysiology

- Smoking (large risk)
- Occupational exposure (toxins, smoke)
- Most common cause of cancer deaths

Signs and Symptoms

- Hemoptysis (coughing up blood)
- Dyspnea (shortness of breath)
- May lead to an airway problem (ABC)

Diagnostics

- Bronchoscopy with biopsy

Interventions

- Chemo, radiation
- Surgery

Oropharyngeal Cancer (Throat Cancer)

Pathophysiology

- HPV virus
- Smoking, alcohol
- Fairly curative, higher recurrence rates

Signs and Symptoms

- Dysphagia
- Hoarseness of voice
- Lump in the throat

Diagnostics

- Bronchoscopy with biopsy

Interventions

- Remove risk factors.
- Surgical resection
- Chemo, radiation
  - Treat mouth ulcerations (stomatitis) with saline solutions; do not use anything alcohol-based.

Colorectal Cancer

Pathophysiology

- Risk factors:
  - Obesity/sedentary lifestyle
  - Inflammatory bowel disease
  - African American
  - Smoking/alcohol use
  - Dietary fat intake/processed foods/red meats
- Highly curable if caught early

Signs and Symptoms

- Rectal bleeding
- Abdominal cramping

Diagnostics

- Colonoscopy with biopsy (preventative at age 50)
  - Bowel prep with polyethylene glycol (GoLYTELY)
  - Diarrhea with liquid stool normal for prep
  - NPO before the procedure (8–12 hours)
  - Moderate sedation for procedure (midazolam)
  - Anterograde amnesia is the goal (forget the procedure).
  - Monitor respiratory rate and vitals.
- Sigmoidoscopy
- Fecal occult blood test (guaiac test)
  - No vitamin C (ascorbic acid) before; may cause a false positive

Interventions

- Chemo, radiation
- Surgery
- Targeted therapy (pharmacological)

Pancreatic Cancer

Pathophysiology

- High incidence of metastases
- High mortality rate
- Often linked to smoking and alcohol

Signs and Symptoms

- Abdominal pain possibly radiating to the back
- Weight loss
- Jaundice (biliary involvement)

Diagnostics

- CT/MRI/ultrasound

Interventions

- Pancreatoduodenectomy (Whipple surgery)
- Chemo, radiation

Gallbladder Cancer

Pathophysiology

- Fairly uncommon, but curative
- Commonly caused by cholecystitis/cholelithiasis

Signs and Symptoms

- Nausea and vomiting
- Jaundice
- Porcelain gallbladder

Diagnostics

- Ultrasound
- Cholangiopancreatography (MRCP) with biopsy

Interventions

- Cholecystectomy

Pheochromocytoma (Adrenal Cancer)

Pathophysiology

- Occurs in the medulla of the adrenals
  - Abnormal secretion of catecholamines (adrenalin)
- Relatively rare

Signs and Symptoms

- Sympathetic responses (fight or flight)
- Hypertension possibly leading to crisis (systolic above 180)
  - Headaches and blurred vision
- Hyperglycemia

Diagnostics

- Blood tests
- CT/MRI
- PET scans

Interventions

- Surgery
- Pharmacological (phentolamine)

Prostate Cancer

Pathophysiology

- Most common cancer in older men
- Very curable when caught early

Signs and Symptoms

- Elevated PSA level (higher level means poorer outcome)
- Hematuria

Diagnostics

- PSA levels and digital rectal exams (secondary prevention – screening)
- Begins at age 45 in men
- Never palpate before drawing a PSA level.
- Cystoscopy
- Biopsy

Interventions

- Chemo, radiation
- Transurethral resection of the prostate (TURP)
  - Post-op continuous bladder irrigation (CBI)
  - Pink (serosanguinous) is good; red (sanguineous) is bad.
  - Irrigation input must come out (bladder could rupture).
  - 2 L of input must yield 2 L of output.

Testicular Cancer

Pathophysiology

- Very curable
- Most common type of cancer in younger men

Signs and Symptoms

- Lumps
- Testicular pain
- Gynecomastia (male breasts)
  - Due to increase in human chorionic gonadotropin (hCG)

Diagnostics

- Ultrasound
- Blood
- Urine test for hCG (same as pregnancy test)

Interventions

- Prevention (self-examination in the shower)
- Surgery (orchiectomy)
- Chemo, radiation

Breast Cancer

Pathophysiology

- Leading cancer deaths in women
- Highly metastatic
- Risk factors:
  - BRCA genes
  - Early first menstruation
  - Hormonal contraceptive use

Signs and Symptoms

- Lumps in the breast tissue
- Lymph involvement in the armpit
- Nipple inversion
- Peau d'orange breast tissue

Diagnostics

- Mammography
  - Preventative beginning at age 40, then every 2 years
- Biopsy

Interventions

- Self-examination (three middle fingers apply pressure in circular motion)
- Chemo, radiation
- Surgery
  - Radical mastectomy (removes lymph tissue)
  - Peripheral lymphedema (elevate the extremities)
  - No blood draws or blood pressure on affected extremities
- Pharmacological
  - Anti-estrogens (tamoxifen)

Ovarian Cancer

Pathophysiology

- Commonly metastatic
- Risk factors:
  - Hormonal contraceptives
  - No children
  - Early first menstruation
  - Polycystic ovarian syndrome

Signs and Symptoms

- Often asymptomatic in the beginning
- Symptoms vary greatly.

Diagnostics

- Blood tests
- Transvaginal ultrasound

Interventions

- Chemo, radiation
- Surgery (oophorectomy)
  - Unilateral: no hormone replacement needed
  - Bilateral: hormone replacement needed (especially if young in age)

Endometrial Cancer

Pathophysiology
- Most common after menopause
- More common in women who have never been pregnant (nullipara)
- Large risk in hydatidiform molar pregnancies

Signs and Symptoms
- Vaginal bleeding

Diagnostics
- Biopsy with dilation and curettage (D&C)

Interventions
- Hysterectomy
  - Radical (removal of ovaries) will induce menopause (hormone replacement likely).
- Chemo, radiation

Nx Tip: A hydatidiform molar pregnancy, a false pregnancy with a mass of cells (not a fetus), carries a very large risk for post-evacuation endometrial cancer. The patient MUST NOT get pregnant within 1 year. Levels of hCG will be drawn to show if the cancer is spreading. If the woman becomes pregnant, the pregnancy would mask the cancer growth.

Cervical Cancer

Pathophysiology
- HPV virus known to cause (vaccinate)

Signs and Symptoms
- Asymptomatic in the beginning
- Vaginal bleeding
- Pain during sexual intercourse

Diagnostics
- Pap smear/biopsy
  - Diagnostic or screening
  - Screening typically begins at age 21, then every 3–5 years, depending on risk.
  - Dysplasia: abnormal growth of cells but not necessarily cancerous yet
- CT/MRI

Interventions
- Chemo, radiation
- Surgery
- Cesium isotope procedure (brachytherapy)
  - Vaginal spotting normal
  - Patient may stand up and shower if order allows; monitor for bleeding.
- Radium implant (brachytherapy)
  - Frequent rotation of staff to avoid radiation exposure over time (family not included)
  - Pregnant healthcare workers cannot take care of these patients.
  - Dosimeter use (calculates exposure)
  - Bedrest (implant could dislodge upon standing)
  - Patient to avoid persons for 3–5 days or keep distance (6 feet)
  - Use separate bathrooms as family members.

Chemotherapy

Adjuvant Therapy
- After radiation or surgery to destroy what cancer is left
- Prevent recurrence

Neoadjuvant Therapy
- Before surgery or radiation to minimize the size of the tumor
- Tumor may be in dangerous territory.

Tumor Lysis Syndrome

Pathophysiology

- Occurs due to cancer treatment
- Lysis (to destroy or break up)

Signs and Symptoms

- Hyperkalemia (cardiac dysrhythmias)
- Hyperuricemia
- Hypocalcemia
- Acute kidney injury

Interventions

- Hemodialysis

End of Life Care

Hospice

- Provides end of life care to terminal patients
- If the patient improves (unlikely), they will be discharged.
- Includes bereavement services for the family for 1 year

Palliative

- Comfort care
- Not thinking about curing anymore; focus is on providing comfort
- May start oxygen if the patient is short of breath
- No IV fluids necessary; dehydration is a normal process of death
- Question orders from HCPs that contradict end of life care.

Post-Mortem Care

- Leave dentures in.
- Allow family to help if they want.
- Keep head of bed elevated.
- Close eyelids.
- Leave in lines and devices if an autopsy is ordered.
  - Suicide
  - Crime related (gunshot, etc.)
  - Family requested
- Do not touch a deceased Muslim patient (if not a Muslim yourself).

Nx Tip: Do not confuse palliative care with hospice care. *Palliative* simply means comfort care. While it is commonly related to end of life care, it could be used for a patient who requires that level of care without death necessarily being in the near future.

DSM Manual

- How psychiatric disorders are diagnosed
- A collection of symptoms

Nx Tip: Pathology exists when the disorder affects patient lives to the point where they cannot keep up with basic ADLs (work, dressing, feeding, etc.).

Anxiety/Panic Disorders

Pathophysiology

- Common in other mental illnesses (depression, bipolar)
- Gamma-aminobutyric acid (GABA)
  o Inhibitory neurotransmitter
  o Excitability, speed of thought
- Generalized anxiety disorder (GAD)
  o Chronic (6 months or more)
  o Can lead to other problems (phobias, etc.)

Signs and Symptoms

- Anxiety
  o Increased focus
- Panic attacks
  o Loss of control, focus
  o Loss of peripheral vision
  o Tremors, palpitations, shortness of breath
  o Feelings of dread or dying
- Social anxiety disorder
  o Irrational anxiety
  o Self-consciousness
  o Fear of judgment/embarrassment
- Phobias
  o Agoraphobia: open spaces, situations, environments
  o Acrophobia: heights
  o Claustrophobia: enclosed spaces (common in CT/MRI scans)

Interventions

- Rule out underlying medical causes (hyperthyroidism).
- Benzodiazepines, antidepressants
- Non-pharmacological
  o Therapy (cognitive behavioral, psychotherapy)
  o Lifestyle factors (caffeine, stress)
  o Biofeedback
  o Desensitization therapy (phobias)

Kübler-Ross Stages of Grief

- Denial
- Anger
- Bargaining
- Depression
- Acceptance

Obsessive Compulsive Disorder

Pathophysiology

- Family history
- Child abuse

Signs and Symptoms

- Obsessions: repeated thoughts leading to anxiety
- Compulsions: repeated acts to alleviate
- Fatigue

Interventions

- Inpatient
  - Do not interrupt compulsions (allow time to complete)
- Behavioral therapy
- Pharmacological (anxiolytics, antidepressants)

Nx Tip: Focus on short-term versus long-term goals. What is realistic in your patient? If the patient was just admitted, it will be different than if they are near discharge. TIME PROXIMITY strategy here. Read questions carefully.

Post-Traumatic Stress Disorder (PTSD)

Pathophysiology

- Traumatic events
  - Wartime
  - Gunshot victims
  - Abuse
- Child abuse
- Attacks often trigger episodes (tire popping, music, etc.).

Signs and Symptoms

- Feelings and thoughts rehashing the traumatic event
- Acute anxiety
- Suicide risk

Interventions

- Inpatient
- Psychosocial needs (assess patient feelings – ADPIE strategy)
- Therapy (group or individual)
- Pharmacological

Nx Tip: If the patient is violent, wait until they calm down to initiate anything; it is important to use de-escalation principles. Shift intervention method from a show of force to a show of support.

Dissociative Identity Disorder

Pathophysiology
- Two or more personalities
- Often caused by trauma (abuse)

Interventions
- Therapy
- Pharmacological

Signs and Symptoms
- Multiple personalities
- Memory lapses
- Often in combination with other psych disorders

Somatic Symptom Disorder

Pathophysiology
- No medical reason for symptoms
  - Diagnosis of exclusion
- Anxiety related to symptoms
- Chronic (6 months or more)

Signs and Symptoms
- Conversion disorder
  - Losing body operation (loss of vision or senses, limb function)
- Hypochondriasis
  - Constant worrying of serious illness
- Social anxiety disorder
  - Viewing oneself in a negative way (poor self-image)
- Malingering
  - Conscious creation, manipulation of symptoms to receive care or sympathy
- Munchausen syndrome
  - Unconscious manipulation of symptoms
  - By proxy – making up an illness or injury or causing in another person (oftentimes a child, an elderly adult, or a person with a disability)

Interventions
- Rule out medical causes.
- Therapy (group or individual)
- Pharmacological

Sleep Disorders

Pathophysiology
- Somnipathy
- Diagnosed by polysomnography (sleep study)
  - Similar to an electroencephalogram (EEG)

Signs and Symptoms
- Narcolepsy
  - Daytime sleepiness
  - Cataplexy (acute loss of muscle strength resulting in potential collapse)
- Sleep apnea
  - Common in obese patients
  - Apneic episodes at night
  - CPAP often used
- Sleepwalking
  - Potential safety issue
- Night terrors

Interventions
- Monitor for symptoms affecting safety.
- Pharmacological
- Assess for potential underlying causes (medical).

Mood Disorders

Dysthymic Disorder

Pathophysiology
- Often undiagnosed for many years
- Patients typically think feeling this way is normal.

Signs and Symptoms
- Chronic feelings of unhappiness (melancholy)
- Often none of the larger depression symptoms (insomnia, anorexia)

Interventions
- Antidepressants

Major Depression

Pathophysiology

- Decrease in serotonin (mood neurotransmitter)
- Decrease in dopamine (secondary mood neurotransmitter)

Signs and Symptoms

- Lack of motivation
- Insomnia, anorexia, sadness
- Anhedonia (lack of pleasure from things that used to give pleasure)

Suicidal Thoughts (thinking)	Suicidal Ideation (planning)
<ul><li>Psychosocial needs</li><li>Explore thoughts and feelings if the patient expresses them</li><li>Assess first</li><li>Giving away valuables</li><li>Assess any suicide plan</li><li>Admission not warranted yet</li></ul>	<ul><li>Medical emergency (requires admission, involuntary if need be)</li><li>Suicide precautions (no metal silverware, no trash bags, no phone cords, etc.)</li><li>Suicide contract (person expresses some small piece of hope for the near future)</li><li>Highest risk for suicide is older men and teenagers</li></ul>

Nx Tip: Do not confuse anorexia with anorexia nervosa. The word *anorexia* simply implies that the patient either has no appetite or is not currently eating. Technically an NPO person is anorexic (unless they have tube feedings).

Interventions

- Antidepressants
- Therapy
- Electroconvulsive therapy (ECT)
  - Last resort
  - Contraindicated if the person is on meds for osteopenia/osteoporosis
  - Post-procedure memory loss is normal; patient safety is key.

Bipolar Disorder

Pathophysiology

- Mania versus hypomania (depression)
- Comorbid psych disorders common
- Substance abuse, psychosis, depression

Signs and Symptoms

- Mania (a crisis, assist the patient in ADLs)
- Hyperactivity, unfocused mood with poor sleep
- Delusions of grandeur (inflated self-worth)

Interventions

- Mood stabilizers, antipsychotics
- Therapy
- If manic, provide finger foods (even if they sound unhealthy; input is input)

Psychotic Disorders

Schizophrenia

Pathophysiology

- Often undiagnosed for many years
- May be seen as early as adolescence

Signs and Symptoms

- Disorganized thinking (1 + 2 = cat)
- Positive affective
  - Delusions (thoughts)
  - Hallucinations (sensory)
- Negative
  - Depression, social withdrawal, flatness of mood
- Paranoid
- Catatonic
  - Waxy flexibility (remains in the same position)
  - Be sure to put the patient back the way you found them.

Interventions

- Antipsychotics
- Therapy

Nx Tip: If the patient is hallucinating, it is not appropriate to necessarily ground them in reality; however, you should not encourage the false reality either. Focus on assessing how the patient feels about their reality in that moment. It is real for them.

Nx Tip: When dealing with patients in acute stages of difficulty or trouble, be sure to focus on a therapeutic response. They do not have the cognitive ability at this moment to hear what you are saying. You must physically take them to do something, such as escorting them back to their room.

Cognitive Disorders

Mental Status Assessment

- Alert and oriented (person, place, time, situation)
- Appearance (clean, disheveled)
- Mood (affect)
- Thought process (judgment)
- Mini–mental state examination (MMSE) to assess dementia

Down Syndrome (Trisomy 21)

Pathophysiology

- Added chromosome
- Leads to degrees of mental retardation

Signs and Symptoms

- Intelligence quotient
  - 40 to 60: Provide task delegation (occupations).
  - Below 40: Provide ADL assistance.

Interventions

- Special education
- Assess the degree of help needed.

Dementia

Pathophysiology

- Chronic progressive
- Alzheimer's (most common type)
- No cure
- Risk factors:
  - CVA/TIA
  - Tertiary syphilis
  - AIDS
  - Parkinson's
  - Huntington's
  - Brain tumor

Signs and Symptoms

- Progressive loss of memory
  - Minor (forgetfulness)
  - Moderate (planning and judgment)
  - Severe (memory, ADLs)
- May progress to changes in mood and motor skills
- Confabulation (creating a story to fill in blanks in memory)

Interventions

- Pharmacological to slow progression
  - If the patient refuses medication, come back in 15 minutes.
- Geropsychiatric units
- Focus on patient safety (flight, elopement risk)
  - Room close to the nurses' station
  - Seclusion (may lock door)

Delirium

Pathophysiology

- Acute reversible
- Temporary loss of cognition typically due to an underlying medical cause such as
  - UTI in the elderly
  - Hypoxia
  - Renal failure
  - Hepatic encephalopathy/hepatic coma
  - Alcohol withdrawal

Signs and Symptoms

- Alert but loss of orientation

Interventions

- Treat the underlying condition.

Substance Abuse

Alcohol	Cannabis	Cocaine
<ul><li>Sedative</li><li>Depressant</li></ul>	<ul><li>THC oil commonly used in chemo/seizure patients</li></ul>	<ul><li>Stimulant</li><li>Vasospastic MI</li><li>Prinzmetal's angina</li></ul>
Special K/PCP	**Opioids**	**Methamphetamines**
<ul><li>Sedative</li><li>Depressant</li><li>May cause hallucinations</li></ul>	<ul><li>Heroin/prescription pain pills</li><li>Most commonly abused drug in the U.S.</li><li>Usage<ul><li>May lead to overdose (naloxone needed)</li><li>Pinpoint pupils</li><li>Respiratory depression</li></ul></li></ul>	<ul><li>CNS stimulant</li><li>Weight loss</li><li>Skin and teeth issues</li></ul>
LSD		**Inhalants**
<ul><li>Causes hallucinations</li><li>May cause future relapses (drug sits in the spine)</li></ul>	<ul><li>Withdrawal<ul><li>Muscle pain</li><li>Dilated pupils</li><li>Coughing and sneezing</li></ul></li></ul>	<ul><li>May cause hallucinations</li><li>Leads to brain damage</li></ul>

Delirium Tremens

Pathophysiology

- Alcohol withdrawal
- Chronic alcohol abuse
- Abrupt stop in use

Signs and Symptoms

- Shaking, diaphoresis, nausea
- Hallucinations
- Hyperthermia and seizures
  - Medical emergency

Interventions

- Benzodiazepines
- Remove stimuli.
- Fluids
- Trend blood alcohol content

Benzodiazepine Overdose/Toxicity

Pathophysiology

- Fat-soluble medication
  - Absorbs into the adipose tissue and can lead to a dangerous build-up
  - Obese patients and the elderly are specifically at risk.
- Chronic benzo use can lead to dependency and withdrawal similar to alcohol withdrawal.

Signs and Symptoms

- Loss of cognition (delirium)
- Respiratory depression/CNS depression
- Coma

Interventions

- Strict monitoring (Glasgow Coma Scale, vitals)
- Titration off benzos
- Antidote (flumazenil)

Nx Tip: Do not confuse a substance overdose with a substance withdrawal. It is impossible for someone to go through withdrawal if they currently are using the drug.

Drug Rehab/Psych Unit

Goals

- Just admitted: get the patient out of the room
- Middle admission: participation in something
- Late admission: running an activity (group leader)

Enforcing Unit Policy

- Focus on strict but polite communication.
- Patients require structure.

Subjective Versus Objective Improvement

- Expected outcomes or goal setting for psych patients
- Focus on the factual answer.
- Feelings and emotions from patients are subjective responses.

Milieu Environment

- Calming

Eating Disorders

Anorexia Nervosa

Pathophysiology

- Low self-esteem
- Body image issues

Signs and Symptoms

- Malnourishment
  - Skinny
  - Emaciated (severe)

Interventions

- Therapy
- Dietary consult
  - Improvement is weight gain (factual objective answer).
- Inpatient
  - Monitor meals (1–2 hours after meals – avoid purging).

> **Nx Tip:** Maslow's hierarchy says physiological needs are priority. While the need for nutrition is physiological, an anorexia nervosa patient would only be a priority if he or she was emaciated. Simply being underweight does not make the patient a priority.

Bulimia Nervosa

Pathophysiology

- Low self-esteem
- Body image issues
- Stress

Signs and Symptoms

- Binge eating followed by throwing up
- Scarred knuckles
- Dental caries (cavities)
- Bad breath (halitosis)
- Mallory-Weiss tears (esophagus)
  - May lead to bleeding

Interventions

- Therapy
- Pharmacological
- Inpatient
  - Monitor meals (1–2 hours after meals – avoid purging).

Restraints

Violent Use

- Patient is at risk for self-harm or harm to others.

Non-Violent Use

- Patient is pulling at lines or tubes.
- Endotracheal intubation
- Elopement

If the patient is threatening to kill someone, they must be admitted. Homicidal or suicidal ideation warrants an admission, either voluntary or involuntary. If a patient is threatening a singular person, it is necessary to contact that person. It is not a breach of HIPAA.

Nx Tip: Restraints are warranted when the patient is at risk of committing violent acts against themselves or other people. Be sure to read questions about using restraints carefully and assess if this person is simply being verbally abusive or if the behavior transfers into a physical act.

Hostile Patients (Verbal or Physical)

- Verbal hostility does not warrant restraints; it warrants secluding the patient and talking to them.
- Physical hostility:
    - In the presence of others but no physical contact, safely remove everyone from the vicinity of the hostile patient and stay with them near the door. Attempt to calm the patient.
    - Safety is the priority; protect the other patients and yourself.
    - The RN may call security when the situation cannot be controlled or if the situation is anticipated to escalate.

Types of Restraints

- Chemical/medical (haloperidol, lorazepam)
- Posey vest (dementia) – prevents sitting too far up in bed
- 4-point leather (all limbs)
- One-to-one supervision (RN may begin without order)
- Soft restraints (RN may begin without order)
- Soft mitts (RN may begin without order)
- Four side rails (RN may begin without order)
- Seclusion (RN may begin without order)

Nx Tip: When initiating one of the restraints without an order, the RN must have assessed the situation and within his or her judgment found restraints to be necessary for safety. The RN must document the need, then call the physician to obtain the order immediately.

Documenting Use of Restraints

- Spot checks
  - o Every 15–30 minutes
  - o Can be delegated to UAP
  - o If patient is sitting up, assess if the patient needs something (water).
  - o Does the patient need to be upgraded or downgraded to a different level of restraint?
- RN assessment
  - o Every 2 hours
  - o Assess skin integrity.
  - o Assess peripheral blood flow (two-finger test).
- New orders from HCP
  - o Every 24 hours
  - o Family must be notified.

Crisis Management

Phase One

- Confronted by a problem or situation
- Increased anxiety leading to problem solving and defense mechanisms

Phase Two

- Increasing discomfort and anxiety
- Disorganized coping begins.

Phase Three

- Increasing anxiety leading to panic
- Trial and error solving
- Patient withdraws (fight or flight).

Phase Four

- Violence
- Suicidal behavior
- Loss of control

Coping Mechanisms

- Assess the patient's ability to cope.
- Is it healthy or maladaptive?
- Sublimation: the act of transferring energy into a positive form of coping

Pediatrics

Med-Surg for Little People

Focus on the age of the child. What is appropriate for this age? Many times answer choices can be eliminated simply because they do not make sense for the age, such as positioning for assessment of an infant. Why click on an answer choice about sitting or standing when the patient is not old enough to do either?

Remember to focus on the med-surg component of the question first. The heart is the heart, the liver the liver; there are certainly special considerations for children, but it is still the human body. Do not complicate this matter. Rely on the underlying anatomy and physiology knowledge.

Remember, dosing is much smaller. Large formats of medications typically do not exist on pediatric floors for safety reasons. A large dose would hardly ever be needed.

Infant (birth–1 year)	Toddler (1–2 years)	Preschooler (2–4 years)
■ Solitary play	■ "No" is a normal response ■ Ignore the child during temper tantrums (this is the only time "ignore" is a correct answer). ■ Finicky eaters ■ Separation anxiety ■ Parallel play	■ Cooperative play
School-age (4–12 years) ■ Mimicking of behavior	**Adolescent (13–18 years)**	

Pediatric Vital Signs

Heart Rate

- Higher at birth; lowers during childhood
- Starts at 100–160 bpm

Blood Pressure

- Lower at birth; elevates during childhood
- Starts at 70/40 to 90/60

Respiratory Rate

- Higher at birth; lowers during childhood
- Starts at 40–60 RR

Temperature

- Does not change based on age

Denver Developmental Screening Test (DDST)

A DDST tests cognitive and behavioral problems in children, typically preschoolers. If an NCLEX question is talking about just a developmental test, it is likely they are referring to physical development, whereas a DDST has more to do with mental growth. Do not confuse the two.

Milestones

2–3 Months

- Holds neck up
- SIDS risk may be reduced.
- Crossed eyes disappear.
- Grasp reflex
- Smiling

6 months

- Teething (start with rice cereal)
- Moro reflex (startle) disappears (not a true milestone, but rather a physiological reflex).
- Sits upright with support
- Can roll over

9–12 months

- Cow's milk can be introduced at 1 year of age (enzyme present).
- Object permanence
  - Object exists even if it cannot be seen.
  - Peek-a-boo
- Babinski reflex (fanning of toes) disappears
- Monosyllabic words (*mama, dada*)
- Can grasp and pull
- Cannot push or build (block towers)
- Stands with support

14–16 months

- Two- to three-word sentences
- Push-pull toy appropriate (firetruck)
- Walking alone

24 months

- If not walking, a developmental delay (refer to physical therapy)
- If not talking (mute), a developmental delay (refer to speech therapy)
- Begin potty training if the child is ready (vocalizes needs).
  - Parents have enough time to help.
  - Child can sit still for at least 5 minutes.
- Builds a six-block tower

Nx Tip: Do not marry yourself to a milestone month. The numbers above are the points when it would be typically considered a delay if not seen. For example, many children teethe before 6 months, but they really should be teething by that time. If they are not, it warrants further investigation.

Tanner Stages

- Secondary sex characteristics during puberty
- Stage 1: pre-pubescent
- Stages 2–5: puberty; starts around age 13

Pediatric Growth

95th Percentile

- Obese child
- Begin with diet and exercise

5th Percentile

- Failure to thrive

Nx Tip: Anything between the 5th percentile and the 95th percentile is fine and normal.

Failure to Thrive

Organic

- Known physical or mental causes
  - GI dysfunction
  - Cystic fibrosis
  - Celiac disease

Inorganic

- Unknown or not having to do with medical issues
  - Poor access to food
  - Lack of knowledge (parents)
  - Not necessarily child abuse (unless food is deliberately restricted)

Fontanelles

Posterior Fontanelle

- Closes at 2–3 months

Anterior Fontanelle

- Closes at 18 months

Fontanelle Considerations

- If the child is mobile and fontanelles are open, there is a SAFETY risk.
  - Child wears helmet.
- Sunken fontanelle shows dehydration.
- Bulging fontanelle is normal during crying.
- Bulging fontanelle at rest indicates ICP issue.

Pediatric Safety

Seat Belts and Car Safety

- Rear-facing car seat (back seat of car)
  - Birth to 25 lbs and 2 years of age
- Forward-facing car seat (back seat of car)
  - 25–50 lbs and 2–5 years of age
- No car seat (back seat of car)
  - 50 lbs and 5 years of age
  - Booster seat needed if seat belt does not cross the chest
- Passenger side (front seat of car)
  - 80 lbs and 12 years of age

Sudden Infant Death Syndrome (SIDS)

- Leading cause of death in infancy
- Aspiration and suffocation
- Sleep safety:
  - Sleep on back
  - Nothing in the crib (no blankets, no toys, no bottles, no stuffed animals, etc.)
  - Sleep sack is okay (just the baby and whatever they are wearing)
- Avoid secondhand smoke.
- Bereavement support for parents in the event of a death

Illness in Children

Assessment of Pain in Children

- Infant
  - NIPS (Neonatal Infant Pain Scale)
  - FLACC pain scale (face, legs, activity, cry, consolability)
- Toddler/preschool
  - May believe pain is a form of punishment
  - Changes in behavior
  - May vocalize area
  - Guarding of injury
- School-age
  - FACES pain scale
- Adolescent
  - Numeric pain scale
  - Behavior changes (decrease in anger is a good sign)
  - Offer privacy.

Relieving Anxiety in Children

- Infant
  - Parents
  - Swaddling
  - Sucrose orally
- Toddler/preschooler
  - Parents
  - Distraction
- School-age
  - Education
  - Doll to display procedures
  - Allow them to touch medical devices.
  - Visualize the environment as a child.
- Adolescent
  - Maintain freedom.
  - Maintain privacy.
  - Allow peer involvement (online if need be).

Congenital Defects

Tetralogy of Fallot

Pathophysiology

- Cyanotic heart defect
- May cause blue baby syndrome

The Tetralogy	
Pulmonary Stenosis - Narrowing of the pulmonary vasculature - Leads to pulmonary hypertension ○ R-Sided HF if untreated	**Overriding Aorta** - Systemic blood pressure issues - Stronger pulse in one side of the body
Ventricular Septal Defect - Shunting of blood from side to side, causing poor blood oxygenation	**Right Ventricular Hypertrophy** - May lead to cardiomyopathy in the infant (R-Sided HF)

Nx Tip: There are different degrees of severity of Tetralogy of Fallot; not all infants have the worst cases that you typically hear about.

Signs and Symptoms

- Cyanosis
- Heart failure
- Failure to thrive
- Increased risk of upper respiratory infections

Interventions

- Tet spell: knee-to-chest positioning (helps oxygenation)
- Surgery
  - Typically performed in infancy
  - May require multiple surgeries
  - May cause valvular issues later in life

Neural Tube Defects

Pathophysiology

- Poor folic acid intake during pregnancy (1st trimester)
- Unclosed neural tube (near opening to the outside of the body)
- Spina bifida (four types):
  - Occulta (mildest and most common form; *occulta* means "hidden")
  - Closed neural tube defects
  - Meningocele (*ocele* means "outside of the body")
  - Myelomeningocele

Signs and Symptoms

- Encephalocele (deformity or sac protrusion of the brain)
- Hydrocephalus (excessive fluid in the brain; common comorbidity)
- Tuft of hair at base of spine (spina bifida)

Interventions

- Surgery
  - Multiple surgeries during aging are common.
  - Pre-op (prone positioning with moist sterile cloth to protect sac)
  - Post-op (prone or supine positioning; monitor for meningitis)

Hydrocephalus

Pathophysiology

- Abnormal collection of fluid in the cranium
- Common in infants with neural tube defects

Signs and Symptoms

- Bulging fontanelle (at rest, not during crying)
- Increased intracranial pressure
  - High-pitched crying
  - Irritability
- Can lead to brain damage and death

Interventions

- Ventriculoperitoneal shunt
  - Drains fluid (CSF) to the abdomen
  - Monitor ICP post-op.

Cleft Lip/Palate

Pathophysiology

- Opening in the lip and/or palate (roof) of the mouth

Signs and Symptoms

- Often no symptoms
- May cause upper respiratory problems (nasal)
- Benign defect, cosmetic

Surgical Intervention

- Pre-op
  o Sucking (feeding) ability is of concern.
  o Partial occlusion of the nipple is okay (feeding).
  o Upright sitting during feedings
  o Frequent burping (baby will swallow more air)
- Post-op
  o Prone positioning with the head to the side (to facilitate drainage)
  o Sterile normal saline to clean suture lining
  o Elbow restraints (to avoid suture damage)
  o Logan bow (holds lip and sutures together; wear continuously)
  o Feeding by bulb syringe into the cheek (no sucking yet)

Talipes Equinovarus (Club Foot)

Pathophysiology

- Congenital defect

Signs and Symptoms

- Internal rotation of the ankle
- Unilateral or bilateral

Interventions

- Initial surgery (may break the bone)
- Multiple casts to correct the deformity

Nx Tip: Think of the casting used for club foot as being similar to braces to correct teeth. Multiple casts are used over time to slowly correct the defect.

Tracheoesophageal Fistula

Pathophysiology

- Abnormal tunneling (fistula) between the trachea and esophagus
- Esophageal atresia

Signs and Symptoms

- Frequent coughing during feedings
- Cyanosis during feedings

Interventions

- NPO until surgery
- Surgical correction

Pediatric Med-Surg

Foramen Ovale

- Normal in utero
- Opening between right and left atria
- Shunting of blood bypassing lungs

Ductus Arteriosus

- Normal in utero
- Connection between pulmonary artery and aorta
- Shunting of blood bypassing lungs

Nx Tip: Foramen ovale and ductus arteriosus openings typically close after birth. If they do not close, it may lead to cyanotic problems in the baby. Surgery may be indicated to correct the opening.

Nephritic/Nephrotic Syndrome

Pathophysiology

- Similar to glomerulonephritis
- Dysfunction of the glomerulus (thin membrane)

Signs and Symptoms

- Hypertension
- Proteinuria
- Edema
  - May lead to pleural effusion (dyspnea)
  - Puffiness around the eyes
  - Ascites
- Hypoalbuminemia
- Hematuria (nephritic)
- Risk for abnormal clotting (DVT)

Interventions

- Reduce salt and potassium intake.
- Anti-inflammatories
- Anti-hypertensives

Reye's Syndrome

Pathophysiology

- Begins with a viral infection
  - o Chickenpox
  - o Flu
- Concurrent administration of aspirin during the viral infection

Signs and Symptoms

- Liver and brain dysfunction

Interventions

- Avoid aspirin

Kawasaki's Disease

Pathophysiology

- Autoimmune disorder
- Inflammation of the vessels (vasculitis)
- Typically in young children (5 years old)

Signs and Symptoms

- Irritability
  - o May last up to 6 months
- Fever
  - o Must come back to the ED if it comes back
- Swollen red tongue
- Infection

Interventions

- Corticosteroids
- Cyclosporin
- Intravenous immunoglobulins (IVIG)
  - o Prevent further damage to the heart
  - o Do not confuse with antibiotics.

Hirschsprung's Disease

Pathophysiology

- Genetic
- Poor or no nervous system innervation to the GI tract
- Leads to poor peristalsis

Signs and Symptoms

- Failure to pass meconium in the first 24 hours after birth
- Constipation
  - o May lead to obstruction and perforation
  - o Monitor for increasing distention.

Surgical Intervention

- Resection of part of the intestine
- Temporary colostomy
- Anastomosis of the intestine (once healed)

Lead Poisoning

Pathophysiology

- Children playing outside and not washing hands
- Lead typically ingested (soil, paint, water)

Signs and Symptoms

- Behavioral changes
- Elevated blood lead levels
- Abdominal pain
- Confusion
- Brain damage

Interventions

- Chelation therapy
  - o Oral (succimer)
  - o IV

Hip Dysplasia

Pathophysiology

- Typically congenital
- Trochanter may sit outside the socket.

Signs and Symptoms

- Affected leg shorter than the other
- Ortolani's sign
  - Abnormal clicking in hip at birth
- Barlow's maneuver
  - Performed in infancy
- Trendelenburg's sign
  - Do not confuse with the position.
  - Performed later when walking begins
  - May also be seen with muscular issues

Interventions

- Pavlik harness
  - Worn over the diaper
  - Worn continuously
  - Inspect skin (never use powder)
  - Specialty car seat
- Spica cast
- Bryant's traction (legs up)

Wilms' Tumor

Pathophysiology

- Tumor in the abdomen

Signs and Symptoms

- Hypertension

Interventions

- DO NOT palpate (leads to hypertensive crisis).

Duchenne Muscular Dystrophy

Pathophysiology

- X-linked recessive disorder (genetic)
- Affects boys more than girls
- No cure

Signs and Symptoms

- Progressive loss of muscle function
- Gain and loss of milestones
- Gower's sign: lack of hip and thigh muscle strength
  - Uses hands and arms to "walk" up their own body to a standing position

Interventions

- Assistive devices
  - Braces
  - Wheelchair
- Respiratory aid
  - Loss of diaphragm use
  - Intubation necessary (end-stage)

Tonsillitis

Pathophysiology

- Inflammation of the tonsils
- Typically secondary to another infection

Signs and Symptoms

- Visual enlargement (+1, +2, etc.)
- Airway crisis
  - Drooling

Interventions

- Tonsillectomy
  - Bleeding risk (drooling blood, frequent swallowing)

Child Abuse

What appears like child abuse does not always mean healthcare providers should jump to conclusions. Get the story. If it matches the injuries, continue to assess. Nurses are mandatory reporters. If child abuse is suspected, you must call police or the proper authorities. On the NCLEX, a correct answer to an abuse question will NOT be to reach out to your hierarchy, such as a charge nurse or nurse manager. You are required to call authorities.

Types of Abuse

Neglect	Emotional
■ Failure to provide the child with basic life needs: food, shelter, medical care, etc. ■ A parent does not have the right to refuse medical treatments to minors in life-threatening situations, such as meningitis. Religious freedom does not apply here.	■ Behavioral problems (acting out, withdrawal, low self-esteem) ■ Psychiatric problems
Physical	**Sexual**

■ Failure to thrive (potentially)
■ Abnormal injuries
  ○ Bruising in multiple stages of healing
  ○ Bruising in abnormal patterns (straight lines, circles, imprint of hand)
■ Changes in story or mismatching stories
■ Not reacting to pain
	■ Swollen genitals
	■ Inappropriate behavior/touching in school-age children
	  ○ Normal in toddlers and adolescents

HIPAA and Minors

There are occasions when the parents do not have to be notified about problems in minors. In most cases consent laws apply to minors 12 and older. Laws vary by state; some states have no policy, and physicians will treat if minors are deemed mature.

Pregnancy	Psychotherapy
■ Automatic emancipated minor ■ Minor controls pregnancy and baby	■ Therapy or mental health services ■ Parents may be the cause of the problem
STDs/HIV	**Substance Abuse**
■ Health department has to be notified to track epidemics; parents do not have to be notified	■ Referral of services and help can be offered without notifying parents

Gynecology

Menstruation

Amenorrhea	Dysmenorrhea	Menopause
■ Absence of periods ■ Causes 　○ Pregnancy 　○ Breastfeeding 　○ Extreme weight loss 　○ Stress 　○ Medical conditions	■ Painful periods ■ Causes 　○ Often normal 　○ Fibroids 　○ Endometriosis	■ No more ovulation ■ Causes 　○ 45–55 years of age 　○ Hysterectomy 　○ Illness

Toxic Shock Syndrome

Pathophysiology

- Caused by improper use of tampons
  - Replace tampons q4–6 hours.
  - Rotate between pads and tampons.
- Bacteria leading to a cytokine storm (overreaction of the immune system)

Signs and Symptoms

- Hyperthermia
- Hypotension
- Progresses to coma and/or multiple system organ failure (MSOF)

Interventions

- Immediate removal of the tampon
- Treat the underlying infection.
- Hospitalization likely (ICU)

Anovaginal Fistula

Pathophysiology

- Abnormal tunneling between vagina and anus
- May occur after perineal tear repair or in older age

Signs and Symptoms

- Stool leaking from vagina

Interventions

- Surgical repair

Polycystic Ovarian Syndrome

Pathophysiology

- Elevated testosterone in women
- Genetic (familial)

Signs and Symptoms

- Amenorrhea
- Acne
- Hirsutism (hair in typically male areas—face, neck, chin)

Interventions

- Weight loss
- Progesterone
- Surgery

Salpingitis

Pathophysiology

- Inflammation/infection of the fallopian tubes
- Precursor to ectopic pregnancy
- Insemination occurs in beginning third of tube.

Signs and Symptoms

- Abdominal pain (ovulation or after sex)
- Fever

Interventions

- Antibiotics

Endometriosis

Pathophysiology

- Tissues grow outside the uterus.
- Genetic (familial)

Signs and Symptoms

- Infertility
- Pelvic pain

Interventions

- Pharmacological
  - Hormones
  - Pain medications
- Surgery

Uterine Fibroids

Pathophysiology

- Benign tumors
- Obesity may cause
- Genetic (familial)

Signs and Symptoms

- Commonly none
- Painful periods
- Heavy periods

Interventions

- Commonly nothing
- Myomectomy/hysterectomy

Diagnostics/Procedures

Papanicolaou Smear

- Assess for cervical dysplasia.
  - Abnormal cell growth (squamous cells)
  - Cells sent to pathology for analysis.
- Screening to begin at 21 years of age (secondary prevention)

Colposcopy

- Vaginal exam (may include biopsy)
- Lithotomy position/semi-recumbent/ dorsal-recumbent
  - If the patient is uneasy about assuming this position, assess for the reason why.
  - Psychosocial strategy (assess feelings)

Colpopexy

- Surgical fix of vaginal prolapse

Hysterosalpingogram

- X-ray examination typically using contrast
  - Assess for adverse effects of contrast.
  - Fluoroscopy (continuous x-ray)
- Visualizes the uterus (hystero) and fallopian (salpingo) tubes

Transvaginal Ultrasound

- Ultrasound (US) inserted through the vagina
- Does not require anesthesia

Dilation and Curettage (D&C)

- Surgical removal of uterine contents
  - Anesthesia used
- Indicated for multiple medical disorders
- 1st trimester abortions
  - 20 weeks or less
  - Legal in United States
- Spontaneous abortion (miscarriage)
  - Loss of pregnancy without outside intervention before 20 weeks gestation
  - D&C traditional surgical option or manual vacuum aspiration

Tubal Ligation ("Tubes Tied")

- Surgical severing or blocking of the fallopian tubes
- Leads to sterility
  - Utilize contraception for 3–4 days post-op to avoid unwanted pregnancy.
- Potentially reversible
- Female equivalent of a vasectomy in male (Males should use a condom for 2 weeks after a vasectomy; sperm are resilient.)

Obstetrics

When answering NCLEX questions about pregnancy, it is very important to focus on how far along the mother is, as the trimester or week of pregnancy will change the nature of the question. Time proximity is crucial; the mother may be postpartum, but is she immediately postpartum or 4 hours postpartum? Pay close attention.

Pregnant teenagers (typically a minimum of 14–16 years of age) are considered legally emancipated from their parents. Once the baby is born, the responsibility for decisions around the baby lies with the teenage mother.

Pregnancy

GTPAL History Assessment

The NCLEX exam would very rarely ask you to build out the full assessment as an answer to a question; it is much more likely that you would need to infer information from a GTPAL assessment given to you in a question and then base your response on the analysis of the GTPAL.

Gravidity

- Number of times pregnant
- Nulligravida (never)
- Primigravida (first)
- Multigravida (multiple)

Term

- Term births (36–40 weeks)

Parity

- Number of pregnancies carried to viability (20–24 weeks)
- Nullipara (never)
- Primipara (once)
- Multipara (multiple)

Nx Tip: Multiparous women have much quicker stages of labor. Be aware of quick assessments for women closing in on 6 cm or more. These patients may be a priority. The baby may be coming, especially if the woman is losing control or vocalizing distress such as "help!"

Abortion

- Pregnancies lost due to abortion or miscarriage (spontaneous abortion)

Living

- Living children

Naegele's Rule

- Calculating pregnancy due dates
- Last menstrual period (LMP) + 1 year – 3 months + 7 days
- Example: LMP on July 4
  - July 4 + 1 year – 3 months + 7 days = April 11

Ectopic Pregnancy

Pathophysiology

- Pregnancy outside of the uterus
- Risk factors:
  - Salpingitis
  - Pelvic inflammatory disease (PID)
  - Artificial insemination/IVF

Signs and Symptoms

- Lower abdominal pain
- Vaginal bleeding
- Fever
- Rupture (medical emergency)
  - Hypotension (shock)
  - Rebound tachycardia

Interventions

- Prior to emergency
  - Induced miscarriage (methotrexate)
- During emergency
  - Surgery (stop the bleeding)

Prepartum

Signs of Pregnancy

Presumptive	Probable	Positive
■ Amenorrhea	■ Goodell's sign	■ Audible fetal heart sounds
■ Quickening	■ Chadwick's sign	■ Ultrasound visualization
■ Nausea/vomiting	■ Hegar's sign	■ Leopold maneuvers
■ Urinary frequency	■ Positive pregnancy test	

Prepartum Considerations

Pregnancy Test

- Tests for human chorionic gonadotropin (hCG)
- Blue (positive)
- Also used to assess for testicular cancer in men

Uterine Growth

- 2nd and 3rd trimesters: majority of growth
  o 1 pound a week
- Fundal growth
  o 22 weeks at the umbilicus

Multiples

- Twins, triplets, etc.
- May lead to gallstone formation in mother
- Risk for preterm labor

Bimanual/Two-Hand Exam

- Evaluation of the womb by entering the vaginal cavity
- Not an RN assessment
- Potential pregnancy confirmation

Prenatal Diet

- Increase 500 calories per day.
- Increase unsaturated fatty acids.

Gestational Diabetes/Diabetes Mellitus

Pathophysiology

- New onset (pregnancy) or previous diabetes

Signs and Symptoms

- The 3 P's of hyperglycemia
- Elevated serum fasting glucose
  o Tested multiple times throughout pregnancy

Interventions

- Oral antidiabetic agents
- Insulin

Hyperemesis Gravidarum

Pathophysiology

- Not morning sickness (morning sickness is typically only in the 1st trimester)

Signs and Symptoms

- Severe nausea and vomiting
- Weight loss
- Dehydration

Interventions

- Rehydrate (oral and IV if needed)
- Pharmacological

Nx Tip: Gestational diabetes/diabetes mellitus often leads to hydramnios/polyhydramnios and LGA (large for gestational age) babies. Whenever you have a change in fetal size, glucose regulation often results in the baby; commonly hypoglycemic.

Prenatal Screening Tests

Triple/Quad Test

- Drawn from maternal blood
- Test for genetic abnormalities (Down syndrome, trisomy, neural tube defects)
  - Alpha-fetoprotein (AFP) test
  - Higher or lower AFP – bad
- Performed in the 2nd trimester (14–16 weeks)

Amniocentesis

- Removal of amniotic fluid
- Tests for genetic abnormalities and sex of the baby
  - Down syndrome
  - Turner syndrome
- Performed at 14–16 weeks
- Complications
  - Preterm labor
  - Miscarriage
  - Chorioamnionitis

Non-Stress Test

- Biophysical profile
- Tests for fetal well-being during pregnancy
- Assess for fetal accelerations (movements).
  - Reactive = normal and good
  - Non-reactive = abnormal and bad

Stress Test

- Tests for fetal ability to handle labor
  - Administration of oxytocin
- Assess fetal heart rate when term.
  - Positive = bad
  - Negative = good

Percutaneous Umbilical Cord Sampling/Fetal Blood Sampling

- Removal of blood from the umbilical cord
- Test if serious risk of genetic defects exists.
- Performed when all other tests are inconclusive
- Complications
  - Hemorrhage
  - Cord damage
  - Miscarriage

Pre-Labor Ultrasound

- Test for cephalopelvic disproportion.
- The birth canal cannot physically allow a vaginal birth.
- Causes
  - Small birth canal
  - Large fetus
  - Multiples (twins, triplets, etc.)
- C-section likely

Prenatal Complications

Teratogenic Issues (Congenital Abnormalities)

1st Trimester

- Neural tube defects (folic acid requirements)
- Fetal alcohol syndrome
  - Similar issues to Down syndrome
- Vertical transmission (mother to child)
- TORCH infections
  - Toxoplasmosis (cats)
  - Other (syphilis, Zika)
  - Rubella (rhinoviruses and noroviruses)
  - CMV (rhinoviruses and noroviruses)
  - Herpes

Nx Tip: Pregnant healthcare workers cannot work with patients who have TORCH infections or patients who may be radioactive due to treatments.

2nd Trimester

- Medications could affect growth.
- Oligohydramnios may begin.
- Ultrasound used to monitor growth

3rd Trimester

- Cocaine abuse
  - May lead to preterm labor
  - Tox screen of the baby
  - If positive, call authorities/police (child abuse)
  - If negative, get social work involved
  - May lead to SGA (small for gestational age) baby (glucose regulation issues at birth)

Preeclampsia

Pathophysiology

- Typically a problem in the 3rd trimester
- If left untreated, may lead to eclampsia

Signs and Symptoms

- Hypertension (blurred vision, headache)
- Proteinuria
- Edema (feet, face, hands)
  - A certain level of ankle edema is normal in late pregnancy.
  - Pitting edema not good

Interventions

- Bed rest
- Pharmacological
  - Antihypertensives
  - Magnesium sulfate (prevent seizures)
    - Watch for hypermagnesemia (decrease in deep tendon reflexes).

Nx Tip: Preeclampsia may lead to HELLP syndrome (hemolysis, elevated liver enzymes, low platelet count).

Eclampsia

Pathophysiology

- Severe complication of preeclampsia
- Medical emergency

Signs and Symptoms

- Seizures
- Death

Interventions

- Emergency delivery (crash c-section)

Braxton Hicks Contractions (False Labor)

Pathophysiology
- Uterus preparing itself for labor
- Not true labor

Signs and Symptoms
- Intermittent, painless, or mild cramping contractions
- Increase in frequency as pregnancy progresses

Interventions
- Monitor to rule out true labor.

Nx Tip: If a woman who experienced Braxton Hicks contractions is discharged, she must be instructed to come back to the ED if symptoms come back. You cannot rule out true labor until she is assessed.

Placenta Previa/Placenta Accreta

Pathophysiology
- Abnormal implantation of the placenta
  - Partial previa (incomplete covering of the cervix)
  - Total previa (complete covering of the cervix)
- Total previa is much riskier.

Signs and Symptoms
- Painless, bright red bleeding

Interventions
- Bed rest, vaginal rest
- HCP will attempt to deliver the baby first.
- C-section may be needed.

Abruptio Placentae

Pathophysiology
- Placenta tearing away from uterine lining
- Medical emergency

Signs and Symptoms
- Rigid, boardlike abdomen
- Painful bleeding

Interventions
- Crash c-section

Nx Tip: Baby has 5 minutes to survive without oxygen from mom. Death or permanent brain damage likely after.

Preterm Labor

Pathophysiology
- Labor before 36 weeks

Signs and Symptoms
- Dull low back pain
- Vaginal discharge (spotting)

Interventions
- If labor is inevitable:
  o Steroid administration to mother to stimulate lung development in fetus
- If attempting to stop the labor:
  o Push fluids.
  o Bed rest
  o Tocolytics (labor suppressants)
  o Trendelenburg position
  o Cerclage (cervical stitch)

Post-Term Pregnancy/Labor

Pathophysiology
- Post 40 weeks of gestation
- Will begin to affect mother's health

Signs and Symptoms
- LGA (large for gestational age) baby
  o Glucose regulation issues after birth (hypoglycemia)
  o Baby has more hair and more creases on hands and feet.

Interventions
- Induce labor (oxytocin).
- C-section likely

Intrapartum

Caesarean Section (C-Section)
- Surgical operation with spinal block anesthesia
- 999 mL of blood loss or less okay (1 L or more = hemorrhage)
- Subsequent pregnancies and labors
  o C-section likely, however a vaginal birth after c-section (VBAC) is possible
- Adhesions (internal scar tissue)
  o May complicate recovery

Vaginal Birth After C-Section (VBAC)

- Baby (fetal) position crucial (perform Leopold maneuvers to assess)
- Not always successful; may require another c-section
- Classic incision preferable (bikini line)

Vaginal Birth

- 499 mL of blood loss or less okay (500 mL or more = hemorrhage)
- Shoulder dystocia risk (shoulder gets stuck)
    - Never push on baby (not RN scope).

Pain Management in Labor

Non-Pharmacological

- Massage and acupuncture
    - Lower back pressure
- Relaxation and meditation
- Emotional support
    - Doula, spouse, or other laypersons
    - Laypersons, including doula or spouse, may assist in non-medical interventions.

Pudendal Block

- Anesthesia for the perineal area
- Aids in pain relief from vaginal birth
- Anesthesia available past 6 cm of dilation

Spinal Block (C-Section)/Epidural (Vaginal)

- Typically a 30-minute procedure to administer
- Cannot be performed too early (3 cm or less)
- Blocks pain and function from the injection site downward
- Women will lose bladder function.
    - Assess for urinary retention (can worsen postpartum bleeding).
    - Palpate the bladder first.
    - Bladder scan second
    - One order for straight catheterization exists after labor.
- Affects the newborn (lower Apgar score)

Intrapartum Complications

Breech Positioning/Birth

Pathophysiology

- Bottom first or legs first

Signs and Symptoms

- Frank breech (legs up, butt first)
- Complete breech (legs first)
- Footling breech (one foot first)

Interventions

- C-section likely

Hypotonic Uterine Contractions

Pathophysiology

- Painful but ineffective contractions

Signs and Symptoms

- Labor will not progress.

Interventions

- Augment with oxytocin.

Endometritis

Pathophysiology

- Inflammation of the endometrium (infection)
- Prolonged rupture of membranes (6 hours or more)

Signs and Symptoms

- Maternal vital signs (1st assessment)
  - Fever
- Lower abdominal pain
- Foul-smelling vaginal discharge
- WBC count (later assessment)

Interventions

- Antibiotics (IV to mother)

The First Stage of Labor

- Longest stage
  - o Help progress by ambulation.
- Dilation (0–6 cm)
- Effacement (thinning of) (0–100%)
- Station (descent) (+1 to +4)

> **Nx Tip:** A Bishop score, used during induction of labor (oxytocin), indicates how successful an induction will be. The higher the score, the more likely the induction will be successful.

Rupture of Membranes

- SROM: spontaneous = normal
- PROM: premature = before 36 weeks
- AROM: artificial = induced by amniotomy (HCP)
- Assess if membranes truly ruptured
  - o Nitrazine test (pH of fluid) (blue = positive, green = negative)
  - o Ferning test (fluid observed under microscope)
- Nursing priority
  - o Assess fetal well-being after confirmed rupture of membranes.
  - o Does not matter how they ruptured; assess fetal well-being

Meconium Amnios

Pathophysiology

- Fetus defecates while in the womb.
- May be a sign of fetal distress

Signs and Symptoms

- Greenish-stained amniotic fluid upon rupture of membranes

Interventions

- Assess fetal well-being.
- Respiratory support for the fetus
  - o Required if aspirated

Fetal Heart Rate (FHR) Monitoring

- Acceleration (FHR increases)
  - o Good and normal
  - o Sometimes called tachycardia (okay as long as not above 200 and sustained)
- Early deceleration (FHR decreasing)
  - o Deceleration occurs at the same time as the contraction.
  - o Normal/head compression during labor

- Variable deceleration
  - Deceleration occurs randomly with no correlation to the contraction.
  - Cord compression during labor
  - Turn mother to the left side.
- Late deceleration
  - Deceleration occurs after the contraction.
  - Uteroplacental insufficiency
    - Worst type of deceleration
  - Turn mother to left side.
  - Start oxygen.
  - Start IV fluids.
  - C-section may be needed.
- No deceleration or acceleration
  - Stillbirth likely

Fetal Scalp Electrode

- Assesses fetal heart rate, not contractions

Transitional Phase (8–10 cm)

- Woman screams out or loses control.
  - "Help me, help me!"
  - Vaginal exam – baby may be coming
- Cord prolapse
  - Trendelenburg position
  - Hands and knees position
  - Apply gentle pressure (not hard).
- Multiparous – quicker labors

Nx Tip: Priority questions involving pregnancy may result in the correct answer being a multiparous woman. Since the transitional phase would be much faster, delivery of the infant may be the priority. Read these types of questions carefully.

The Second Stage of Labor

- Delivery of the infant
- Contractions stronger and more frequent
- Good labor (2–3 minutes apart, 45 seconds in length)
  - Labor ineffective if less
  - Infant loses oxygen if more.
- Baby's head presents
  - Confirm no cord around baby's head/neck

The Third Stage of Labor

- Delivery of the placenta (afterbirth)
- Involution of the uterus (clamping down)
  - o Poor involution leads to bleeding.
  - o Void the bladder.

The Fourth Stage of Labor

- Period of recovery after birth
- Refer to postpartum considerations.
- Called puerperium

Postpartum

Postpartum (Puerperium) Considerations

- Bleeding
  - o Massage the fundus.
  - o Blue pad = 100 mL
  - o 100 mL of blood loss (or more) per hour = hemorrhage
- Boggy uterus
  - o Placenta fragment retention
  - o Risk for bleeding
  - o Massage the fundus.
  - o Crede's maneuver (direct pressure to lower abdomen)
- Uterine atony
  - o Weak muscle
  - o Risk for bleeding
  - o Administer uterotonics.

Nx Tip: If the patient believes she urinated on herself or the bed, it may very likely be blood. Assess the situation.

Episiotomy/Perineal Tears

Pathophysiology
- Surgical incision from vagina to anus (episiotomy)
- Stages 1–4 (tear)
  - The higher the stage, the larger the tear.

Signs and Symptoms
- Risks for bleeding and infection

Interventions
- Dietary fiber
- Never scrape, always dab.
- Laxatives (no bowel straining)
- Sitz baths (not immediately after)
- Donut cushion
- Soap and water to clean (possibly half hydrogen peroxide)

Colostrum
- The first feeding
- Contains antibodies/immunoglobulins
  - Newborn has no immune system.
- Concentrated milk (high in nutrients)

Uterine Involution
- Uterus returns to normal size.
- 2 days postpartum – umbilicus
- 2 fingerbreadths per day after

Lochia Rubra
- Red (sanguineous)
- Up to 5 days

Lochia Serosa
- Pink/brownish (serosanguineous)
- 5 to 7 days

Lochia Alba
- White/yellow (serous – clear)
- After 7 days

Nx Tip: Cloudy, foul-smelling, or purulent discharge is likely an infection. Refer to the HCP/MD.

Taking-In Phase

- Immediately after birth
- New mother learning
- Overwhelmed

Taking-Hold Phase

- 10 days after birth
- Begins motherly roles

Postpartum Blues

- Early after birth; symptoms last for about 2 weeks
- More acute and mild
- Assess
  - Lack of interest in the newborn
  - Signs and symptoms of depression

Postpartum Depression

- Symptoms last longer than 2 weeks after the birth and interfere with ADLs.
- Later after birth (2 weeks)
- Assess
  - Lack of interest in the newborn
  - Signs and symptoms of depression

Mastitis

Pathophysiology

- Inflammation of the breast tissue

Signs and Symptoms

- Tenderness

Interventions

- Prevent by washing nipples after feedings.
- Express milk out of bad breast.
  - Feeding (will not harm newborn)
  - Pumping
- Antibiotics
- Warm compress

Apgar Scores

The Apgar test assesses the newborn's appearance, pulse, grimace, activity, and respiration. The Apgar score is based on a scale of 1 to 10. The higher the score, the better. Focus on the key components of Apgar. From there, it is much easier to interpret what is expected versus unexpected.

- The test is performed 1 minute after birth and then repeated 5 minutes later; if the score is less than 7, continue every 5 minutes until stable.
- The test is used to determine the need for medical intervention.
- Most neonates score 8 or 9.

Appearance	Pulse	Grimace
- Acrocyanosis (circumoral) normal at birth (blue limbs) - Improvement at 5 minutes likely	- Slower HR more serious (<100) than increased HR	- Response to stimulation
Activity	**Respiration**	
- Flexed arms and legs - Maternal anesthesia during labor affects neonatal activity.	- Crying	

Nx Tip: When assessing Apgar scores on an NCLEX question, it is best to assume the baby is perfect (a score of 10), and then dock off a point for each problem described in the question. This approach is much easier than trying to count up from 0.

Neonatal Compromise

- Low Apgar scores may indicate neurological damage.
- NICU is likely if score is below 5.
- Breathing is most important.

Neonate Normals

Admission to Nursery

- Unless the Apgar is low, nursery placement is normal.
- Nursery care requires special training (no floating to this unit).

Birth Weight

- Normal for newborns to lose some weight after birth
- Weight loss regained in 7 days
- Doubling of the weight at 5–6 months
- Tripling of weight by 1 year

Guthrie Test (Heel Prick)

- Tests for genetic conditions, especially phenylketonuria
- PKU is recessive genetic.
- Mandated by law in the U.S.
- Performed when the following apply:
  - Minimum 48 hours post birth
  - Have fed for minimum 48–72 hours
  - Not near discharge; otherwise, urine test follow-up at 2 weeks

Vernix Caseosa

- Present (normal) in full-term babies
- Lubricating for birth, protecting after birth
  - Aids in temperature regulation
  - Vernix not washed after birth unless mother has HIV

Milia

- Normal finding in newborns (no matter age)
- White bumps on cheeks and nose
- Will resolve naturally; no treatment needed

Skin Findings

- Stork bites (nevus simplex)
  - Colored birthmark typically on back of neck or forehead between eyes
  - Normally disappears weeks after birth
- Mongolian spots (dermal melanocytosis)
  - Grayish-blue discoloration typically on the sacrum
  - Typically disappears weeks after birth
- Cafe au lait
  - Brownish birthmark (for life)
  - Typically benign (non-harmful) unless large in number; may imply a more serious disorder
- Erythema toxicum
  - Benign rash (non-harmful); however, need to rule out herpes
  - Erythematous vesicles
- Seborrheic dermatitis
  - Yellowish crusty rash (sebum—oil) on top of head (cradle cap)
  - May be caused by fungal infection
  - Typically resolves without treatment; may need antifungal cream

Prematurity

Pathophysiology

- Newborns born before 36 weeks of gestation
  - Viability typically starts at 30 weeks.
  - 25–30 weeks: very high risk
- Admission to the NICU may be required, but not certain.

Signs and Symptoms

- Fewer creases on hands and feet
- Presence of lanugo (fine, downy hair)
- Jaundice (immaturity of liver)

Interventions

- Intrapartum
  - Steroids such as betamethasone IV push to mother; stimulate fetal lungs
- Postpartum
  - Surfactant
    - Increases surface area in lungs to aid in oxygen exchange
    - Typically administered through ET tube
    - Combats respiratory distress syndrome (RDS)
  - IV caffeine
    - Increases respiratory rate

Nx Tip: Focus on the week of pregnancy if the mother goes into labor. The earlier the labor, the higher the risk of complications with the neonate.

Postmaturity

Pathophysiology
- Newborns born after 40 weeks
- Problems with placental function lead to neonatal problems.

Signs and Symptoms
- Newborn may appear thin.

Interventions
- Monitoring and priority to feeding

Nx Tip: Postmaturity typically affects the labor more than the newborn itself. If the mother and baby are medically okay, the priority may focus on feeding the newborn. Babies need food.

Neonatal Med-Surg Illness

Ophthalmia Neonatorum

Pathophysiology
- Caused by passage of newborn by vaginal delivery
- Caused by gonorrhea or chlamydia

Signs and Symptoms
- Discharge from eyes (conjunctiva)

Interventions
- Obtain an order for antibiotic eye drops.
- If detected prior to labor, treat mother with antibiotics

Neonatal Hypoglycemia
- Neonatal glucose level below 40
- Feeding is best.

Transient Tachypnea of the Newborn (TTN)

Pathophysiology
- Often seen in term c-section newborns

Signs and Symptoms
- Tachypnea above 60 breaths per minute

Interventions
- Typically resolves on its own
- Monitor respiratory rate and signs of distress.

Neonatal Bleeding

- Prevented by immediate postpartum administration of vitamin K

Heat Loss in Neonates

Conduction		Evaporation	
■ Heat loss when in contact with a cold surface ■ Warm any objects that will touch the newborn.		■ Heat loss when skin is wet and exposed to air ■ Dry the newborn.	
Convection		**Radiation**	
■ Heat loss when body is exposed to air ■ Keep newborn wrapped.		■ Heat loss from body to other objects ■ Cover areas of heat loss on the body. o Cap on head	

Hemolytic Disease of the Newborn/Erythroblastosis Fetalis

Pathophysiology

- Rh factor incompatibility
- Mother is Rh negative; father is Rh positive.
- Mother forms antibodies against Rh RBCs.
- Mother's antibodies attack baby's RBCs.

Signs and Symptoms

- Positive Coombs test
  - Tests for body attacking RBCs
  - Agglutination (clumping or clotting): displays positive test
  - No agglutination: displays negative test
- Direct umbilical blood collection
  - Hemoglobin levels
  - Bilirubin levels (elevates when RBCs are destroyed)
  - Jaundice

Interventions

- RhoGAM (maternal administration)
- Phototherapy (neonatal administration)
  - Eyes must be covered.
  - Normal for stool discoloration
  - Parents may turn off light to feed.

Neonatal Abstinence Syndrome

Pathophysiology

- Baby withdrawing from drugs delivered while in womb

Signs and Symptoms

- Irritability
- Sneezing
- Muscle shaking
- Refusal to feed

Interventions

- Inpatient stay
- Pharmacological (weaning)
- Non-pharmacological
  - Swaddling

Neonatal Basic Care and Comfort

Umbilical Cord Care

- Clean and dry cord is best.
- Soap and water is best to clean.
- Do not tuck stump into diaper (infection risk).
- No tub baths until cord falls off (typically in 7–14 days)

Neonatal Positioning

- Adduction is okay.

Neonatal Urine Output

- 1–2 mL/kg an hour is normal.

Circumcision

- Advocate anesthesia for neonate.
- Post-procedural bleeding
  - Apply pressure (direct or by diaper).
  - Apply petroleum jelly (Vaseline) to the penis (prevents sticking).
- No tub baths
- Yellowish exudate is normal during healing (2–4 days).

Periods of Reactivity

- Times of alertness of newborn after birth
- Periods where baby is awake and needs to be fed
- Newborns sleep a lot; feeding is priority when medically okay.
- Periods of not eating greater than 4 hours in between is cause for further investigation.

Pharmacology

When reviewing medications for the NCLEX, there are many things to keep in mind. First and foremost, it is not necessary to know everything about everything. You are a nurse, not a clinical pharmacologist; do not go overboard. It is vastly more important to grasp the underlying pathophysiology of an illness and reasons behind the need for the medication in the first place.

It is incredibly difficult to memorize all medications, and it is not the nurse's job to do so. What is important is to understand the safe practice and administration of these medications and when to seek help. Having said that, there are three rules that can be applied to make learning this difficult subject monumentally easier. Each medication is built with these three rules in mind. Follow the 1-2-3:

1. **What is it?**
   o Memorize the generic name and class when specified.
   o Pay attention to nomenclature (suffix, prefix).
2. **What does it do to the body?**
   o Memorize the reaction within the body (example: causes urination, increases serotonin).
   o Do not overlearn mechanism of action.
3. **Why do we give it?**
   o What illnesses or disorders is the drug used for?

With these tools, the brain can work smarter. It bears repeating: Do not overdo it. Do not take the brain to medical school. No one person can memorize everything, and nurses are no different. Focus on the hard-hitting, most important components. The pharmacology listed in this chapter is specifically directed toward the NCLEX. Pay close attention to the Nx Tips in this chapter; they contain important additional information.

Pharmacology Terminology

Enteral: Oral or NG/OG route

Parenteral: IM, SQ, and IV

Intrathecal (anesthesia managed): Into the CNS

Intra-articular (HCP managed): Into a joint

First Pass Effect: When digested, oral medications must first pass through the liver before entering the systemic circulation of the body. This greatly reduces the amount of drug to reach the intended target. Special consideration must be given to patients with liver and/or kidney issues; dosing should be closely monitored.

P-450 System: Endogenous and exogenous chemicals are metabolized by this system. You, as the nurse, should understand the breaking down of toxic substances, such as drugs and bilirubin within the liver.

Agonist drugs: Stimulate a reaction.

Antagonist drugs: Inhibit or stop a reaction.

Black Box Warnings: The Food and Drug Administration forces this labeling warning when serious harm and/or death can occur when the drug is taken.

Side Effects/Adverse Effects (SE/AE)

The NCLEX may test on specific SE/AE; however, it is recommended that you do not overly focus on these things unless specifically addressed in the medication in this chapter. It is more important to focus on the 1-2-3. Most questions revolve around understanding what the drug will end up doing to the body. Consider a patient with hypertension and fluid overload who is prescribed furosemide. It is altogether possible that this patient could lose too much fluid too quickly and fall into hypotension.

Side effects generally refer to the more minor effects that may happen after a medication is taken, such as nausea or dizziness. A patient would not die from a side effect. Adverse effects generally refer to more serious effects. These could include anything from ototoxicity to respiratory depression. Adverse effects could seriously harm a patient if not monitored closely.

> Nx Tip: There are only four medications important to remember for the NCLEX that need to be taken on an empty stomach. They are antacids, iron, levothyroxine, and tetracycline. It is best to park this information in the brain and then say everything else is safe to give with food and water.

Toxicities

- **Neurotoxicity:** Drowsiness, auditory and visual disturbances, restlessness, seizures
- **Hepatotoxicity:** Hepatitis, jaundice, elevated liver enzymes
- **Nephrotoxicity:** Decreased urinary output, elevated creatinine and BUN, acid-base imbalances
- **Ototoxicity:** Tinnitus, hearing loss, lightheadedness, vertigo
- **Cardiotoxicity:** Cardiac dysrhythmias, changes in BP

Pediatric/Elderly Specific

In infants and elderly patients, there are special considerations. An immature or weakened nature of some bodily systems can cause a dangerous increase in the serum (blood) level of the drug. It is crucial to understand that the patient's metabolism (liver function) and excretion (kidneys) may not operate like those of a normal healthy adult. Dosing is typically lower in these patients to avoid complications.

Intramuscular (IM) Administration Sites

Ventrogluteal (Hip)

- Palm of hand on greater trochanter

Dorsogluteal (Buttocks)

- No longer utilized (danger for damage to sciatic nerve)

Deltoid (Arm)

- Avoid proximity to shoulder.

Vastus Lateralis (Thigh)

- Site for babies and toddlers

Right to Refuse

Is the medication necessary for life?

- Yes
  - o Educate (first).
  - o Document the refusal.
  - o Notify the MD/HCP.
  - o Example: antibiotic for infection
- No
  - o Document the refusal.
  - o Reassess in 30 minutes to 1 hour.
  - o Example: pain medication
- No (psych patient)
  - o Leave and try again in 15 minutes.

Cardiovascular Medications

Cardiac pharmacology is fairly intricate when it comes to understanding exactly what is going on inside of the body when these medications are used. Pay close attention and think about the larger reasons these medications are needed in the first place. Understanding the underlying anatomy and physiology of the cardiovascular system will make the process much easier.

Antihypertensives

metoprolol	verapamil, diltiazem, nicardipine	captopril
1. Beta blocker; suffix "lol" 2. Lowers heart rate and decreases force of contraction 3. Hypertension, dysrhythmias **Nx Tip:** ■ **May mask signs of hypoglycemia** ■ **Check glucose q4hr.** ■ **Careful with asthma patients** ■ **Contraindicated in bradycardia and heart block**	1. Calcium channel blocker; suffix "dipine" 2. Decreases force of contraction 3. Hypertension, angina, cardiac dysrhythmias **Nx Tip:** ■ **No grapefruit juice**	1. Angiotensin-converting enzyme (ACE) inhibitor; suffix "pril" 2. Decreases retention of water and sodium 3. Hypertension **Nx Tip:** ■ **Side effect: cough** ■ **Hyperkalemia risk**
losartan	clonidine	hydralazine
1. Angiotensin receptor blocker; suffix "sartan" 2. Decreases retention of water and sodium 3. Hypertension and diabetic nephropathy **Nx Tip:** ■ **Used if ACE inhibitor cannot be tolerated** ■ **Hyperkalemia risk**	1. Alpha agonist 2. Lowers heart rate, vasodilates 3. Hypertension **Nx Tip:** ■ **Side effect: dry mouth**	1. Vasodilator 2. Smooth muscle relaxation (blood vessels) 3. Hypertension **Nx Tip:** ■ **Oral or IV**
pentoxifylline	nitroglycerin, isosorbide dinitrate	nitroprusside
1. Vasodilator 2. Smooth muscle relaxation (blood vessels) 3. Pain due to PAD (intermittent claudication)	1. Nitrate 2. Vasodilator, decreases preload 3. Hypertension and angina **Nx Tip:** ■ **Sublingual: 3 times, 5 minutes apart** ■ **If second dose fails, head to ER.** ■ **Risk for orthostatic hypotension** ■ **Risk for headache; treat with acetaminophen** ■ **Do not take with erectile dysfunction meds (sildenafil).** ■ **Given via IV for severe HTN**	1. Nitrate 2. Strong vasodilator, decreases preload 3. Hypertensive crisis **Nx Tip:** ■ **Slowly lower BP or MAP (too quickly may cause body to go into shock).** ■ **May cause cyanide poisoning (caution)**

Vasopressors

Inotropic: contractility (dopamine)

Chronotropic: time (digoxin, atropine)

Dromotropic: conduction (nervous system of heart)

dopamine	dobutamine	epinephrine	norepinephrine
1. Catecholamine/ vasopressor 2. Increases force of contraction and heart rate 3. Shock **Nx Tip:** ■ **Close hemodynamic monitoring necessary (ICU)** ■ **Renal dose: low dose to increase GFR**	1. Adrenergic agonist/ vasopressor/positive inotrope 2. Increases force of contraction and heart rate 3. Shock, heart failure **Nx Tip:** ■ **Intake/output** ■ **Weight changes** ■ **Electrolyte imbalances**	1. Catecholamine/vasopressor/ adrenergic agonist 2. Cardiovascular and CNS stimulant, increases force of contraction 3. Shock, cardiac emergency **Nx Tip:** ■ **EpiPen for anaphylaxis; head to ER after administration** ■ **Injection can go through clothes.** ■ **Close hemodynamic monitoring** ■ **Risk for hyperglycemia**	1. Catecholamine/ vasopressor/ adrenergic agonist 2. Strong vasoconstrictor 3. Shock **Nx Tip:** ■ **May cause limb ischemia (purple toes, necrosis)**

Diuretics

hydrochlorothiazide	furosemide, bumetanide	triamterene, eplerenone, spironolactone
1. Thiazide diuretic 2. Increases urine production (makes you pee) 3. Hypertension, fluid overload **Nx Tip:** ■ **Intake/output** ■ **Weight changes** ■ **Electrolyte imbalances**	1. Loop diuretic 2. Increases urine output including sodium and potassium 3. Fluid volume excess, edema, pulmonary edema, hypertension **Nx Tip:** ■ **Contraindicated in chronic kidney disease (CKD)** ■ **Risk for hypokalemia** ■ **Push slowly; risk for ototoxicity**	1. Potassium-sparing diuretic 2. Increases urine output with retention of potassium 3. Fluid volume excess, edema, hypertension **Nx Tip:** ■ **Risk for hyperkalemia (avoid salt substitutes, avoid bananas)**
mannitol	acetazolamide	
1. Osmotic diuretic 2. Increases urine output 3. Increased intracranial pressure and intraocular pressure **Nx Tip:** ■ **Contraindicated in CKD**	1. Carbonic anhydrase inhibitor 2. Increases urine output with sodium, potassium, and bicarb 3. Glaucoma, pulmonary edema **Nx Tip:** ■ **Risk for orthostasis**	

Heart Failure

Diuretics, beta blockers, calcium channel blockers, and ACE inhibitors are also used to treat heart failure.

digoxin
1. Cardiac glycoside
2. Lowers heart rate, increases force of contraction
3. Symptomatic heart failure, atrial fibrillation

Nx Tip:
- **Do not administer if HR is below 60.**
- **Risk for digitalis toxicity (anorexia, N/V/D, fatigue, headache); hypokalemia may trigger toxicity**

Antihyperlipidemic

lovastatin	fenofibrate	niacin
1. Statin; suffix "statin"	1. Fibrate	1. Nicotinic acid (vitamin B3)
2. Increases HDL, lowers LDL, lowers cholesterol	2. Increases HDL, lowers LDL, lowers cholesterol	2. Increases HDL, lowers LDL, lowers cholesterol
3. Hypercholesterolemia and hyperlipidemia	3. Hypercholesterolemia and hyperlipidemia	3. Hypercholesterolemia and hyperlipidemia
Nx Tip: - **Contraindicated in liver disease** - **Risk for rhabdomyolysis (medical emergency)**		**Nx Tip:** - **Over-the-counter supplement** - **Added to other therapies**

Coagulation

Hypocoagulation: thin blood

Hypercoagulation: thick blood

Heparin, enoxaparin	warfarin	clopidogrel, aspirin
1. Anticoagulant; suffix "parin"	1. Anticoagulant	1. Antiplatelet
2. Blocks mechanisms in clotting cascade	2. Blocks mechanisms in clotting cascade	2. Blocks platelet aggregation
3. Prevention of blood clots (DVT)	3. Prevention of blood clots (atrial fibrillation)	3. Prophylaxis for clotting events (MI, PE, CVA)
Nx Tip: - **Lab values: aPTT** - **Antidote: protamine sulfate** - **SQ injection: Rotate injection site; never massage.** - **For inpatient use** - **Risk for heparin-induced thrombocytopenia (HIT)**	**Nx Tip:** - **Lab values: PT/INR** - **Antidote: vitamin K** - **For outpatient or inpatient use** - **Take warfarin while going off of heparin (use will overlap).**	**Nx Tip:** - **Risk for salicylate poisoning (aspirin)** - **Risk for bleeding (assess)**

alteplase, tissue plasminogen activator (tPA)	aminocaproic acid	
1. Thrombolytic/fibrinolytic 2. Enzyme that breaks down clots 3. Diagnosed acute ischemic stroke, myocardial infarction, pulmonary embolism **Nx Tip:** ■ **Given within the golden window (3 hours)** ■ **Hemorrhagic stroke must be ruled out (obtain CT of head).** ■ **Caution in the elderly**	1. Hemostat 2. Aids in clotting cascade, prevents breakdown of formed clots 3. Hemorrhage, DIC, controlling bleeding, overdose of fibrinolytics **Nx Tip:** ■ **Commonly used post-op to prevent hemorrhage**	

Cardiac Dysrhythmia

This list includes atropine; however, that medication is also listed with the cholinergic agents in the "Motor Neurons and Glands" section.

quinidine, procainamide	lidocaine	amiodarone
1. Antiarrhythmic 2. Decreases conduction 3. Atrial dysrhythmias	1. Antiarrhythmic 2. Decreases threshold or membrane response 3. Ventricular dysrhythmias (V. Fib) **Nx Tip:** ■ **Lidocaine toxicity: CV/CNS**	1. Antiarrhythmic 2. Prolongs action potential duration 3. Life-threatening dysrhythmias **Nx Tip:** ■ **Prophylaxis for fatal rhythms** ■ **Risk for pulmonary toxicity**
adenosine	sodium polystyrene sulfonate	
1. Antiarrhythmic 2. Decreases conduction through AV node 3. Supraventricular tachycardia (SVT) and ventricular tachycardia **Nx Tip:** ■ **Hemodynamic monitoring required (keep crash cart close)** ■ **Central preferred, peripheral allowed** ■ **Push fast followed by 10 mL NS flush (FAST).**	1. Potassium-removing resin 2. Causes excretion of potassium in stool 3. Hyperkalemia **Nx Tip:** ■ **Slow onset** ■ **Assess for constipation (will not work).** ■ **Hypokalemia risk** ■ **Oral or by enema**	

Motor Neurons and Glands

Cholinergic agents can be a confusing realm of medications to learn. Refer to the "Motor Neurons and Glands" chapter in this book to refresh your memory on anatomy and physiology. Understanding the difference between what a cholinergic agonist does and what an anticholinergic agent does is crucial.

bethanechol	tolterodine, oxybutynin	acetylcholine	pilocarpine, carbachol
1. Cholinergic agonist	1. Anticholinergic	1. Cholinergic agonist/miotic agent	1. Cholinergic agonist
2. Stimulates bladder	2. Blocks cholinergic function	2. Constricts iris	2. Constricts iris
3. Urinary retention	3. Urinary incontinence	3. Ophthalmologic surgeries	3. Glaucoma, dry mouth
Nx Tip:	**Nx Tip:**		**Nx Tip:**
■ **Rule out obstructive causes of retention first.**	■ **Anticholinergic side effects (SLUDD acronym)**		■ **Risk for cholinergic crisis (medical emergency)**
methacholine	neostigmine	atropine	
1. Cholinergic agonist	1. Cholinergic agonist	1. Anticholinergic	
2. Inhaled causing bronchoconstriction	2. Increases available acetylcholine	2. Blocks cholinergic function	
3. Asthma, bronchial disease	3. Myasthenia gravis, paralytic ileus, antidote for paralyzing agents	3. Symptomatic bradycardia	
Nx Tip:		**Nx Tip:**	
■ **Used for diagnostic assessment**	**Nx Tip:**	■ **Anticholinergic side effects (SLUDD)**	
	■ **Risk for cholinergic crisis (medical emergency)**		

Respiratory Medications

The majority of upper respiratory tract medications can be obtained over-the-counter (OTC); lower respiratory tract medications are typically prescribed.

Administration

Metered-Dose Inhaler

- Aerosolized medication in specific amounts
- Commonly self-administered
- Spacer used to increase delivery amount

Dry-Powder Inhaler

- Strong, forceful inhalation for proper delivery
- Alternative to metered-dose inhaler
- Commonly self-administered

Nebulizer

- Mist delivery method for medication
- Often more effective than inhalers
- Commonly given by respiratory therapist

dextromethorphan
1. Antitussive
2. Suppresses cough reflex
3. Nonproductive cough

Nx Tip:
- **Do not use in cough for asthma or emphysema.**
- **Patients should cough up the production.**
- **May cause drowsiness**

pseudoephedrine
1. Decongestant
2. Constricts nasal arterioles
3. Common cold, sinusitis, rhinitis

Nx Tip:
- **May cause CNS stimulation**
- **Abuse potential (meth production)**
- **ID required at pharmacy to acquire**

fexofenadine
1. Antihistamine
2. Blocks action of histamines to decrease inflammation
3. Seasonal allergies

Nx Tip:
- **No grapefruit juice**
- **Contraindicated in glaucoma**

diphenhydramine, scopolamine, dramamine
1. Antihistamine; suffix "amine"
2. Blocks action of histamines to decrease inflammation
3. Allergies (urticaria, angioedema, hypersensitivities), motion sickness

Nx Tip:
- **May cause drowsiness (common in sleep aids)**

guaifenesin
1. Expectorant
2. Decreases viscosity of secretions
3. Common cold, acute bronchitis, influenza

Nx Tip:
- **Perform pulmonary hygiene (deep breathing and incentive spirometry).**

acetylcysteine
1. Mucolytic
2. Thins out thick secretions to be coughed up
3. COPD, pneumonia, tuberculosis, cystic fibrosis

Nx Tip:
- **Antidote to acetaminophen toxicity**
- **Common in nebulizer treatments**

albuterol, terbutaline
1. Bronchodilator
2. Stimulates smooth muscle in lungs causing relaxation and dilation
3. Asthma: rescue inhaler

Nx Tip:
- **May cause sympathetic stimulation (tachycardia, anxiety, tremors, elevated BP)**
- **PRN medication for attacks (exacerbations)**
- **May be taken prophylactically before a stress event (sport, etc.)**

salmeterol
1. Long-acting bronchodilator
2. Stimulates smooth muscle in lungs causing relaxation and dilation
3. Asthma as scheduled dose

Nx Tip:
- **Do not confuse with albuterol.**
- **Not a rescue inhaler**

ipratropium bromide
1. Anticholinergic; suffix "tropium bromide"
2. Slows down effects of acetylcholine, stops bronchoconstriction
3. COPD, asthma

Nx Tip:
- **Anticholinergic side effects (SLUDD)**
- **Scheduled dose, not PRN**
- **Often delivered by nebulizer**

theophylline
1. Bronchodilator; suffix "phylline"
2. Affects smooth muscle in bronchioles causing dilation
3. COPD, asthma

Nx Tip:
- **Toxic medication, monitor lab values (normal: 10–20)**
- **Trough 30 minutes to directly before dose, peak 1–2 hours after**
- **Toxicity (CNS, CV effects)**

flunisolide, beclomethasone
1. Anti-inflammatory, inhaled glucocorticosteroid
2. Reduces inflammation in respiratory tract
3. COPD, asthma

Nx Tip:
- **Wash mouth out after each use.**
- **Utilize nystatin (swish and swallow) to prevent oral candidiasis (thrush).**
- **Long-term side effects:**
  - **Immunosuppression**
  - **Weight gain (water)**
  - **Hyperglycemia**
  - **Osteoporosis**

cromolyn sodium
1. Mast cell stabilizer
2. Prevents underlying causes of allergic or environmental physiological damage
3. Asthma, bronchospasm

Nx Tip:
- **Takes a while to work**

zafirlukast, montelukast
1. Leukotriene receptor antagonist
2. Blocks inflammatory response
3. COPD, asthma

Endocrine Medications

Endocrinology as a whole can be very difficult to understand in the beginning. There are multiple directions of considerations, especially hyper versus hypo issues. It is important to understand the underlying pathophysiology of a disease before a medication can truly make sense.

prednisone, hydrocortisone	aminoglutethimide
1. Glucocorticosteroid, mineralocorticosteroid, hormone agonist	1. Steroid hormone antagonist
2. Replacement hormone, anti-inflammatory agent, suppresses immune system	2. Slows down the production of adrenal steroids
3. Adrenal insufficiency (Addison's disease), inflammation, organ transplants	3. Hypercortisolism (Cushing's syndrome)
Nx Tip:	**Nx Tip:**
■ **Short-term side effect: CNS stimulation**	■ **Short-term therapy until surgery**
■ **Long-term side effects:**	■ **May cause orthostatic hypotension**
○ **Immunosuppression**	
○ **Weight gain (water)**	
○ **Hyperglycemia**	
○ **Osteoporosis**	

Insulins

Primary hormone in the metabolism of glucose

All type 1 diabetes, type 2 diabetes uncontrolled by diet and oral antidiabetics

It is not necessary to memorize the exact peak times and durations of all of the insulins. Remember the ballpark times below on when the insulin begins to work; that is far more important. For example, if NPH was given at breakfast, when would the RN be most concerned about hypoglycemia? Answer: at lunch. Critical thinking is key, rather than sheer memorization of random numbers.

- ■ Fast-acting: 30 minutes or faster
- ■ Intermediate: 2–4 hours
- ■ Long-acting: 6–8 hours

Here's a summary:

aspart (very fast)	lispro (fast) glulisine (fast) regular insulin (fast)	NPH/isophane (intermediate)	detemir (long) glargine (long)
1. Insulins			
2. Cause glucose to move into cells			
3. Type 1 diabetes (always); type 2 diabetes (uncontrolled by diet and oral meds)			
Nx Tip: Insulin risks:			
■ **May cause hypokalemia**			
■ **May be pushed with D5 for hyperkalemia**			
■ **Risk for hypoglycemia**			

glyburide, glipizide	metformin	exenatide	glucagon	somatropin
1. Sulfonylurea 2. Stimulates pancreatic cells to release insulin, decreases sugar release by liver 3. Type 2 diabetes **Nx Tip:** ■ **Cross hypersensitivity (allergy) with sulfa antibiotics (SMZ TMP)** ■ **Contraindicated in severe liver and renal disease**	1. Oral antidiabetic agent 2. Decreases sugar release by liver, increases cell sensitivity to insulin 3. Type 2 diabetes **Nx Tip:** ■ **Nephrotoxic, hold dose for diagnostics with contrast (CT, cardiac cath, etc.)** ■ **Contraindicated in severe liver and renal disease**	1. Antidiabetic agent 2. Increases release of insulin from pancreas, decreases release of glucagon by pancreas 3. Type 2 diabetes **Nx Tip:** ■ **SubQ injection**	1. Glucose elevator 2. Stimulates the release of glucose by the liver 3. Severe hypoglycemia **Nx Tip:** ■ **May be given IM for outpatient emergencies (similar to EpiPen, stick through clothes into thigh)**	1. Growth hormone 2. Stimulates growth when epiphyses of bones not closed 3. Low intrinsic GH in children, Turner's syndrome **Nx Tip:** ■ **Joint and muscle pain common**
vasopressin	levothyroxine (T4)	propylthiouracil (PTU), iodine, methimazole	calcitonin, alendronate, risedronate	calcitriol, vitamin D
1. Antidiuretic hormone 2. Retention of fluid, vasoconstricts 3. Diabetes insipidus, code situations	1. Thyroid hormone 2. Stimulates metabolism 3. Hypothyroidism **Nx Tip:** ■ **Take in a.m. on empty stomach** ■ **Lifelong therapy** ■ **Watch for thyroid storm.**	1. Antithyroid compound 2. Inhibits thyroid hormones (T4 and T3) 3. Hyperthyroidism, thyrotoxic crisis, Grave's disease **Nx Tip:** ■ **Iodine may be radioactive (destroys tissue), but not a cure.** ■ **If radioactive, caution to surrounding people for 72 hours** 　○ **Caution in bodily fluids (bathroom use)** ■ **Risk for neutropenia with PTU**	1. Antihypercalcemic, bisphosphonates 2. Inhibits body's ability to pull calcium from bones, releases calcium from the kidneys 3. Hyperparathyroidism, hypercalcemia, Paget's disease, osteopenia, osteoporosis **Nx Tip:** ■ **Do not lie down after taking (GERD risk).** ■ **Take bisphosphonates on empty stomach.** ■ **Bisphosphonates commonly taken in postmenopausal women**	1. Antihypocalcemic 2. Stimulates bone growth 3. Hypoparathyroidism, hypocalcemia, bone disease **Nx Tip:** ■ **UV light (sunlight) needed to work**

Gastrointestinal Medications

Gastrointestinal medications are easiest to memorize when split into what affects the upper and lower GI tracts. The information is separated below for ease of study. Remember the anatomy and physiology of the body parts that are affected by these medications.

Upper GI Tract

aluminum hydroxide, sucralfate	ondansetron	omeprazole	ranitidine
1. Antacid 2. Increases pH within stomach 3. GERD, esophagitis, hiatal hernia, peptic ulcers **Nx Tip:** ■ **Take separate from other drugs, food, etc. (30 minutes before or after).** ■ **Coats the stomach**	1. Antiemetic 2. Decreases the stimulation causing nausea and vomiting 3. Post-operative and chemo-related nausea and vomiting	1. Proton pump inhibitor; suffix "prazole" 2. Suppresses acid production in the stomach 3. GERD, peptic ulcers **Nx Tip:** ■ **Common for prophylactic prevention of aspiration pneumonia** o **NG tube, tracheostomy, intubated patient** ■ **May lead to osteoporosis**	1. H2-receptor antagonist; suffix "tidine" 2. Suppresses acid production in the stomach 3. GI ulcers, GERD, esophagitis
metoclopramide	pancrelipase, amylase	ursodiol	
1. Prokinetic agent 2. Increases GI peristalsis 3. Gastroparesis, nausea/vomiting post surgery or chemotherapy **Nx Tip:** ■ **Commonly used post-op to prevent constipation (opioids)**	1. Digestive enzymes 2. Breaks down food into nutrient components for absorption 3. Enzyme replacement for cystic fibrosis or pancreatic insufficiency **Nx Tip:** ■ **Do not crush or chew tablets.** ■ **Take with meals (no need if not eating).**	1. N/A 2. Breaks down cholesterol-formed gallstones 3. Cholesterol gallstones	

Lower GI Tract

simethicone	loperamide	magnesium hydroxide, lactulose	sulfasalazine
1. Antiflatulent	1. Antidiarrheal	1. Laxatives	1. Aminosalicylate
2. Decreases gas production	2. Suppresses GI peristalsis	2. Softens stool, induces bowel movements	2. Decreases acid and inflammation in colon
3. Pain and discomfort from GI upset	3. Diarrhea	3. Constipation, hepatic encephalopathy	3. Inflammatory bowel disease (IBD)
Nx Tip:	**Nx Tip:**	**Nx Tip:**	**Nx Tip:**
■ **Take after meals.**	■ **Risk for abuse**	■ **Lactulose used to discard ammonia through stool**	■ **Contains salicylate (aspirin)**
		○ **Assess for constipation first (it may not work).**	○ **Avoid in children (Reye's syndrome).**
		■ **Castor oil contraindicated in pregnancy**	○ **Bleeding risk**
		○ **May lead to preterm labor**	

Immunology Medications

Immunology covers a wide array of considerations including autoimmune treatments and antibiotics. It is important to not confuse which medications are used to treat which infection. Reminder: Antiviral for viruses. Remember to always draw a culture before administering an antibiotic. Immunizations are covered in the "Immunology" chapter. Information about specific infections is covered in the "Safety and Infection" chapter.

cyclosporin, tacrolimus	adalimumab	methotrexate, etanercept	penicillin	cefazolin
1. Immune modulator	1. Immune modulator	1. Disease-modifying antirheumatic drugs (DMARDs), tumor necrosis factor (TNF)	1. Penicillins; suffix "cillin"	1. Cephalosporin; prefix "cef"
2. Suppresses immune response	2. Suppresses immune response	2. Causes immunosuppression (T cells)	2. Inhibits bacterial replication	2. Inhibits bacterial replication
3. Autoimmune diseases, organ transplants, graft versus host	3. Ulcerative colitis, Crohn's disease, rheumatoid arthritis	3. Rheumatoid arthritis, ectopic pregnancy	3. Infections by bacteria	3. Infections by bacteria
Nx Tip:	**Nx Tip:**	**Nx Tip:**	**Nx Tip:**	**Nx Tip:**
■ **Nephrotoxicity**	■ **Risk for infections (TB, etc.)**	■ **Contraindicated in pregnancy or those thinking about getting pregnant, as well as men**	■ **Cross hypersensitivity (allergy) with cephalosporins**	■ **Cross hypersensitivity with penicillins**
■ **Neutropenia risk**		■ **Used to induce spontaneous abortion in ectopic pregnancies**	○ **Assess specific reaction first.**	○ **Assess specific reaction first.**

continued

vancomycin

1. Vancomycin
2. Inhibits bacterial replication
3. Resistant bacterial strains, bacterial meningitis

Nx Tip:

- **Toxic drug**
  - **Trough level 30 minutes or directly before dose**
  - **Peak levels 1–3 hours after**
  - **Ototoxic, nephrotoxic**
- **Risk for red man syndrome (rash)**

gentamicin, clindamycin, erythromycin, neomycin

1. Aminoglycoside; suffix "mycin"
2. Inhibits bacterial replication
3. Infections by bacteria

Nx Tip:

- **Ototoxic, nephrotoxic, neurotoxic**
- **Peak levels drawn 30 minutes after for gentamicin**
- **Used for burns, minor skin issues (neomycin)**

mafenide acetate

1. Sulfamylon
2. Inhibits bacterial replication
3. Prophylaxis or treatment for skin infections from burns

linezolid

1. Antibiotic
2. Inhibits bacterial replication
3. Resistant bacterial strains (VRE, MRSA)

Nx Tip:

- **Thrombocytopenia risk**

tetracycline

1. Tetracycline
2. Inhibits bacterial replication
3. Chlamydia, rickets, acne

Nx Tip:

- **Take on an empty stomach.**
- **May cause discoloration of teeth**
- **Photosensitivity**

chloramphenicol

1. Antibiotic
2. Inhibits bacterial replication
3. Meningitis

Nx Tip:

- **Risk for blood dyscrasias (anemia)**
- **May lead to gray baby syndrome**

ciprofloxacin

1. Broad spectrum antibiotic; suffix "floxacin"
2. Inhibits bacterial replication
3. Infections by bacteria

Nx Tip:

- **Risk for tendonitis or tendon rupture**
- **Commonly used for UTIs**

sulfamethoxazole trimethoprim (SMZ TMP)

1. Sulfonamide
2. Inhibits bacterial replication
3. Urinary tract infections

Nx Tip:

- **Cross hypersensitivity (allergy) with other "sulfa" medications**
  - **glyburide, glipizide**
- **Push fluids.**
- **Risk for Stevens-Johnson syndrome**

isoniazid, rifampin

1. Antitubercular
2. Inhibits mycobacterial proliferation
3. Tuberculosis (active or latent)

Nx Tip:

- **Long-term therapy (9–12 months)**
- **Hepatotoxic (isoniazid)**
- **Toxic to eyes (rifampin)**
- **Rifampin turns urine orange.**
- **Risk for vitamin B6 (pyridoxine) deficiency in isoniazid therapy**

phenazopyridine

1. Pyridine analgesic
2. Produces analgesic effects topically during excretion
3. Pain from UTI

Nx Tip:

- **Turns urine orange/red**

nitrofurantoin	amphotericin B	nystatin	fluconazole	acyclovir
1. Aseptic 2. Inhibits bacterial replication 3. Urinary tract infections **Nx Tip:** ■ **Contraindicated in renal impairment (CKD, ESRD)**	1. Antifungal 2. Inhibits fungal proliferation 3. Severe fungal infections (tinea—ringworm) **Nx Tip:** ■ **Risk for infusion reactions** ■ **IV is orange/ yellow.**	1. Antifungal 2. Inhibits fungal proliferation 3. Candidiasis (thrush), skin fungal infections **Nx Tip:** ■ **Swish and swallow.** ■ **Comes in powder for skin**	1. Antifungal 2. Inhibits fungal proliferation 3. Fungal infections	1. Antiviral 2. Inhibits viral proliferation 3. Herpes, Epstein-Barr, CMV **Nx Tip:** ■ **Nephrotoxic**
oseltamivir, amantadine	**lamivudine**	**zidovudine, tenofovir, maraviroc**	**hydroxychloroquine**	**permethrin**
1. Antiviral 2. Inhibits viral proliferation 3. Influenza (H1N1, avian, etc.)	1. Antiviral 2. Inhibits viral proliferation 3. Hepatitis	1. Antiretroviral therapy 2. Inhibits HIV proliferation 3. HIV, AIDS **Nx Tip:** ■ **Hepatotoxic, nephrotoxic, hyperlipidemia, osteoporosis, lipodystrophy**	1. Antimalarial 2. Inhibits parasite proliferation 3. Malaria **Nx Tip:** ■ **Common in prophylaxis** ■ **Risk for macular or corneal damage**	1. Antiectoparasitic 2. Inhibits pediculosis proliferation 3. Lice, scabies, crabs **Nx Tip:** ■ **The bug is called pediculosis.** ■ **All family members should be treated.** ■ **Shampoo or lotion (repeated doses may be necessary)** ■ **Linens must be bagged and sealed for 2 weeks.** ■ **Hot water to clean, not warm**

Hematology Medications

epoetin alfa	filgrastim	iron	vitamin B12
1. Erythropoiesis stimulating	1. Colony-stimulating factor	1. Ferrous sulfate	1. Cobalamin
2. Stimulates bone marrow for RBC production	2. Increases WBC formation	2. Increases iron for heme development	2. Increases B12 in the body
3. Anemia	3. Neutropenia	3. Iron deficiency anemia	3. B12 deficiency, pernicious anemia
Nx Tip:	**Nx Tip:**	**Nx Tip:**	**Nx Tip:**
■ **Risk for clotting events (assess CBC)**	■ **Commonly used in cancer patients**	■ **Take on an empty stomach (with a little vitamin C).**	■ **Given by injection if no stomach exists**
■ **Assess for increase in reticulocyte count (means it is working).**		■ **Given orally or by injection**	
■ **Normal RBC lifespan: 90–120 days**		■ **Turns stool black (it is not melena)**	
		■ **Drink through straw (may turn teeth black).**	
		■ **Do not take with tea.**	

Oncology Medications

Oncology is one of the easier pharmacology sections to learn for the NCLEX. That's because if the name of the medication is memorized, the rest of the question is typically easy. Mistakes happen from not recognizing the medication. Do not go overboard on this section though; the most important thing to learn is simply the name. The individual drugs are purposefully short and vague for this reason.

interferon alfa	thalidomide	ever sirolimus
1. Cytokine	1. Anti-angiogenic	1. mTOR inhibitor
2. Inhibits growth of cancer cells	2. Inhibits angiogenesis (capillary growth)	2. Inhibits cancer growth
3. Cancer	3. Cancer	3. Breast cancer
rituximab, imatinib, 5-fluorouracil (5-FU), carmustine, cyclophosphamide	**doxorubicin**	**tamoxifen**
1. Chemotherapy	1. Antitumor antibiotic	1. Antiestrogen
2. Inhibits cancer growth	2. Inhibits cancer proliferation	2. Inhibits cancer proliferation
3. Cancer	3. Cancer	3. Breast cancer
Nx Tip:	**Nx Tip:**	**Nx Tip:**
■ **May cause infusion reactions (fever, chills, angioedema)**	■ **Black box warning: cardiotoxic**	■ **Induces menopause symptoms (hot flashes)**
■ **Special certification required to handle (specialized RN or pharmacy)**	■ **Alopecia reversible**	
○ **Not an LPN or UAP**	■ **Vesicant: Monitor closely.**	

Musculoskeletal and Pain Medications

Orthopaedic and pain management considerations fall under this section. Remember to perform a follow-up pain assessment within 1 hour of giving a pain medication. Pain is much easier to prevent when it is treated early on. The goal is to avoid giving pain medications for breakthrough pain. Prevent it from happening in the first place.

Patient-Controlled Analgesia (PCA) Pump

- Monitor pump utilization q4hr.
  - Document doses.
  - Patient demand requests above max
- Patient complains of unrelieved pain.
  - Start at patient and work way up technology or machinery.
  - Is the tubing connected? Is it kinked? Is machine working?
  - Does patient understand how to use PCA?
  - Is pain properly managed?

colchicine, allopurinol	morphine, fentanyl, hydromorphone, meperidine, oxycodone, tramadol	codeine, hydrocodone
1. Antigout	1. Strong opioid narcotics	1. Mild opioid narcotics
2. Decreases inflammation, decreases hyperuricemia	2. Decreases pain	2. Decreases pain
3. Acute and chronic gout	3. Moderate to severe pain	3. Mild to moderate pain, cough suppressant
Nx Tip:	**Nx Tip:**	**Nx Tip:**
• **Acute gout: colchicine**	• **Side effect: constipation**	• **Common PO medications**
• **Chronic gout: allopurinol**	• **Adverse effects: respiratory depression, hypotension**	• **Risk for falls**
◦ **Push fluids (2–3 L per day).**	• **Risk for dependence and addiction**	• **Do not use codeine in patients where cough is desired (productive cough).**
	• **Risk for falls**	
pentazocine	naloxone	ibuprofen, naproxen, ketorolac, indomethacin, meloxicam
1. Narcotic agonist—antagonist	1. Narcotic antagonist	1. NSAIDs
2. Decreases pain	2. Reverses effects of opioid narcotics	2. Decreases inflammatory response
3. Moderate to severe pain	3. Opioid overdose	3. Mild to moderate pain
Nx Tip:	**Nx Tip:**	**Nx Tip:**
• **Similar to narcotic effects**	• **Repeat doses may be required.**	• **Risk for bleeding (all NSAIDs)**
	• **Risk for bleeding**	• **Risk for ulcer formation**
		• **Risk for asthma exacerbation (careful use in asthma patients)**
methadone, buprenorphine	acetaminophen	sumatriptan
1. Anti-dependency	1. NSAID, antipyretic	1. NSAID; suffix "triptan"
2. Used in maintenance therapy for drug abuse	2. Decreases inflammatory response, decreases fever	2. Decreases inflammation
3. Drug withdrawal, rehab	3. Mild pain, fever	3. Migraine headaches
Nx Tip:	**Nx Tip:**	**Nx Tip:**
• **Common in sublingual or PO format**	• **Risk for hepatotoxicity**	• **Take during aura phase (do not wait until headache).**
	• **Risk for acetaminophen toxicity (acetylcysteine as antidote)**	
	• **Used for nitroglycerin-related headaches**	
	• **4g daily max**	

Neurology Medications

This section covers a wide array of medications, from neuromuscular diseases and spasticity to anesthesia.

phenytoin, carbamazepine, valproic acid, gabapentin	propofol, ketamine, dexmedetomidine	phenobarbital	baclofen	isoflurane
1. Antiepileptic 2. Decreases sodium influx into cells (sodium-potassium pump) 3. Seizure disorders **Nx Tip:** ■ **Phenytoin (toxic): therapeutic level 10–20 mcg/mL** ■ **Side effect: vision changes** ■ **Risk for gingival hyperplasia (phenytoin)** ■ **Additional contraception needed if on birth control (risk for pregnancy)**	1. Parenteral anesthetic agents 2. Induces loss of consciousness and sedation 3. Sedation in ICU, induction and maintenance of anesthesia **Nx Tip:** ■ **Appears white like milk (propofol)** ■ **Risk for hypotension and respiratory depression** ■ **Contains soybean oil, glycerol, and egg (assess for allergy)** ■ **May need to replete zinc (propofol)**	1. Barbiturate 2. Increases effects of GABA 3. Seizures, sedation **Nx Tip:** ■ **Risk for dependency (highly addictive)**	1. Centrally acting spasmolytic 2. Reduces musculoskeletal activity 3. Spasm disorders (MS, cerebral palsy, TBI, SCI) **Nx Tip:** ■ **May be used in pump (continuous delivery)** ■ **Risk for sedation (fall risk)** ■ **Risk for hallucinations**	1. Inhaled agent; suffix "flurane" 2. Induces loss of consciousness and sedation 3. Anesthesia **Nx Tip:** ■ **Irritates the throat (cough)—paralyze patient first** ■ **Risk for hypotension and respiratory depression (intubate)**
lidocaine, bupivacaine	**vecuronium, succinylcholine**	**amantadine**	**cyclobenzaprine, metaxalone**	**dextroamphetamine, methylphenidate**
1. Local anesthetic 2. Inhibits nerve function (temperature, pain, touch, proprioception, skeletal muscle tone) 3. Local and regional anesthesia, nerve blocks, dental procedures **Nx Tip:** ■ **Also used IV for ventricular dysrhythmias**	1. Neuromuscular blocking agents, paralyzing agents 2. Blocks nerve impulses (acetylcholine) causing paralysis 3. Intubation, surgical procedures **Nx Tip:** ■ **Risk for malignant hyperthermia (assess family history)** ■ **Reversal agent: neostigmine**	1. Dopaminergic agent 2. Increases level of dopamine in synapse 3. Parkinson's disease **Nx Tip:** ■ **Risk for orthostatic hypotension** ■ **Risk for Parkinsonian crisis (similar to neuroleptic malignant syndrome)**	1. Centrally acting muscle relaxants 2. Alleviates muscle spasms through CNS 3. Muscle spasms **Nx Tip:** ■ **Risk for sedation (increase in fall risk)**	1. Centrally acting CNS stimulants; suffix "tamine" 2. Decreases the inflammatory response 3. ADHD **Nx Tip:** ■ **Risk for abuse** ■ **Risk for too much weight loss (1 lb per week allowed)**

carbidopa-levodopa, ethosuximide	glatiramer, interferon beta	riluzole	neostigmine	dantolene
1. Antiepileptic 2. Decreases calcium influx into cells 3. Seizure disorders	1. Anti-MS 2. Inhibits demyelination 3. Multiple sclerosis (reduce frequency or progression)	1. Anti-ALS 2. N/A 3. Slows the progression of ALS	1. Cholinergic agent; suffix "stigmine" 2. Increases levels of acetylcholine 3. Myasthenia gravis, paralytic reversal	1. Peripherally acting spasmolytic 2. Reduces muscle activity 3. Spasticity, malignant hyperthermia
sibutramine 1. Anorectic agent 2. Decreases appetite 3. Obesity **Nx Tip:** ■ **Risk for abuse**	**caffeine** 1. Respiratory stimulant 2. Stimulates respiratory center 3. Slow respiratory rate in preterm neonates **Nx Tip:** ■ **Natural diuretic** ■ **Often combined with acetaminophen for headaches**			

Psychiatry Medications

Psychiatry is incredibly important to understand for the NCLEX. It is a popular question topic. The side effect profile for these classes of medications tends to be more important than those for other medications.

Anxiety Disorders

lorazepam, alprazolam, chlordiazepoxide	buspirone	trazodone	zolpidem
1. Benzodiazepine, anxiolytic; suffixes "pam," "lam" 2. Increases inhibitory effects of GABA 3. Anxiety disorders, sedation, alcohol withdrawal, benzo withdrawal, seizures **Nx Tip:** ■ **Risk for respiratory depression and sedation (fall risk)** ■ **Elderly and obese patients are at higher risk for adverse effects and overdose.** ■ **Risk for addiction, dependence, and withdrawal** ■ **Strong version: Midazolam is commonly used for twilight/moderate sedation.**	1. Anxiolytic, nonbenzodiazepine 2. N/A 3. Anxiety disorders **Nx Tip:** ■ **Takes 3–4 weeks to show therapeutic effects** ■ **Preferred with patients with addiction and the elderly**	1. Atypical antidepressant 2. Induces sedation as a side effect 3. Insomnia	1. Hypnotic 2. Induces sleep 3. Insomnia **Nx Tip:** ■ **Risk for hallucinations**

continued

sertraline, citalopram, fluoxetine, paroxetine

1. Antidepressant, selective serotonin reuptake inhibitor (SSRI)
2. Increases serotonin in synapse
3. Depression, OCD, panic disorder, PTSD

Nx Tip:

- **Side effects: insomnia, sexual dysfunction, weight gain**
- **Adverse effect: serotonin syndrome (medical emergency)**
- **Black box warning: increased risk for suicide in first 3 weeks**

venlafaxine

1. Serotonin and norepinephrine reuptake inhibitor (SNRI)
2. Increases serotonin and norepinephrine in synapse
3. Depression, OCD, panic disorder, PTSD

Nx Tip:

- **Similar side effects and adverse effects as SSRI**

nortriptyline

1. Tricyclic antidepressant; suffixes "line," "mine"
2. Increases serotonin and norepinephrine in the synapse
3. Depression

Nx Tip:

- **Risk for TCA toxicity (CV, liver)**
- **Risk for suicide in beginning of regimen**
- **Side effect: anticholinergic (SLUDD)**

lithium, valproic acid, aripiprazole

1. Mood stabilizer
2. N/A
3. Bipolar disorder, manic episodes

Nx Tip:

- **Monitor sodium intake (do not increase or decrease).**
- **Adhere to steady fluid intake (2–3 L/day).**
- **Risk for lithium toxicity**
  - **Therapeutic range: 0.6–1.2 mEq/L**
  - **Early signs and symptoms: slurred speech, weakness, confusion, twitches**
  - **Late signs and symptoms: delirium, arrhythmias**

phenelzine

1. Monoamine oxidase inhibitor (MAOI)
2. Inhibits breakdown of dopamine, epinephrine, norepinephrine, and serotonin
3. Depression unresponsive to other treatment

Nx Tip:

- **Follow tyramine diet: no aged cheeses, wine, salami (risk for HTN crisis).**
- **Risk for photosensitivity (protect eyes and skin)**
- **Medication reconciliation (high priority): multiple drug interactions**
- **Contraindicated in liver and kidney diseases**

haloperidol, perphenazine, chlorpromazine

1. Typical antipsychotics
2. N/A
3. Schizophrenia, psychosis

Nx Tip:

- **Side effects: extrapyramidal symptoms (EPS), tardive dyskinesia**
- **Risk for photosensitivity (protect eyes and skin)**
- **Risk for neutropenia**
- **Risk for neuroleptic malignant syndrome (medical emergency)**
  - **Fever, diaphoresis, tachycardia, muscle rigidity**

olanzapine, clozapine, risperidone

1. Atypical antipsychotics
2. N/A
3. Schizophrenia, psychosis

Nx Tip:

- **Preferred over typical antipsychotics (less chance of side effects)**
- **Risk for neutropenia**
- **Risk for neuroleptic malignant syndrome (medical emergency)**

rivastigmine, donepezil

1. Acetylcholinesterase enzyme inhibitor
2. Increases acetylcholine in synapse
3. Dementia

Nx Tip:

- **Acetylcholine may be responsible for cognition.**
- **Cannot cure dementia; goal is to preserve function**

disulfiram	naltrexone		
1. Aldehyde dehydrogenase inhibitor 2. Induces "hangover"-like symptoms upon ingestion of alcohol 3. Alcoholism **Nx Tip:** - **Cooking with alcohol is okay (burns off).** - **Avoid other products containing alcohol (mouthwash, etc.).**	1. N/A 2. Decreases urge to drink 3. Alcohol dependence		

Men's Health Medications

testosterone, oxandrolone	sildenafil	finasteride, minoxidil, prazosin

1. Androgens, anabolics; suffix "one"
2. Repletes decreased testosterone
3. Hormone replacement
 	
Nx Tip:
- **Monitor for secondary male sex characteristics (body hair, muscle mass, libido, vocal changes).**
- **If intradermal, remove old patch or lotion before applying more; rotate skin sites.**
- **Side effect: gynecomastia**
- **Adverse effect: hepatotoxicity**
	1. N/A; suffix "fil"
	2. Promotes vasodilation in corpus cavernosum of penis, vasodilates pulmonary vasculature
	3. Erectile dysfunction, pulmonary hypertension
	
	Nx Tip:
	- **Contraindicated in men taking nitrates (nitroglycerin), causes serious drop in BP**
	- **Risk for priapism**
	  - **Medical emergency**
	  - **Prolonged erection lasting longer than 4 hours**
		1. N/A; suffix "zosin"
		2. Restores hair loss, improves ability to urinate
		3. Male pattern baldness, benign prostatic hyperplasia
		
		Nx Tip:
		- **Risk for orthostasis (zosins)**

Women's Health Medications

estrogen	progesterone, medroxyprogesterone	oxytocin
1. Estrogen 2. Repletes decreased estrogen 3. Hormone replacement, menopausal symptoms **Nx Tip:** - **Short-term therapy** - **Contraindicated in most breast cancers and clotting disorders**	1. Progestins 2. Regulates gonadotropins inhibiting ovulation 3. Birth control (contraception) **Nx Tip:** - **Education to include healthy lifestyle (diet, exercise, no smoking)** - **Contraindicated in clotting disorders** - **Black box warning: increases risk of ovarian and breast cancer**	1. Uterotonic 2. Increases the contractions of the uterus, stimulates milk production 3. Induction or augmentation of labor **Nx Tip:** - **Titrated drug by RN to achieve good labor (contractions 2–3 minutes apart, 45 seconds in length)** - **Monitor intake and output.** - **Risk for uterine atony (tired muscle)—slow down the drip** - **Risk for uterine rupture (medical emergency)—stop the drip** - **May be used intranasally to increase milk production**
ergonovine, carboprost 1. Uterotonic; suffix "ovine" 2. Constricts blood vessels in the uterus 3. Prevention of postpartum bleeding	**terbutaline, magnesium sulfate** 1. Tocolytic 2. Reduces and ceases contractions 3. Prevents preterm labor, prevents seizures **Nx Tip:** - **Magnesium sulfate may lead to hypermagnesemia (loss of deep tendon muscles).**	

Contraceptives

- Condoms
  - Leave space at tip.
  - Primary prevention of STDs and pregnancy
  - Contraindicated in latex allergy
- Emergency oral (Plan B)
  - Most effective if taken within 24 hours of intercourse
  - May be taken up to 72 hours after intercourse
- Transdermal
  - Applied to clean, dry skin
  - Rotate skin sites.
  - Wipe off old before applying new.
- Vaginal rings
  - Steady delivery of medication over weeks
- Diaphragm
  - Placed 30 minutes before intercourse, left in 6 hours after
  - Must be resized if weight changes
- Intrauterine device (IUD)
  - May last up to 5 years (copper or synthetic progesterone)
  - Risk for pelvic inflammatory disease and ectopic pregnancy

Genetics

The NCLEX may ask about probability genetics. To analyze genetic probability, you use a Punnett square, as illustrated below. It is also important to understand the basics about genetics and to be familiar with the terminology. It is not, however, necessary to memorize the different types of genetic disorders, as the disorder would be identified in the NCLEX question. For example:

A 26-year-old male was recently diagnosed with Marfan syndrome, an autosomal dominant disorder, . . .

A 32-year-old male with hemophilia, an x-linked recessive disorder, . . .

Punnett Square

	H	h
H	HH	Hh
h	Hh	hh

The parents' alleles are placed on the top and left sides of the Punnett square (one parent on the top, the other on the left side). From there, utilize a simple cross-multiplying mentality to reach each probable child allele. In the example above, if both parents are heterozygous for the trait (Hh), the child has a 25% chance of being homozygous dominant (HH), a 50% chance of being heterozygous (Hh), and a 25% chance of being homozygous recessive (hh).

Heterozygous

- Hh
- Mixed combination allele

Homozygous

- HH, hh
- Same combination allele

Autosomal Recessive Disorder

- hh
- Must be homozygous recessive for the disorder

Autosomal Dominant Disorder

- HH, Hh
- Any dominant combination results in the disorder.

X-Linked Recessive Disorder

- xx, xy
- Hemophilia, Duchenne muscular dystrophy
- More common in boys than girls

X-Linked Dominant Disorder

- Xx, Xy
- Any dominant "X" will result in the disorder.

Motor Neurons and Glands

Acetylcholine is involved in a large number of bodily functions. When these functions fail, certain diseases and dysfunctions can arise. Diseases like myasthenia gravis come into play, as does the nature of how anesthesia paralyzes a patient with neuromuscular blocking agents. Understanding the underlying anatomy and physiology is crucial to tackling this difficult subject. It is not just the pathophysiology that is important; a series of medications exist and an understanding of these medications is needed for the NCLEX. For a list of these medications, see the "Motor Neurons and Glands" section of the "Pharmacology" chapter.

Acetylcholine

Acetylcholine is the neurotransmitter responsible for the movement of muscles and actions by glandular tissue. Neuromuscular junctions are all over the human body, innervating muscles and glands.

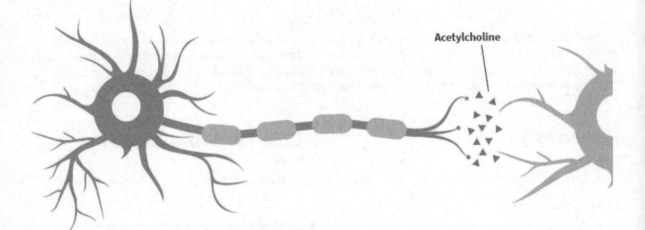

Neuromuscular Connections

Skeletal Muscle

- Voluntary muscle movement
- Movement of body
- Diaphragm for breathing

Cardiac Muscle

- Involuntary muscle movement
- Force of contraction

Smooth Muscle

- Involuntary muscle movement
- Blood vessels, bronchioles, bladder, pupils
  o Contraction and dilation
- GI peristalsis

Neuroglandular Connections

SLUDD Acronym

The SLUDD acronym will help you remember the responses of the parasympathetic nervous system:

- Salivation
- Lacrimation
- Urination
- Digestion
- Defecation

Anticholinergic (Dry)

- Dry mouth
- Dry eyes
- Urinary retention
- Constipation
- Difficulty defecating

Cholinergic Agonist (Wet)

- Increased saliva production
- Increased tear production
- Increased need to urinate
- Increased peristalsis
- Increased urge to defecate

Cholinergic Crisis

Pathophysiology

- Dangerous increase in acetylcholine
- May occur due to cholinergic agonists
- Sarin gas (nerve-blocking agents)

Signs and Symptoms

- The "wet" symptoms above (muscarinic symptoms)
- Increase in SLUDD signs and symptoms
- Muscular involvement (nicotinic symptoms)
  - Muscle cramps, tachycardia, weakness, tremors, shaking
  - Leads to muscle paralysis (death)

Interventions

- ICU admission (frequent monitoring)
- Mechanical ventilation if needed
- Time heals (no pharmacological intervention for breathing problems).

Gravity

When confused about what may or may not be the best positioning for the patient, think of gravity. Gravity will pull the body and organs in certain directions. This is the main reason why the healthcare team may recommend a specific position for a patient. Other reasons may rely on anatomy alone or be due to safety. The various patient positions are detailed below, along with the common reasons for each.

High-Fowler's

90 degrees; head elevated
- Respiratory happy place—gravity pulls the diaphragm downward, allowing for chest/lung expansion
  - Dyspnea, desaturation, cyanosis
  - Tripod position (leaning forward)
  - Pleuritic chest pain
  - Pleurocentesis (leaning forward)

Semi-Fowler's

15–45 degrees; head elevated
- Neuro, respiratory, and cardiac happy place
  - ICP issues and brain trauma
  - Optimal for patients who have a nasogastric tube in place
- Occasionally respiratory if high-Fowler's not tolerated
  - Ascites causing dyspnea

Supine

Flat on back
- Spinal injuries
- Post lumbar puncture (spinal tap)
- Dorsal recumbent (knees bent, feet flat on surface)
  - Similar to lithotomy for pelvic exam
- Pericardiocentesis

Prone

Flat on stomach; head turned to one side
- Meningocele and neural tube defects
- ARDs
- Post-op cleft palate repair
  - Facilitates secretion removal
  - Same for post-op tonsillectomy
  - Only position that allows for full extension of hip and knee joints

Sims

On stomach; right leg bent up
- Enema, suppository, rectal temp
- Pregnant women (3rd trimester)

Trendelenburg

Head lower than body
- Prolapsed cord in labor
- Preterm labor
- Shock/hypotension (assists preload back to heart)
- Air embolism (Trendelenburg and to left)

Left-Side Lying

On left side
- Variable or late decelerations
- Dumping syndrome
- Facilitates bowel movements
- GERD
- Relieves pressure on sacrum and heels

Right-Side Lying

On right side
- Post liver biopsy
- Facilitates digestion (aids gastric emptying)

This practice exam contains 75 questions, the minimum number of questions on the computer-adaptive NCLEX exam. Do not concern yourself with time for the purpose of this exercise. While the NCLEX itself is timed at 6 hours, a well-prepared student will rarely run out of time. Make sure to take the time to read each question and answer choice very carefully. Focus on word choices, especially the adjectives used by the writers. The difference between a minor or major problem can change the nature of the answer.

At the end of this practice exam, you'll find an answer key and the rationale for each correct answer, including what chapters to refer to in this book.

Certain components on the NCLEX, such as Prioritization and Safety and Infection, are more important than others. It is impossible to pass the NCLEX without mastering these topics. Pay close attention to Prioritization questions and the strategies taught in the book.

The goal of the practice exam is to achieve a score of 60% or higher. While students who perform below this level often pass the NCLEX, it is a benchmark to keep in mind and will help you determine if additional study and practice questions would help in your overall preparation. Good luck, future nurses! Take a deep breath and begin.

75 Questions

1. The charge nurse on a neurological stepdown unit must assign one of the following patients to a float nurse from the med-surg floor. Which of the following patients would be **most** appropriate to give to this float nurse?

   A. A patient who just returned to the unit after a supratentorial craniotomy. The patient has an epidural catheter.
   B. A patient with increased ICP on mannitol
   C. A patient with a seizure disorder undergoing an EEG
   D. A patient post-op 1 hour sympathectomy

2. After receiving a shift change report, a nurse prioritizes which of the following patients to be assessed **first**?

   A. A patient scheduled for a coronary artery bypass surgery in 1 hour. Multi-vessel occlusions exist.
   B. A patient complaining of increased pain who is due for the next dose of oxycodone/acetaminophen. The patient has received 2 g of acetaminophen so far today.
   C. A COPD patient with a current ABG of pH: 7.31, CO_2: 48, HCO_3: 22, PaO_2: 70
   D. A patient post-op 1 hour from cardiac catheterization complaining of wetness on the bed who believes it to be sweat

3. A physician has ordered an augmentation of a labor using oxytocin. The woman is 40 weeks gestation and has been in labor for 6 hours. The woman has been dilated 2 cm for 3 hours now. While obtaining the supplies, the nurse is remembering key points of oxytocin infusion. What is the **most** important consideration with oxytocin infusion?

   A. Placenta previa formation
   B. Early deceleration
   C. Premature labor
   D. Vaginal bleeding

4. A 22-year-old female patient has recently returned to the unit post-op double lung transplant due to advancing cystic fibrosis. The patient remains intubated and sedated. Which of the following would the nurse expect?

   A. A temperature of 100.5°
   B. A new prescription for tacrolimus
   C. A new prescription for methotrexate
   D. A new prescription for albuterol

5. A nurse working on a telemetry unit has recently been assigned to a patient with frequent PVCs. After recent lab work reveals a potassium level of 6.3 mmol/L, the physician orders sodium polystyrene sulfonate to be administered STAT. Which of the following would the nurse do **first**?

   A. Assess the number of recent bowel movements.
   B. Administer the STAT medication.
   C. Ask if the patient takes any stool softeners at home.
   D. Draw a second potassium to confirm.

6. A patient diagnosed with gout has recently been prescribed allopurinol to reduce uric acid levels in the blood. Aside from encouraging the patient to push fluids, which of the following recommendations is **best** for the nurse to make for this patient?

   A. Avoid shellfish.
   B. Drink 2–3 L of water per day.
   C. Take ibuprofen if pain continues.
   D. Take acetaminophen if pain continues.

7. A nurse in the emergency department receives a call about an incoming patient who fell into a lake while ice fishing. First responders indicate the patient is severely hypothermic and is currently asystole. While preparing for the trauma, notifying all of the appropriate people, it is **most** important for the nurse to understand which of the following key points about this patient?

   A. The patient will be immediately defibrillated.
   B. The patient's outcome will not be known until he or she is warm.
   C. The patient will be kept hypothermic to preserve brain tissue.
   D. The patient will need to be warmed as fast as possible.

8. While a student nurse is drawing up 20 mg of furosemide for an IV push, the preceptor is teaching why we push this medication slowly over 2–3 minutes. Which point is the **most** important for the preceptor to make?

   A. Loss of too much volume
   B. Damage to the ears
   C. Hepatotoxicity
   D. Hypokalemia

9. A nurse is teaching a patient with chronic migraines about potential interventions. Which of the following statements, if made by the patient, requires **further education**?

   A. "I should take my aspirin and sumatriptan together."
   B. "It is best if I lie down and decrease noise and light around me."
   C. "I should avoid alcohol."
   D. "When the headache begins, I should take my sumatriptan medication."

10. A 75-year-old woman is admitted to the hospital from a nursing home. She complains of abdominal pain and steatorrhea. She is confused, and the family cannot be contacted for a medical history. The nursing home is in the process of sending medical history over, but in the meantime, which of the following findings would be the **most** important assessment to note when explaining the admissions assessment via SBAR to the doctor?

    A. A surgical scar in the right upper quadrant (RUQ)
    B. A current prescription of donepezil for dementia
    C. A stage 2 pressure ulcer on the sacrum
    D. A blood pressure of 150/90

11. A nurse is caring for four patients on the post-surgical unit. Which of the following new admissions would the nurse see **first**?

    A. A patient post endoscopic retrograde cholangiopancreatography (ERCP) with lithotripsy complaining of dull abdominal pain
    B. A patient post rhizotomy complaining of an inability to urinate
    C. A patient post coronary artery bypass (CAB) draining 50 mL of sanguinous fluid into the chest tube per hour
    D. A patient post supratentorial craniotomy with a Glasgow Coma Scale (GCS) of 13

12. A 7-year-old child was recently diagnosed with lead poisoning and transferred to a med-surg floor. The nurse receives the patient and begins care immediately. It is important to monitor for continued and worsening signs of lead poisoning, in addition to potential complications of the treatment. Which of the following signs and symptoms would be the **most** alarming?

    A. Violent outbursts
    B. BP of 100/65
    C. Lack of desire to eat
    D. Neutropenia

13. You are a pediatric nurse working in a children's hospital emergency room. Parents bring in a 5-year-old child with pustules around the nose and mouth; some appear honey-crusted in nature. The child is scratching the areas often. What is the priority intervention for the nurse to perform upon these assessment findings?

    A. Instruct the child to use the knuckles and not the fingertips to scratch.
    B. Have the parents restrain the child so he or she cannot scratch.
    C. Place the child in an isolation room.
    D. Immediately draw blood cultures and call the HCP.

14. A nurse is caring for a 65-year-old male newly admitted to the emergency room with a suspected stroke. He is unable to speak but is accompanied by his daughter. What is the **most** important question to ask the daughter before following any orders?

    A. "What are his current medications taken at home?"
    B. "What was he doing when the symptoms began?"
    C. "Is there a family history of stroke?"
    D. "When did the symptoms begin?"

15. A nursing instructor is monitoring the actions of students on a med-surg floor. A patient's cultures come back positive for meningitis. Which of the following is **most** important for the instructor to teach the students at this time?

    A. Monitor the patient immediately for signs and symptoms of increased intracranial pressure.
    B. Obtain an order and place the patient on droplet precautions.
    C. Obtain blood cultures.
    D. Assess the patient for Kernig's sign.

16. A 53-year-old patient was admitted to the medical intensive care unit (MICU) due to suspected septic shock secondary to a MRSA infection. The patient was given fluids, ciprofloxacin, and placed on dobutamine immediately upon admission. After receiving the above hand-off, the nurse walks into the room to find the patient deteriorating and becoming hypotensive. After exhausting the ordered amount allowed for dobutamine, the nurse calls the physician. Which of the following orders from the physician would be performed **first**?

    A. Emergency surgery with exploratory laparotomy
    B. Cefazolin IV STAT
    C. Norepinephrine IV
    D. Abdominal x-ray STAT

17. A 6-year-old boy in your care was admitted 4 hours ago with laryngotracheal bronchitis. Upon assessment you find an HR of 135, RR of 35, and a temp of 98° F. Upon your last assessment, the high-pitched sounds upon inspiration have diminished. What is the priority nursing intervention?

    A. Call the HCP and anticipate giving epinephrine.
    B. Call the HCP and anticipate giving albuterol.
    C. Assess lung sounds bilaterally.
    D. Draw blood cultures and continue to monitor.

18. During an emergency, a patient has not been breathing enough to maintain body function. Which of the following ABGs would be expected in a patient such as this?

    A. pH: 7.55, CO_2: 30, HCO_3: 18
    B. pH: 7.45, CO_2: 35, HCO_3: 22
    C. pH: 7.28, CO_2: 28, HCO_3: 10
    D. pH: 7.30, CO_2: 50, HCO_3: 22

19. A patient in the medical intensive care unit (MICU) is receiving fluid replacement with lactated Ringer's solution after 45% of his body was burned 4 hours ago. The assessment shows the following:

    Temperature: 97.5°

    HR: 135

    BP: 85/60

    Central venous pressure (CVP): 3

    Urine output: 50 mL in 2 hours

    +2 generalized pitting edema

    What would the nurse recommend to the HCP, given these assessment findings?

    A. IV fluid increase and switch to normal saline
    B. Whole blood with normal saline
    C. Increase LR and add albumin.
    D. Furosemide

20. A nurse preceptor in the surgical intensive care unit (SICU) is working closely with a new nurse during the orientation phase. A new patient has returned from surgery an hour ago and is still intubated. The new nurse is working in the room. Which actions by the new nurse would require the preceptor to intervene?

    A. The new nurse is setting up to change a bloody surgical dressing.
    B. The new nurse places the head of the bed at 30 degrees.
    C. The new nurse is preparing to administer pantoprazole IV, as ordered.
    D. The new nurse is suctioning the patient as needed.

21. A nurse on a hepatology floor is reviewing the morning labs of a patient with liver cirrhosis. Which of the following lab values would the nurse expect to be high?

    A. Albumin
    B. Prothrombin time
    C. Platelets
    D. Sodium

22. A patient was recently found unresponsive on the sidewalk of a busy urban street. 911 was called quickly, and CPR was performed on the scene. The patient is brought into the emergency department. V. Fib is currently seen on the monitor. Which of the following interventions would the nurse expect to be ordered at this point in the care? **Select all that apply.**

    A. Atropine
    B. Bicarbonate
    C. Epinephrine
    D. CPR
    E. Synchronized cardioversion
    F. CT scan

23. A patient is recently admitted to the emergency room with a suspected overdose of oxycodone and alcohol. Which of the following signs would the nurse expect specific to opioid use versus other substances?

    A. Dilated pupils
    B. Respiratory depression
    C. Constricted pupils
    D. Tachycardia

24. A community care nurse is assessing risks for pneumonia in a patient population of the elderly. Which of the following patients would have the lowest risk for developing pneumonia?

    A. A male patient diagnosed with atrial fibrillation
    B. A female patient treated post-op perforated bowel
    C. A male patient with a CVA who exhibits signs of dysphagia
    D. A homeless woman who is an alcoholic

25. A patient diagnosed with endocarditis 3 weeks ago had a PICC line placed for long-term antibiotic treatment. The patient came into the emergency room 15 minutes ago complaining of chills and general malaise. Which of the following findings would be especially troubling?

    A. BP 102/70 and an HR of 115
    B. WBC 15,000
    C. Erythema and tenderness around the catheter
    D. Fatigue and a 102° fever

26. A patient is receiving heparin therapy for anticoagulation and prevention of a deep vein thrombosis after surgery. As the nurse is rounding on this patient, pinpoint red spots are found on the skin. During an initial assessment, the nurse finds no complaints of dizziness and the patient's vital signs are stable. What would the nurse do **first**?

    A. Call the physician immediately.
    B. Decrease the dose of heparin.
    C. Confirm an order for PT/INR and draw blood.
    D. Confirm an order for aPTT and draw blood.

27. A nurse is assessing an elderly patient post-operative day 1 who is showing signs of delirium. The patient believes she is back home and in a different year. The bed alarm has been going off repeatedly, as the patient does not stay in bed. What is the priority intervention at this time for this patient?

    A.   Obtain an order for haloperidol STAT.
    B.   Call the family so they can be with the patient.
    C.   Arrange for a nursing assistant (UAP) to stay with the patient.
    D.   Move the patient to a room closer to the nurses' station.

28. A nurse is preparing for an upcoming seminar for education revolving around preventative care. The nurse's main focus is on secondary prevention at this visit. Which of the following topics would be included in this seminar? **Select all that apply.**

    A.   Condom use
    B.   Mammography
    C.   Post-MI cardiogram
    D.   PSA blood levels
    E.   Immunizations
    F.   Exercise and dieting
    G.   Colonoscopy

29. A patient recently admitted to the psych unit is screaming at the nurse, demanding to know his rights even though he has been involuntarily admitted. Which statement would be **true** if said to the patient?

    A.   "You have the right to refuse medication."
    B.   "You have the right to leave whenever you want."
    C.   "You do not have the right to bring in family or friends."
    D.   "You do not have the right to take part in the choices of your care."

30. A nurse is receiving hand-off reports on a med-surg floor. Which findings would the nurse report to the HCP **immediately**?

    A.   A 24-year-old patient with stable vital signs, diagnosed with pancreatitis related to cystic fibrosis. The patient reports cramping pain in the upper left quadrant.
    B.   A 65-year-old male with COPD who reports shortness of breath and displays a pulse ox of 89%. The patient is in high-Fowler's position and on 2 L nasal cannula.
    C.   A 33-year-old intubated patient who has been on NG tube feedings for the past 4 hours. The patient's stomach is distended.
    D.   A 53-year-old female 2 hours post-op cholecystectomy due to gallstones. The patient appears to be sleeping.

31. The nurse walks into a patient's room to find a lit cigarette in a trash can. A fire begins. In **what order** would the nurse complete the following actions?

    A. Pull the fire alarm.

    B. Remove the patient and family members from harm's way.

    C. Close all doors and windows close to the fire.

    D. Locate the fire extinguisher and attempt to put out the fire.

    E. Instruct unnecessary staff and visitors to use the stairs.

32. A 42-year-old female patient is to be discharged home with amitriptyline. You are teaching the patient about the medication. What statement by the patient indicates that your teaching has been **effective**?

    A. "I will wear sunscreen when outdoors."

    B. "I will avoid alcohol."

    C. "It is normal for me to experience heart palpitations; it is nothing to worry about."

    D. "There is no need to call the doctor if my skin begins to change color."

33. When coming back from lunch break, the nurse is asking for any updates that might have transpired while gone. Which statement would the nurse want to follow up with **first**?

    A. "I took care of the incisional dressing in room 18, your post-op day 3 laparotomy. The dressing was beginning to look dirty."

    B. "Room 16, your appendectomy who came in this morning, was complaining of pain, so I gave her the scheduled oxycodone."

    C. "The PICC nurse came by room 15 while you were away. The procedure went well."

    D. "Room 14, your 3-day post-op cholecystectomy, continued to ring the call bell saying he was cold. He appeared to be shaking, so I got him more blankets."

34. A patient who received cardiac catheterization returns to the telemetry unit for frequent monitoring. As the nurse assigned to this patient, you understand it is important to assess which of the following **first**?

    A. An EKG strip for post-procedure rhythm changes

    B. The dressing over the puncture or insertion site

    C. The level of consciousness

    D. Pulses on all extremities

35. An 8-year-old child is admitted to the pediatric cardiac care unit with an exacerbation of heart failure. The parents are not always able to be at the hospital with their child due to another sick child at home. What would the nurse include in the care plan for the child to help **reduce** the stress of being in the hospital?

    A. Have the child participate in activities in the playroom.

    B. Provide the child with a favorite movie.

    C. Play a board game with the child.

    D. Provide the child privacy in her room.

36. Patient lab values recently came back. The A1C (glycosylated hemoglobin) level was found to be 8%. Which statement is the **most** accurate regarding this situation?

   A. It is best to have the patient fast for 6 hours and then redraw.
   B. Assess if the patient ate directly before this lab draw.
   C. Have the patient explain his diet, exercise, and management of the diabetes at home.
   D. Review with the patient how to avoid hypoglycemic attacks.

37. The nurse is caring for a male patient post hip replacement surgery. He is now recovering in the PACU before transferring to a med-surg unit. It is important that the nurse pay attention to potential complications from the surgery. Which findings would indicate a **life-threatening** complication?

   A. Lengthening of the affected extremity
   B. Difficulty when ambulating
   C. Lethargy and confusion
   D. Shortness of breath and tachycardia

38. A patient comes to urgent care stating he "generally does not feel well." The nurse documents malaise and continues the assessment. The patient states he recently traveled to East Asia and has had a chronic cough for a couple of weeks now. His vitals are stable with an elevated temperature of 102°. What illness is this man likely suffering from?

   A. Typhoid fever
   B. Cholera
   C. Malaria
   D. Tuberculosis

39. The nurse is taking care of a post-op patient on oral contraceptives. Her chart reveals she has a history of smoking. During an assessment, the nurse finds a swollen, slightly erythematous right calf. When witnessing the UAP care for the patient, what finding requires immediate intervention?

   A. The UAP is talking about the effects of smoking and why the patient should quit.
   B. The UAP is avoiding putting undo pressure on the swollen area.
   C. The UAP is assisting the patient to the bathroom to urinate.
   D. The UAP is providing more pillows for comfort and assisting the patient in sitting upright.

40. As a nurse on the cardiac stepdown unit, part of your job is to monitor patient rhythm. A patient is post-op valve replacement on his second day of recovery. Upon assessment, new atrial fibrillation is found. Which symptoms would be especially alarming to the nurse? **Select all that apply.**

   A. Shortness of breath
   B. Throbbing headache
   C. Nausea
   D. BP of 95/60
   E. Chest pain
   F. Pulse ox of 91%

41. While outside on a hot summer day, a nurse witnesses a pedestrian collapse while walking down the sidewalk. The nurse walks up to assess. The pedestrian is disoriented and very diaphoretic. When assessing the pulse, the nurse notes it is racing and thready. What would the nurse do **first**?

    A. Offer the pedestrian water.
    B. Remove the pedestrian from the sun.
    C. Call 911.
    D. Allow the patient to relax and regain orientation.

42. After lunch, you are enjoying a conversation with some nurses from different units about upcoming time off. During the conversation, the alarms go off, indicating a Code Pink is occurring. What is the priority nursing intervention for you and your colleagues?

    A. Call your respective units inquiring if help is needed.
    B. Stay in the current location and assess the area for anyone with large bags or coats.
    C. Contact security and notify them of the situation.
    D. Return to your assigned units and assess the situation.

43. A nurse on a hepatology unit is reviewing hospital policy for a pre-op liver transplant patient. Which findings would the nurse expect in the patient at this stage in the liver disease? **Select all that apply.**

    A. Respiratory difficulty and nervousness
    B. Delirium with asterixis
    C. Icterus
    D. Oliguria
    E. Decreased PT/INR
    F. Increased PT/INR

44. A 34-year-old female client comes into her OB/GYN's office. She is found to have vulva candida. The nurse expects the physician to prescribe which drug?

    A. Penicillin
    B. Nystatin
    C. Fluconazole
    D. Acyclovir

45. The nurse is evaluating the outcomes on a number of therapies for a 55-year-old male with heart failure. He was admitted 3 days ago with an acute exacerbation with pulmonary edema and severe hypoxemia. Upon echocardiogram, the patient was found to have an ejection fraction of 25%. With the following therapies, what would indicate **improvement** in the patient's condition?

    Oxygen 2 L NC

    Bumetanide 40 mg BID

    Digoxin 0.5 mg BID

    A. BP of 90/60
    B. PaO_2 of 85%
    C. Patient states "feeling much better."
    D. Increased urine output

46. A 73-year-old female diagnosed with post-streptococcal glomerulonephritis further deteriorates on a med-surg floor with suspected sepsis. The rapid response team (RRT) is called, and it is decided that the patient will be moved to the medical intensive care unit (MICU). As a nurse on the MICU, and understanding the case, which sign would **most** worry you?

   A. Confusion
   B. BP of 95/60
   C. Elevated WBCs
   D. Crackles in the base of the lungs

47. The nurse has received report on four patients in the postpartum unit. Which of the following patients would the nurse see **first**?

   A. A patient complaining of urinating the bed 2 hours after the birth of a healthy 7 lb. 6 oz. boy
   B. A patient 1 hour after the birth of a newborn with an initial Apgar score of 7. She received an epidural during the labor and has yet to urinate.
   C. A patient 3 hours after the birth of an underweight baby with scant lochia and a firm fundus. Patient reporting pain 4 out of 10.
   D. A patient who gave birth to a premature girl. The mother is requesting to see her baby.

48. As a nurse working in Florida, you are very much aware of the Zika virus coming up from South America. You are treating a patient with suspected Zika infection who begins to experience paresthesia and numbness of the toes. Two hours later, the same patient complains of weakness of the feet. What is the nursing priority as presented by the patient's signs and symptoms?

   A. Monitor urine output for discoloration.
   B. Monitor mental status for acute changes.
   C. Monitor respiratory status.
   D. Monitor cardiovascular system.

49. A 78-year-old female with Alzheimer's dementia is admitted to the emergency department (ED) with decreased alertness. The caregivers stated the patient has not been acting like herself lately. They state the patient has been drinking unusually large amounts of water among other behavioral problems. Recently, the patient has been more difficult to arouse, which led to the ED visit today. Given this story and the signs and symptoms of the patient, what would the nurse do **first**?

   A. Assess for signs of stroke.
   B. Pad the side rails of the bed.
   C. Assess intake and output.
   D. Place the patient in a supine position.

50. A patient is admitted to the emergency department due to fainting and severe fatigue. Upon assessment, the nurse notices some abnormal bruising on the body. The patient complains of a sore tongue that appears red. Which of the following would the nurse expect to find in the labs drawn for this patient?

    A.   A platelet count of 50,000
    B.   A white blood cell count of 15,000
    C.   A decreased Shilling test
    D.   A hemoglobin of 12

51. A patient is given chlordiazepoxide for an anxiety disorder. When would the patient be at the highest risk for drug overdose?

    A.   When the patient does not know how the drug works
    B.   When the patient drinks alcohol daily
    C.   When the patient takes the medication on an empty stomach
    D.   When the patient drinks milk with the medication

52. A nurse is caring for an 8-year-old child who has a fever and petechial rash. It is suspected the child may have meningococcal meningitis. Which interventions would the nurse need to implement **first**? **Select all that apply.**

    A.   Place the child in a negative airflow room.
    B.   Initiate NPO status.
    C.   Place a mask on the patient and mother.
    D.   Initiate droplet precautions.
    E.   Administer IV antibiotics, as ordered.

53. A nurse is performing a developmental screening on a child during a checkup visit. Which of the following are risks associated with autism spectrum disorder? **Select all that apply.**

    A.   Family members who have autism
    B.   Receiving vaccinations
    C.   Parents who smoked during pregnancy
    D.   Not speaking by 2 years of age
    E.   Poor diet as a child

54. A patient recently diagnosed with right-sided heart failure returns to the cardiac care unit (CCU) after a minor test. One hour later, you observe that the central venous pressure has risen from 7 to 9. How would you interpret these findings and act?

    A.   The heart failure is improving; continue to monitor.
    B.   The heart failure is worsening; assess the patient.
    C.   The CVP changed due to the procedure; check the machinery.
    D.   Immediately call the physician.

55. A telemetry nurse is rounding on patients when she comes to a 65-year-old male patient who is dizzy and nauseous. When looking at the rhythm, she sees it is displaying sinus bradycardia. When updating the physician, what can the nurse expect to be potentially ordered?

    A. Lidocaine IV STAT

    B. Amiodarone 300 mg IV bolus

    C. Atropine 1 mg IV

    D. Sodium polystyrene sulfonate PO

56. After coronary artery bypass surgery (CAB) 16 hours ago, a patient is complaining of pain 8/10 at the donor site. After assessing for potential complications of the surgery and finding none, how would the nurse intervene on the following orders, assuming any could be used?

    A. Administer oxycodone 10 mg PO PRN as needed for minor pain.

    B. Administer morphine 2 mg IV q4hr.

    C. Administer nitroglycerin PRN for chest pain.

    D. Administer splinting techniques when breathing.

57. A patient with chronic hypertension is being cared for by the nurse on a med-surg floor. Which of the following is a common comorbidity with long-term hypertension?

    A. Damage to kidneys

    B. Development of cataracts

    C. History of diabetes

    D. Raynaud's syndrome

58. While painting a house, a 45-year-old man falls from a ladder and lands on his back. While able to recover relatively quickly, 30 minutes later, his employer drives him to the emergency room. The man complains of severe pain in his lower back along with worsening numbness on the buttocks. The physician orders a CT scan and diagnoses cauda equina syndrome. What does the nurse expect for potential treatment next?

    A. Administer morphine 3 mg IV.

    B. Prepare for emergency surgery.

    C. Ambulate the patient to reestablish blood flow.

    D. Maintain respiratory function with deep breathing and oxygenation if needed.

59. While providing care on a pediatric unit, the nurse realizes that one of the medications due to the patient was late by 1 hour. The nurse immediately administers the medication. What action should the nurse take **first** following this administration?

    A. Notify the charge nurse of the error and fill out an incident report.

    B. Chart the late medication.

    C. Call the physician after assessing for any adverse events.

    D. Immediately call the physician.

60. A patient in the medical intensive care unit (MICU) was diagnosed with septic shock, precipitated by systemic inflammatory response syndrome (SIRS) by an old wound. The physician decides to begin norepinephrine. What is the goal of this pharmacological therapy with the patient?

    A. Reduce WBC to 12,000.
    B. Increase mean arterial pressure (MAP) to above 60.
    C. Maintain consciousness.
    D. Decrease cardiac output to stabilize blood pressure.

61. A patient with suspected anthrax exposure is brought into the emergency room by paramedics. A student nurse is assigned to take the patient. Which statement by the student nurse would need to be **corrected** by their preceptor?

    A. "I am going to assess his breathing frequently."
    B. "I may expect the patient to form a lesion on the skin."
    C. "I am going to isolate the patient right now."
    D. "Anthrax is caused by a bacteria."

62. A patient admitted with pneumonia has had an increasingly bad cough for days and continually saturates into the 80% range. The HCP has ordered piperacillin-tazobactam for the patient and respiratory hygiene. The order also states to provide oxygen via nasal cannula to maintain an SpO_2 above 93%.

    If all of these interventions are utilized, which of the following would indicate an **improvement** in the patient's condition?

    A. SpO_2 of 92%
    B. The patient states a decreasing shortness of breath.
    C. The patient is sleeping quietly.
    D. ABG lab values of pH: 7.36, CO_2: 35, HCO_3: 24

63. A new nurse working in the GI lab is being taught by the nurse preceptor about moderate sedation for procedures. Medications such as midazolam and fentanyl are commonly given. Which of the following would require **further teaching** by the nurse preceptor to the new nurse?

    A. A loss of gag reflex is common.
    B. Anterograde amnesia is common.
    C. If overdose is suspected, flumazenil may be given.
    D. Moderate sedation is given by the RN.

64. While working in the cardiac care unit (CCU), the nurse returns to the patient's room to find the patient's heart rhythm in supraventricular tachycardia (SVT). Which of the following would the nurse do **first**?

    A. Administer adenosine IV bolus.
    B. Instruct the patient on how to perform a valsalva maneuver.
    C. Assess the patient for dizziness and palpitations.
    D. Assess a 12-lead EKG/ECG.

65. A nurse is walking down a hallway of the hospital when she notices a visitor slumped on the floor in a waiting area. After rushing to the visitor's aid, in what order should the nurse take the following steps? Place the following items in the order the nurse would perform them.

    A. Check for a pulse at the carotid artery.
    B. Check to see if the patient is responsive by speaking to him, touching him, or shaking him.
    C. Have a nearby staff member or visitor call for help.
    D. Ensure that the scene is safe to approach.
    E. Begin CPR.
    F. Defibrillate the patient, if needed, by AED.

66. An infection control specialist is rounding on your unit and making suggestions to prevent hospital-acquired infections. Which finding would the specialist likely recommend you to correct or act upon?

    A. An intubated patient receiving pantoprazole
    B. Delegating a sterile dressing change for a central line to an LPN
    C. Utilizing a clean technique when performing a straight catheterization
    D. Placement of a trash can by the door of a MRSA patient

67. A patient is admitted to the emergency room with suspected exacerbation of Crohn's disease. Which of the following HCP orders should the nurse implement **first**?

    A. Obtain a fecal occult blood test.
    B. Administer acetaminophen/oxycodone PO for pain.
    C. Initiate IV normal saline at 100 mL/hr.
    D. Draw blood for a CBC and chem panel.

68. While working on a med-surg floor, the nurse is caring for a patient in liver failure with portal hypertension and esophageal varices. Halfway into the shift, the patient begins to violently vomit blood. The physician is called to the bedside and a Sengstaken-Blakemore tube is inserted. The bleeding stops; however, 30 minutes later the patient begins to have difficulty breathing and is desaturating quickly. Which action would the nurse perform **first**?

    A. Initiate nasal cannula 2 L.
    B. Cut the Sengstaken-Blakemore tube with scissors and remove.
    C. Prepare for intubation.
    D. Auscultate the lungs.

69. A nurse on an oncology unit is in the room when a patient is told by her doctors that she has advanced breast cancer. When the doctors leave the room, the patient appears visibly distraught. Which of the following is the most appropriate to say to the patient at this time?

    A. "Don't worry. We will do everything we can to cure your cancer."
    B. "This must be very shocking for you. What are you feeling?"
    C. "You should fight and beat this cancer."
    D. "Do you have any questions about your diagnosis?"

70. A depressed patient has recently been admitted to a psych unit due to worsening symptoms and strong feelings of hopelessness. The patient has been on SSRIs for years, with frequent switching between medications due to a lack of therapeutic improvement. What does the nurse anticipate the physician to order?

    A. Sertraline

    B. Phenelzine

    C. Electroconvulsive therapy (ECT)

    D. Clozapine

71. A nurse on a psychiatric floor is evaluating the effectiveness of medications given. Which of the following findings requires **immediate** follow-up by the nurse?

    A. A patient with anxiety who was given lorazepam and now has his eyes closed

    B. A patient who was given haloperidol due to violent behavior and is now complaining of feeling very hot and stiff

    C. A patient diagnosed with schizophrenia who has been on risperidone and is complaining of a sore throat

    D. A patient with depression on paroxetine who is complaining of anorexia, nausea, and vomiting

72. What positioning is **best** for a patient who just returned to the unit from a liver biopsy?

    A. Left-side lying

    B. High-Fowler's

    C. Right-side lying

    D. Sims

73. A couple comes into a genetic counseling office asking questions about the odds that their child may have cystic fibrosis (CF), an autosomal recessive disease. Both husband and wife have a family history of the disease. Upon testing, it is found that both parents are heterozygous for the trait. What is the probability that they will have a child with CF?

    A. 100%

    B. 50%

    C. 25%

    D. 0%

74. A 23-year-old unconscious male is brought in by his girlfriend after he overdosed on anti-anxiety pills. The girlfriend states to the nurse that he has recently been depressed and experiencing continuous anxiety. While the nurse is assessing the patient, he awakens. Which question takes priority to ask the patient?

    A. "Can you talk to me about your depressed thoughts?"

    B. "Did you take these pills in an attempt to kill yourself?"

    C. "How much medication did you take?"

    D. "What type of medication did you take?"

75. A patient was recently admitted due to shortness of breath, fever, a productive cough, and severe fatigue. During the history and physical, it is found that the patient has been taking a course of prednisone to treat lower back pain. Which of the following diagnostic findings would the nurse expect? **Select all that apply.**

   A. Elevated fasting glucose
   B. A wider antero-posterior diameter of the thorax
   C. WBC: 3,000
   D. Bacteriuria
   E. Weight gain
   F. Increased edema

Answer Key

1. C	26. D	51. B
2. D	27. C	52. D, E
3. D	28. B, D, G	53. A, D
4. B	29. A	54. B
5. A	30. C	55. C
6. A	31. B, A, C, D, E	56. B
7. B	32. B	57. A
8. B	33. D	58. B
9. D	34. B	59. C
10. A	35. B	60. B
11. B	36. C	61. C
12. A	37. D	62. D
13. C	38. D	63. A
14. D	39. C	64. C
15. B	40. A, B, E, F	65. D, B, C, A, E, F
16. C	41. B	66. B
17. A	42. B	67. C
18. C	43. B, C, F	68. B
19. C	44. C	69. B
20. A	45. B	70. B
21. B	46. D	71. B
22. B, C, D	47. A	72. C
23. C	48. C	73. C
24. A	49. B	74. D
25. A	50. C	75. A, C, E, F

Answer Explanations

Question 1

Answer: C

Review chapter: Delegation; Neurosensory

When delegating to a less experienced nurse, give him or her the same patient you would give an LPN. If it is an ICU nurse, delegate him or her an ABC patient. In this case, the most stable, not requiring any high level neuro assessments or interventions, is the patient undergoing an EEG. A seizure disorder is relatively straightforward; this type of patient management is learned in school. All nurses understand pushing lorazepam is needed to treat all types of seizures. Therefore, choice C is correct.

ICP issues, choice B, automatically make a patient unstable. Fresh post-op patients, choices A and D, are also unstable. Remember time proximity strategy. Be careful on time issues. If the patient in question was more than a day out of surgery, a nurse would worry far less.

Question 2

Answer: D

Review chapter: Cardiovascular; Prioritization

Priority question: What can kill your patient the quickest? A patient complaining of a feeling of "wetness" after a cardiac cath procedure needs to be immediately assessed for bleeding; always check all patient surfaces, lifting covers and turning the patient as needed, especially if there is an underlying risk of a post-op bleed (recent child birth or a patient on blood thinners, for example). Nurses must always do their own assessment, particularly if something stated by the patient, family, LPN, UAP, or other RN is worrisome. Make sure to assess that patient personally. Therefore, choice D is correct.

Scheduled procedures, choice A, would not be a concern; the OR will send for the patient and chart. Pain, choice B, is a psychological need using Maslow's hierarchy; it should definitely be addressed, but it is not considered the highest priority in this case. COPD patients are chronically acidotic and chronically hypoxic; the numbers in answer choice C are acceptable for a COPD patient.

Question 3

Answer: D

Review chapter: Pharmacology; Prioritization

Priority question: What can kill your patient the quickest? It is so much easier answering priority questions when asking that simple question. Out of these four answer choices, which of them would truly kill your patient? And not 5 days from now; think 5 seconds from now. ABC issues and medical emergencies are almost always the correct answer to a priority question. In this case, it is a circulatory medical emergency in the form of vaginal bleeding. Understanding oxytocin and the increased risk for a ruptured placenta is crucial to administering the medication. If this would occur, a c-section is almost certain. Therefore, choice D is correct.

A placenta previa (PP), choice A, forms typically months in advance of a woman going into labor. It is not realistic to think that PP will suddenly appear, nor would it be caused by any medication. Early deceleration, choice B, is normal and expected with any woman in labor; this is not of concern. A woman at 40 weeks gestation would not be in premature labor, choice C; it is normal labor.

Question 4

Answer: B

Review chapter: Immunology; Pharmacology

After transplants, it is typical for patients to begin a cocktail of anti-rejection medications. This typically includes medications like tacrolimus, cyclosporine, and steroids; the goal is to suppress the immune system to avoid rejection. Therefore, choice B is correct.

An above-normal temperature post-op transplant, choice A, is a big red flag for rejection. The nurse would not expect this; it must be reported to the HCP. A prescription for methotrexate, choice C, is expected with rheumatoid arthritis, as well as a few other medications that can be seen in the "Pharmacology" chapter, but not with a lung transplant. A prescription for albuterol, choice D, would be expected for asthma exacerbation or COPD. Cystic fibrosis patients have difficulty with thick secretions, not with the airway.

Question 5

Answer: A

Review chapter: Pharmacology; ADPIE (Nursing Process)

Sodium polystyrene sulfonate is used as a potassium binder for people with hyperkalemia and is excreted in stool. If the patient has not had a recent bowel movement, has not been eating, or is constipated, the medication may not have the desired effect to correct the hyperkalemia. Healthcare professionals, including nurses, do not give medications randomly, presuming they are going to work. Follow ADPIE, and assess first. Remember to acquire an assessment that warrants the intervention. Therefore, choice A is correct.

Simply because an order is STAT, choice B, does not imply nurses skip over the nursing process. If the patient takes stool softeners at home, choice C, they should be included in admission orders, which will help the sodium polystyrene sulfonate do its job. The primary goal for this patient is to have a bowel movement in order to excrete the excess potassium. It is not uncommon for the patient to have diarrhea after this medication has been administered; this is how the nurse knows it is working. There is no reason not to trust a potassium value of 6.3 mmol/L. If a lab value comes back and there are no signs and symptoms that support that value, it may be appropriate to repeat the lab to double-check the results, choice D.

Question 6

Answer: A

Review chapter: Musculoskeletal; Scope of Practice – RN

In this case, avoiding purines is crucial for people with gout. Foods like shellfish, choice A, and organ meats are high in purines and should be avoided. Therefore, choice A is correct.

The question already says to push fluids, so choice B is redundant. The NCLEX will never have a redundancy be the correct answer. You must look for the next best thing, which, in this case, is choice A. It is absolutely always a good idea to push 2 to 3 liters of water a day for any human being on the planet. The most common exception to that rule on the NCLEX would be a patient in heart failure; however, do not restrict things from the patient unless there is a written order. Hydration is especially important in relation to allopurinol to prevent the formation of calculi. Read carefully, though; as noted above, if a response is already stated in the question, it will not be the correct answer. While ibuprofen, choice C, may be administered to help with the pain of gout, it is outside of the scope of practice of the nurse to tell a patient to take a medication without approval from the HCP. Telling the patient to take acetaminophen, choice D, is incorrect for the same reason. Be very careful here. Read the "Scope of Practice – RN" chapter for directions on how to follow the scope of an RN.

Question 7

Answer: B

Review chapter: EKG Interpretation

As the saying goes, a patient is not deceased unless they are warm and deceased. The patient in this question will require slow warming back to a normal body temperature before he is declared deceased. At that point, all of the medical interventions that the medical staff have at their disposal for a situation like this will likely be utilized as a final push through this trauma. If those interventions do not bring the patient back, the physician may then decide to call the time of death. Therefore, choice B is correct.

Asystole is not a shockable rhythm, so immediate defibrillation, choice A, would not be an effective intervention. Induced hypothermia, choice C, is typically used for people who have a typical cardiac arrest. When the brain has been without circulation, the healthcare team may decide to induce hypothermia to preserve the brain tissue. The word *fast*, used in choice D, is likely not a good recommendation for anything medical, unless you are pushing adenosine, which has a very short half-life. Read very carefully. There are many circumstances when an answer choice simply sounds off or wrong because of certain adjectives being used. A good example would be something that includes the word *minor*. It is hard to prioritize something if it is *minor, scant,* or *tinged*. Such adjectives imply that it is not a big deal. At any rate, a patient is never rewarmed fast, choice D. It is always a slow and steady process to bring any tissue in the body up to a normal temperature. The same rule of thumb would apply to a burn or frostbite: slow and steady.

Question 8

Answer: B

Review chapter: Pharmacology

There are many risks associated with administration of furosemide, and ototoxicity (damage to the ears) is a significant side effect that may be transient or permanent. Methods of avoiding ototoxicity include slow infusion, divided oral doses, and blood levels not exceeding 50 mcg/ml. An early sign of ototoxicity is tinnitus; be on the lookout. Therefore, choice B is correct.

Hepatotoxicity, choice C, is not an adverse effect of furosemide. The nurse would not need to look out for this in regard to this medication. Remember though that when administering furosemide, the patient must have functioning kidneys. If the patient is in chronic renal failure or end-stage renal disease, furosemide will not work, and there will be no increase in urine output since the starting point was already anuria. A patient can lose too much volume, choice A, and become hypokalemic, choice D, regardless of how fast the medication is pushed. For example, 20 mg is 20 mg; no matter how the 20 mg is administered, it will react the same way in the body.

Question 9

Answer: D

Review chapter: Neurosensory; Pharmacology

Triptan medications are meant to be taken in the early phases of a migraine, before the actual headache symptoms have evolved. The goal is to either prevent the headache or lessen the headache symptoms when it occurs. That cannot happen if the triptan is held until the pain has heightened. Most patients would describe this period before the headache as the "aura" phase. Refer to the "Neurosensory" chapter for an overview on the phases of migraines. Therefore, choice D is correct.

All of the other answer choices are good behaviors for a person with migraines to implement. A triptan drug can be taken with other medications, choice A, as can aspirin, and they often are. Decreasing stimuli, choice B, is a great idea for someone who is experiencing a migraine; it will help lessen the pain. Alcohol, choice C, is often a trigger for migraines in many people; it is best to avoid it all together.

Question 10

Answer: A

Review chapter: Gastrointestinal; Prioritization

Steatorrhea are white frothy stools, typically the result of excess fat in the stool caused by disease of the pancreas or intestine and characterized by chronic diarrhea and weight loss. This is often seen in people with malabsorption or when the body is not making enzymes or bile needed for digestion. If a patient has had a cholecystectomy in the past, which is what the incision in the RUQ suggests, it would explain the symptoms the patient is experiencing, namely, post-cholecystectomy syndrome. The patient is likely not following a low-fat diet. Therefore, choice A is correct.

Dementia, choice B, would fall under a psychological problem the patient has in her history, but it is not a current priority issue and has nothing to do with the signs and symptoms this patient is experiencing. A stage 2 pressure ulcer, choice C, and hypertension, choice D, are important things the nurse will want to follow up on, but these are secondary to the problem at hand. Remember to focus on the signs and symptoms being displayed in the question and match those to what you believe to be the potential diagnosis. You can use this strategy if the question itself does not give you the diagnosis.

Question 11

Answer: B
Review chapter: Neurosensory; Prioritization

Priority question: What can kill your patient the quickest? Remember, ABCs and medical emergencies tend to be the correct answers to priority questions. In this case, the priority is the risk of organ rupture due to bladder retention. This risk would apply to anyone who has undergone general anesthesia, but given that the surgery also was spinal in nature, it makes it all the more possible. The nurse would want to pay close attention to any potential complications of the surgery, such as loss of bowel or bladder function. Therefore, choice B is correct.

A post ERCP patient may complain of abdominal pain, choice A. Bruising on the back or side where the stone was treated and some pain over the treatment area after a lithotripsy procedure to break up either gallstones or kidney stones are expected. Regarding the patient described in choice C, 100 mL of blood loss per hour or more is considered hemorrhage, so 50 mL in the chest tube per hour is allowed for a CAB, especially if the patient is directly out of surgery. A GCS of 13, choice D, is slightly depressed, but without anything to compare it to, it makes it almost impossible to prioritize. With that in mind, a GCS of 13 is fine. It would be expected as well for someone coming out of anesthesia from surgery.

Question 12

Answer: A
Review chapter: Pediatrics

Depending on the level of lead in the blood and the overall severity of the poisoning, the signs and symptoms may vary. When the poisoning is severe, however, the patient may begin to exhibit behavioral changes, such as violent outbursts or cognitive changes. This would be considered a red flag for severe poisoning. Therefore, choice A is correct.

Choices B (BP of 100/65), C (lack of desire to eat), and D (neutropenia) may be seen in patients with lead poisoning, but this is a priority question. It is asking what is the "most" alarming. Therefore, choices B, C, and D are incorrect.

Question 13

Answer: C
Review chapter: Safety and Infection

Honey-crusted lesions are indicative of impetigo, a highly contagious disease caused by bacteria. Impetigo requires contact isolation of the patient, which is the priority answer. Typical priority questions rely on ABC issues and medical emergencies; however, there are other priorities such as isolation protocol and fall risk. If there is not an immediate ABC or physiological issue, Maslow's hierarchy will allow priority to move to other needs, such as safety and psychological needs. Therefore, choice C is correct.

We often teach patients to use their knuckles for scratching, choice A, to avoid damaging their skin, but that is not what this question is asking. A priority question should always be about "what can kill your patient the quickest." This mantra is repeated throughout this book because medical emergencies will almost always be the correct answer to a priority question. Parents do not make good restrainers for their own kids, choice B. If you need to restrain a child for a procedure, a papoose is used, not a parent. In this case, restraint is not warranted. Blood culture results (choice D) take time to come back from the lab, 24 hours or more. A priority question is about what we can do right this very second. Remember to focus on the present.

Question 14

Answer: D
Review chapter: Neurosensory

You need to know when the symptoms began. There is a golden window of 3–4 hours for an ischemic stroke patient to receive tPA, which acts as a thrombolytic to break up the clot. Outside of this window, the options to treat the infarction are reduced. This patient would receive a CT scan without contrast first to rule out a hemorrhagic stroke, then receive tPA. Therefore, choice D is correct.

All of the other questions are perfectly valid to ask the patient's daughter, but they are NOT the priority. Priority focuses on the presenting symptoms and important interventions here and now, which is where most dangers lie for this patient regarding his survival and recovery.

Question 15

Answer: B
Review chapter: Prioritization; Safety and Infection

Refer to the "Prioritization" chapter. There is a lot on Maslow's hierarchy in a question like this. There are times when you may feel the NCLEX prioritizes things strangely, but they do make sense. In a case like this, the priority falls to the integrity and safety of the entire hospital. The patient will not die in the next 5 minutes; however, every second a contagious patient has not been put on appropriate isolation precautions, another human being is put at risk for that infection. Starting droplet precautions is the priority. Therefore, choice B is correct.

Choice A, intracranial pressure (ICP) issues, is a potential risk of meningitis, but without signs and symptoms leading to ICP, it is a stretch. Focus on what is in front of you. Choice C, obtain blood cultures, has already been performed in the question. A redundancy is never a correct answer on the NCLEX. Do not repeat yourself. Choice D, Kernig's sign, would likely be present since the patient is diagnosed with meningitis. Be cautious and read carefully. Is the patient diagnosed with a disease or problem or is it suspected? There is a difference.

Question 16

Answer: C
Review chapter: Pharmacology; Cardiovascular

Septic shock involves an infection that reaches the bloodstream and may affect multiple organs. In this case, the patient is in septic shock from a MRSA infection. Appropriately, IV fluids, antibiotics, and dobutamine have been initiated in this case. Dobutamine can be used initially for patients in septic shock who have low cardiac output. In this case, another vasopressor is needed to increase the mean arterial pressure (MAP). The patient is getting worse; the blood pressure is still dropping. This can lead to respiratory or heart failure or, even worse, organ failure and death. Norepinephrine should be given as an additional first-line vasopressor. Norepinephrine causes vasoconstriction and increases the mean arterial pressure, with little effect on heart rate, stroke volume, and cardiac output. Therefore, choice C is correct.

Neither the exploratory laparotomy, choice A, nor the abdominal x-ray, choice D, would be warranted at this time. The patient will not die if these are not performed immediately, but the decreasing blood pressure could kill him. Cefazolin, choice B, is incorrect for similar reasons. The patient will die from organ failure long before the antibiotic begins to work. The first priority here is to focus on what you are trying to prevent or promote. In this case, you are trying to prevent further condition deterioration and promote an increase in blood pressure.

Question 17

Answer: A
Review chapter: Respiratory

The child in this question is losing his airway due to the infection. The nurse needs to prioritize this ABC risk and respond accordingly with an intervention that will fix the problem right now. Laryngotracheal bronchitis (croup) can get worse if left untreated. Treatment is similar to treatment for a patient who is losing his or her airway due to an allergic reaction: Administer epinephrine. Therefore, choice A is correct.

If the patient in question has asthma, albuterol, choice B, would be a better answer as an immediate rescue inhaler. The child in this question, however, is losing his airway due to severe inflammation, not bronchoconstriction. Epinephrine and albuterol do different things to the human body. Look them up in the "Pharmacology" chapter and focus on the second rule: What does it do to the body? Choice C is redundant; the nurse already assessed lung sounds in this question; they were found to be diminished. Remember, a redundancy will not be the correct answer. Blood culture results, choice D, take time to get back from the lab, sometimes a day or longer. A priority question is about what you can do right now. Focus on the present.

Question 18

Answer: C
Review chapter: Arterial Blood Gases (ABGs)

When patients do not breathe (ventilate) adequately to maintain body functions, anaerobic respiration begins to take over to create energy needs. The by-product of anaerobic respiration creates a build-up of lactic acid in the blood, which leads to lactic acidosis, a type of metabolic acidosis. Choice C is the only answer with ABG results confirming this diagnosis. Therefore, choice C is correct.

Choice A is indicative of combined alkalosis. Choice B is a normal ABG. Choice D shows respiratory acidosis.

Question 19

Answer: C
Review chapter: Fluid and Electrolytes; Critical Care

This patient is hypovolemic. The assessment displays a low blood pressure with rebound tachycardia attempting to compensate. The low CVP displays a fluid volume deficit, and a low urine output is indicative of shock-induced pre-renal acute kidney injury. All of these problems are corrected by administration of IV fluids, isotonic (same as blood), and typically lactated Ringer's solution in a burn victim, rather than normal saline (choice A). When 45% of the body is burned, it is a medical emergency that can cause hypovolemic shock. Albumin also aids in maintaining the osmolality of the blood. When a patient is burned, the cell membrane becomes highly permeable, causing fluid to the third space. The patient's blood pressure will drop, and they will form edema due to the movement of the fluid out of the vessels and into the third space. The goal is to get the fluid back where it belongs, the vasculature. This is accomplished by isotonic solutions and albumin. Therefore, choice C is correct.

Whole blood, choice B, is not needed in this patient, as the patient is not bleeding; it is a fluid shift. Furosemide, choice D, would likely kill a patient in this condition; it would cause him to lose even more fluid from the diuretic effect.

Question 20

Answer: A

Review chapter: Safety and Infection

The first surgical dressing change post-op is performed by the surgical team, not the RN. In this case, the patient is only 1 hour post-op, so the dressing should not be changed by the nurse. At the 24-hour mark, the nurse can assume the first dressing change has occurred, if part of the question. The preceptor would intervene on this anticipated dressing change. Therefore, choice A is correct.

Raising the head of the bed, choice B, is appropriate and important in most post-op patients and even more important in an intubated patient due to ventilator-associated pneumonia. For the same reason, it is common to administer a PPI such as pantoprazole for intubated patients, choice C, and that's why suctioning is necessary. It is important, however, to only suction when it is needed, choice D. New research shows that excessive suctioning can damage tissues.

Question 21

Answer: B

Review chapter: Gastrointestinal

This question requires an understanding of the liver and the functions of the liver that will begin to fail in liver cirrhosis. If the liver is not producing the right amount of blood-clotting proteins, the clotting process takes longer, as indicated by a high prothrombin time (PT). A high PT is indicative of liver cirrhosis. Therefore, choice B is correct.

All of the other lab values listed in this question (albumin, platelets, and sodium) are likely to decrease in liver failure, not increase.

Question 22

Answer: B, C, D

Review chapter: EKG Interpretation

A patient in V. Fib will not have a pulse. This is immediate criteria for CPR, choice D. Even if the patient has a rhythm where a pulse may be expected, if no pulse is present, CPR is called for. Epinephrine, choice C, is a drug utilized during a Code Blue such as V. Fib or pulseless V. Tach, along with compressions and defibrillation. Bicarbonate, choice B, is given at the discretion of the physician directing the code—it helps buffer acidosis produced by low perfusion states and inadequate oxygenation that occurs in cardiac arrest. Therefore, choices B, C, and D are correct.

Atropine, choice A, is used for symptomatic bradycardia. Synchronized cardioversion, choice E, is used during SVT if adenosine is not effective. A CT scan, choice F, may be performed at some point, but during a Code Blue, it is not a priority. Remember, focus on the immediate needs of the patient.

Question 23

Answer: C
Review chapter: Psychiatry

Opioid use results in constriction of the pupils, choice C, whereas opioid withdrawal causes a dilation of the pupils. Therefore, choice C is correct.

Another component of the question that requires careful reading is that the answer must be independent of other substances. The question states "specific to opioid use." Dilation of the pupils, choice A, can happen with a number of substances, not just opioids. The same applies to respiratory depression, choice B; while this may occur with alcohol and opioids, it is not specific to just opioid use. Likewise, tachycardia, choice D, is a sign that would be seen in a multitude of substances.

Question 24

Answer: A
Review chapter: Respiratory; Safety and Infection

There are multiple risks for pneumonia, but a common factor is when something is aspirated into the lungs that does not belong there. The male patient diagnosed with atrial fibrillation is at the lowest risk. Therefore, choice A is correct.

A patient post-op, choice B, is always at increased risk for pneumonia; that is why nursing encourages deep breathing, coughing, and incentive spirometry in all post-op patients. The patient with a CVA, choice C, is likely to be at the highest risk for pneumonia due to the dysphagia. Food or water can slip into the lungs very easily. The fact that a person is homeless, choice D, may increase the risk for infections, but the alcohol abuse is likely a much higher risk factor due to suppressed awareness when swallowing and concern for aspiration.

Question 25

Answer: A
Review chapter: Cardiovascular

The blood pressure itself at 102/70 is not hugely worrisome, but add that to the rebound tachycardia, and you have the beginning signs of a worsening infection and possible sepsis. Therefore, choice A is correct.

Another red flag in this case would be a decrease in urine production (oliguria), raising a concern for organ hypoperfusion or renal failure, but this is not an answer choice. An elevated WBC count, choice B, would be expected with an infection, but the count in this case does not display a large difference between a minor or major infection. It simply tells us "yes, there is an infection" versus "no, there is not." The same train of thought applies to erythema and tenderness at the central line site, choice C, and fatigue and a fever, choice D; these findings would all be expected with an infection, but together they may be a concern for sepsis. Remember when prioritizing, ABCs should consistently be the first thought and focus.

Question 26

Answer: D

Review chapter: Lab Values; ADPIE (Nursing Process)

The lab value affected by heparin is the aPTT. Since the patient is stable, the best action by the nurse is to follow ADPIE: assess first. The nurse should confirm an order for aPTT and draw blood, choice D, to check if the aPTT is dangerously elevated. Once the level is confirmed, it is likely that the physician will decrease the heparin (choice B), hold the dose, or order protamine sulfate if the bleeding risk is high. Therefore, choice D is correct.

The nurse should not call the physician immediately, choice A. The first question the physician is likely to ask is "What is the aPTT?" so this should be done first. It's also worth noting assessment before intervention for ADPIE strategy. As indicated in the question, the nurse notes pinpoint red spots on the skin known as petechiae. Infections and reactions to medications are two common causes of petechiae. The skin assessment can provide initial signs of multiple systemic or autoimmune problems. It is likely that this patient has been hypocoagulated with heparin and is beginning to show early signs of bleeding, but do not assume. PT/INR, choice C, is affected by warfarin, not heparin.

Question 27

Answer: C

Review chapter: Psychiatry

The priority risk for this patient is safety. The patient is a high risk for falls, which could also damage anything done by the surgery. The only way to ensure that the patient does not fall at this point is to assign a one-to-one supervision sitter. Therefore, choice C is correct.

A chemical restraint such as haloperidol, choice A, would be a huge overreaction to this situation and borderline patient battery. Family, choice B, cannot be used for safety measures; they are not trained staff and the hospital would be liable if anything should happen. Moving the patient closer to the nurses' station, choice D, sounds like it may fix the problem, but that assumes someone is at the nurses' station to answer a bed alarm. A bed close to the nurses' station would be better for a patient who is a fall risk, but is currently listening to nursing direction; the patient in this question is delirious and getting out of bed.

Question 28

Answer: B, D, G

Review chapter: Safety and Infection

Secondary prevention is about screenings and catching the problem early if it exists. Mammography (choice B), PSA blood levels (choice D), and colonoscopy (choice G) are screenings performed for this purpose. Therefore, choices B, D, and G are correct.

Condom use (choice A), immunizations (choice E), and exercise and dieting (choice F) fall under primary prevention. A post-MI cardiogram (choice C) is a tertiary prevention.

Question 29

Answer: A
Review chapter: Psychiatry

Unless he is at risk for self-harm or harm to others, the patient technically has the right to refuse medications. This right can be eventually revoked, but that requires a ruling in a court of law. Therefore, choice A is correct.

The patient was admitted involuntarily, so until the physician feels the patient is safe outside of the hospital, he cannot leave against medical advice (AMA), choice B. Patients, whether voluntary or involuntary, are typically allowed to see family, choice C, after they are stabilized. Patients in any circumstance are always encouraged to voice their concerns about the plan of care that has been established for them, choice D. It is often frustrating that most psych patients do not become involved in their care, but this does not mean they lose their right to take part in and make requests regarding their care.

Question 30

Answer: C
Review chapter: Gastrointestinal; Critical Care

If a patient is not tolerating tube feedings, it becomes an aspiration risk. The feedings will sit in the stomach and accumulate. This occurs when the food is not being properly digested in the small intestine. It is important to check for a residual volume before you provide additional fluid to the tube feeding. Aspiration of stomach contents can lead to pneumonia or an immediate Code Blue situation because of respiratory compromise. Remember priority strategy: "What can kill your patient the quickest?" Aspiration could potentially kill this patient. Therefore, choice C is correct.

Cramping pain is expected with pancreatitis, choice A; that patient also has stable vital signs. A pulse ox of 89% is expected for a patient with COPD, choice B. The post-op cholecystectomy patient, choice D, appears to be recovering nicely and is sleeping.

Question 31

Answer: B, A, C, D, E
Review chapter: Basic Care and Comfort

Here's the proper order:

> **B.** Remove the patient and family members from harm's way.
> **A.** Pull the fire alarm.
> **C.** Close all doors and windows close to the fire.
> **D.** Locate the fire extinguisher and attempt to put out the fire.
> **E.** Instruct unnecessary staff and visitors to use the stairs.

Utilize the acronym RACE: R for rescue, A for alarm, C for contain, and E for extinguish or evacuate.

Question 32

Answer: B
Review chapter: Pharmacology

On the NCLEX, it is an easy rule to simply say all patients should avoid alcohol. The board exam does not allow for a moderate use of alcohol to be a good idea. It is considered all or nothing. The same rule would apply for people who are smokers. In the eyes of the board exam, no amount of smoking is good, so if a person reduces his smoking from one pack a day to, say, five cigarettes a day, that is NOT considered to be an improvement. Improvement is zero cigarettes. There are many other medications, such as antibiotics, where consuming alcohol while on them is a bad idea, as alcohol can reduce the efficacy of the medication. Therefore, choice B is correct.

Photosensitivity, choice A, is a fairly rare side effect; you may see it when tetracycline is used. Photosensitivity is also a symptom of lupus. TCA toxicity is a very real thing. It is important to monitor for signs and symptoms such as palpitations, choice C, or dry skin, as well as other physical findings confirming toxicity. A change in skin color should absolutely be discussed with the physician, so choice D is incorrect. Brush up on your psychiatry pharmacology in the "Pharmacology" chapter.

Question 33

Answer: D
Review chapter: Safety and Infection

The 5 W's (wind, water, wound, walking, wonder drugs) is an easy strategy for distinguishing general post-operative complications, including infection. It can help determine which risks apply to which patients, depending on how many post-op days they are. In this case, it is possible that the patient in choice D who is cold and shaking has an infected wound that is advancing to sepsis and potentially septic shock if left untreated. Remember, the priority is always "what can kill your patient the quickest." Therefore, choice D is correct.

A dressing change, choice A, is not going to kill anybody in the next 5 minutes. Pain, choice B, is not a priority unless it is associated with a medical emergency, such as sickle cell crisis or a heart attack; follow Maslow's hierarchy. If you are being told a procedure went well, choice C, and no alternate information is available, it is completely fine to trust that information and reassess during routine rounding.

Question 34

Answer: B
Review chapter: Cardiovascular

Prioritization calls for a focus on ABCs and medical emergencies. All of these answer choices will be performed, but the question is asking about the priority. The priority risk after a cardiac cath procedure is bleeding at the insertion site, so the dressing should be assessed. Therefore, choice B is correct.

A loss of level of consciousness, choice C, is absolutely a risk and a possibility with this patient, but it would be after the bleeding occurs. Performing neurovascular exams like checking the pulses on all extremities, choice D, is important, but a loss of life medical emergency, such as an ABC issue, has a higher priority than a loss of limb medical emergency (loss of distal pulse). The same rule applies to EKG changes, choice A; while important, an ABC issue such as bleeding is the priority.

Question 35

Answer: B
Review chapter: Pediatrics

This child will not have much energy, so aside from the medical constraints that certain activities may pose, providing a favorite movie is the best option given the fact the child will be fatigued physically and mentally. Therefore, choice B is correct.

Playroom activities, choice A, would require too much physical energy. A board game, choice C, requires mental energy. An 8-year-old is too young to be left alone, choice D; that would be more appropriate for a teenager.

Question 36

Answer: C
Review chapter: Endocrinology

An A1C measures long-term adherence to the overall diabetes management of the patient. It includes all measures that are being used to treat the patient's condition. An A1C higher than 6% likely shows some level of non-adherence to the clinical plan of care. Such results are not always indicative of a patient who is deliberately not listening to physician orders; these results can also stem from a lack of education. It is the job of the nurses to make sure patients understand how to adhere to their plan of care. Therefore, choice C is correct.

It is important to explain to patients that an A1C lab value will not change based on behavioral changes in the last 24 hours, making choices A and B incorrect. The test measures long-term adherence, typically a 3-month outlook. Hypoglycemic attacks, choice D, will not alter the A1C.

Question 37

Answer: D
Review chapter: Musculoskeletal

A pulmonary embolism, indicated by shortness of breath and tachycardia, is a breathing (ABC) medical emergency. The patient is at risk for immediate loss of life. Therefore, choice D is correct.

A lengthening of the affected extremity, choice A, would be an abnormal finding and the surgeon needs to be notified, but this finding will not kill the patient. Lethargy and confusion, choice C, would be an expected finding for any patient coming out of anesthesia, as would difficulty ambulating, choice B. That is why it is all the more important to monitor fall risk in patients post-op, particularly if the surgery involves the hip.

Question 38

Answer: D
Review chapter: Safety and Infection

Third-world countries or areas with a large population concentrated in small, cramped living spaces are at increased risk for tuberculosis (TB) transmission and exposure. It is not uncommon to see blood-tinged sputum and night sweats as symptoms of active tuberculosis. If this patient has TB, it is important to isolate him immediately. He is an airborne risk for transmission, and personnel require an N95 disposable face mask to protect themselves. Do not use the yellow or blue face masks; they will not provide an appropriate filter effectiveness. Therefore, choice D is correct.

View the "Safety and Infection" chapter to brush up on typhoid fever (choice A), cholera (choice B), malaria (choice C), and other infections. It is important to have a general understanding of a great many types of infections for the NCLEX.

Question 39

Answer: C
Review chapter: Obstetrics/Gynecology

Oral contraceptives increase the risk of a DVT. Considering the patient is already post-operative, she is at increased risk for a DVT; the oral contraceptive use increases that risk, along with her history of smoking. The immediate concern is that a clot from the DVT can break off and cause an embolism, which will lead to a clotting event and a medical emergency. Remember, priority questions are about "what can kill your patient the quickest." Getting out of bed will increase the risk of a clot breaking off. Therefore, choice C is correct.

It is important to teach about ways to quit smoking, choice A, but your patient won't die in the next 5 minutes if this is not taught. The same reasoning applies to providing pillows for comfort, choice D. Avoiding pressure on the affected extremity, choice B, is a good behavior. Remember, this is a negative question (immediate intervention or clarification); we are looking for the bad answer to intervene and stop. Comfort technically falls under a psychological need from Maslow's hierarchy and should be addressed, but the physiologic concern for death by embolism is the immediate priority.

Question 40

Answer: A, B, E, F
Review chapter: EKG Interpretation

The rhythm in question is atrial fibrillation. It is not an uncommon complication of valve replacement surgery, but it should be a concern for any nurse taking care of a post-op open-heart surgery patient. Clotting events are the immediate risk of atrial fibrillation. These clotting events can be a myocardial infarction, pulmonary embolism, or ischemic stroke, so when looking at the answer choices, know that the correct answers are all signs and symptoms associated with one of these clotting events. Shortness of breath, choice A, and a decreasing pulse ox, choice F, would be related to a pulmonary embolism. Chest pain, choice E, would be associated with a myocardial infarction, as could shortness of breath. A throbbing headache, choice B, could be a symptom of a potential ischemic stroke. Therefore, choices A, B, E, and F are correct.

Nausea (choice C) and a BP of 95/60 (choice D) are not symptoms of clotting events.

Question 41

Answer: B
Review chapter: Cardiovascular

This patient is likely suffering from heatstroke. The immediate concern is that the problem could get worse, so the nurse must remove the person from that risk by getting him or her out of the sun. Therefore, choice B is correct.

All of the listed interventions are likely appropriate, but the priority is the immediate concern of life. Once the patient is removed from the heat, the nurse should assess the patient as well as can be expected in the field. If the patient does not improve, calling 911 is the next logical step since this patient will likely need medical intervention.

Question 42

Answer: B
Review chapter: Safety and Infection

During a Code Pink situation, a missing baby, the immediate risk is that the baby could be taken off property. The hospital, in essence, shuts down automatically. The nurse in this situation should lock down the unit and scan for suspicious individuals or areas where a child of that size may be hiding. The same thought process applies to other code situations, such as a Code Red (fire). The immediate job of the nurse is to secure the area he or she may be in at that exact moment. Therefore, choice B is correct.

Security is automatically notified, so a phone call to them, choice C, is redundant. The staff back on unit will take care of the unit; therefore, choices A and D are incorrect. Focus on the immediate area and the safety of the patients in that immediate area.

Question 43

Answer: B, C, F
Review chapter: Gastrointestinal

The liver is responsible for quite a few actions in the human body. If you need to, it is wise to brush up on anatomy and physiology of the liver. Delirium, choice B, is brought on by hepatic encephalopathy. The same applies to asterixis or "liver flap," a characteristic jerking movement of the limbs as the patient progresses into a hepatic coma. The movement disappears as somnolence worsens. Icterus (jaundice), choice C, is seen due to elevated bilirubin levels in the blood. The liver is responsible for creating clotting factors for the blood; if these are deficient, the coagulation lab values will increase (choice F), leading to a bleeding risk in the patient. Therefore, choices B, C, and F are correct.

Respiratory difficulty and nervousness, choice A, are hallmark signs of hypoxia or other types of respiratory distress. Oliguria, choice D, is not seen in liver failure, but more so with kidney failure. As noted above, coagulation indicators such as aPTT and PT/INR would increase, not decrease, choice E.

Question 44

Answer: C

Review chapter: Safety and Infection; Pharmacology

Vulva candida, a yeast infection, is a fungal infection of the vagina. Vulva candida is treated with an antifungal, such as fluconazole. It is applied to the fingers and placed inside the vaginal walls to treat the infection. Therefore, choice C is correct.

Penicillin, choice A, is used for bacterial infections, not yeast infections. Do not confuse vulva candida, also sometimes called candida albicans, with candidiasis (thrush) of the mouth. Nystatin, choice B, is used in candidiasis. Acyclovir, choice D, is an anti-viral. Pay attention to the pharmacology associated with antibiotics. It is important to be able to differentiate between the different types of infections and which medications are used to treat them.

Question 45

Answer: B

Review chapter: Arterial Blood Gases (ABGs); Cardiovascular; ADPIE (Nursing Process)

A PaO_2 is drawn from an ABG with a normal range of 80%–100% in a non-COPD individual. A PaO_2 of 85% tells you the severe hypoxemia has improved, along with the other issues of the heart failure. When the diuretics work by removing fluid from the lungs, the alveoli have an easier time oxygenating the body; therefore, the PaO_2 and SpO_2 begin rising. The patient will also need less and less supplemental oxygen when more lung tissue can work effectively. The heart will also pump more effectively with digoxin aiding in the decreasing pulmonary edema. Therefore, choice B is correct.

A blood pressure of 90/60, choice A, is technically stable, but it is nearing the point of 89 or lower, which would begin to cause concern. We do not base improvement of heart failure on a lowered blood pressure alone. If a diuretic was being given for hypertension, then a drop in blood pressure would be the desired outcome. A patient stating he is "feeling much better," choice C, is a subjective interpretation. It is important to focus on objective answers and measures for outcome evaluations. Evaluations are about good or positive outcomes. An increase in urine output, choice D, is an expected finding for the medication bumetanide, but that alone does not necessarily show us improvement in this case. That could be a separate NCLEX question in its own right.

Question 46

Answer: D

Review chapter: Prioritization

An advancing infection that begins to affect the patient's breathing is likely the beginning of acute respiratory distress syndrome (ARDS). It is a relatively common complication of septic shock and/or hypovolemic shock. With ARDS, it is likely that the patient will have to be intubated until the infection improves. The other way to look at this question is from a simple priority standpoint. ABCs would dictate that a blood pressure of 95/60, choice B, looks like a circulatory problem with the low blood pressure value, but crackles in the base of the lungs, choice D, looks like a breathing problem. Airway trumps breathing trumps circulation. Therefore, choice D is correct.

Confusion, choice A, and elevated WBCs, choice C, would be expected in a 73-year-old patient with an infection.

Question 47

Answer: A
Review chapter: Obstetrics/Gynecology; Prioritization

The immediate risks are ABCs and medical emergencies. This holds true for all priority questions. Review the "Prioritization" chapter for a breakdown of the order of operation. It is possible that the patient in choice A is confusing urinating in her bed for bleeding. It is important for the nurse to rule out the bleeding first. Is it possible that she urinated in her bed? Of course, but you have to rule out an emergency before you assume that one does not exist. Therefore, choice A is correct.

A patient who received an epidural during labor, choice B, automatically has an order for a straight cath in the chart. If the patient cannot void within 4 hours after the labor, the order is to palpate for the level of the bladder, bladder scan, then straight cath if there is retained urine. This patient is only 1 hour post labor, so it is not yet a big deal. A patient with scant lochia and a firm fundus, choice C, is the picture-perfect postpartum patient. The woman who wants to see her newborn, choice D, presents a psychological need by the mother, not a physiological one. While seeing her baby is important for bonding and feeding, she is not the priority in this case. The physiological stability of the mother comes first.

Question 48

Answer: C
Review chapter: Neurosensory

Guillain-Barre syndrome can be triggered by viral infections, including the flu or even Zika. Most people associate the infection with microcephaly of newborns, but the virus can also trigger other problems in the human body such as Guillain-Barre or a myasthenia gravis crisis. It is important that the nurse pay attention to potential complications of Guillain-Barre; the destruction of the nerves can travel centrally to the diaphragm, affecting the breathing. The patient may need to be intubated during this period of time until the body can heal. Therefore, choice C is correct.

None of the other body systems listed here are affected by Guillain-Barre. It is a neuromuscular syndrome.

Question 49

Answer: B
Review chapter: Lab Values; Neurosensory

This patient is likely suffering from water intoxication due to drinking the large amounts of water. It is not an uncommon occurrence in dementia populations. It is called psychogenic polydipsia. It occurs in certain types of psychiatric patients when they drink too much water because of the desire to, or as in this case, the patient likely does not remember when she drank water, so she continues. It leads to severe hyponatremia, also known as water intoxication. When this occurs, the brain tissue swells, increasing the intracranial pressure (ICP). The immediate risk is seizure activity, so the priority is to pad the side rails. Therefore, choice B is correct.

Signs and symptoms of a stroke, choice A, are different from those of the patient in this question; think hemiplegia and a throbbing headache. Assess intake and output, choice C, is redundant because it is already included in the care of a patient such as this. Something cannot be the priority for the nurse if it is already a standard part of the care plan. That is like saying you're going to prioritize turning your patient every 2 hours. You already should have been doing that. Supine, choice D, is not the correct position; semi-Fowler's is the neurological happy place. You can read more about this in the "Positioning" chapter.

Question 50

Answer: C
Review chapter: Hematology

A Schilling test is an obscure test most nurses do not learn in school. There is no such thing as an increased Schilling test; however, when it is decreased, it is indicative of pernicious anemia resulting from a vitamin B12 deficiency. The described symptoms of a sore red tongue and fatigue may also lead you to expect a vitamin B12 deficiency. Therefore, choice C is correct.

A patient would not faint due to a low platelet count, choice A, which is indicative of thrombocytopenia, at least not unless there is underlying bleeding; and it would not explain the sore tongue. A white blood cell count of 15,000, choice B, indicates an infection, but none of the patient's other symptoms would lead you to expect an infection. A hemoglobin of 12, choice D, is technically normal.

Question 51

Answer: B
Review chapter: Pharmacology

On the NCLEX, it is an easy rule to simply say all patients should avoid alcohol. The board exam does not allow for a moderate behavior of alcohol to be a good idea. It is considered all or nothing. No amount of alcohol is a good idea when taking a multitude of medications. The combination can be dangerous and sometimes fatal. Therefore, choice B is correct.

The patient's knowledge of how a medication works, choice A, is not really important. Some patients may want to know, but generally speaking, most people are not aware of exactly how the medication that they are taking works. (There is a difference between knowing "why" they are taking a medication and "how" it works. Do not be tripped up by the wording.) Most medications are taken on an empty stomach, choice C, but that does not change the total milligram amount ingested. Milk, choice D, would typically inhibit absorption of a medication, not make it more powerful.

Question 52

Answer: D, E
Review chapter: Neurosensory; Prioritization

This is a priority question, so refer to Maslow's hierarchy in the "Prioritization" chapter. Safety can be a priority for infection protocol. This child should be immediately placed in droplet precaution, choice D, to prevent the spread of the illness. Treating the dangerous infection with antibiotics, choice E, is also important before complications arise. Therefore, choices D and E are correct.

Meningitis is a droplet precaution, not airborne, so a negative airflow room, choice A, is not needed. An NPO status, choice B, is needed for many medical conditions, but typically only if there is a risk for aspiration (dysphagia), for GI-related issues, or for impending surgery. This patient will likely be okay. If the child begins to become fatigued or too sleepy to eat, that would be a red flag. Placing a surgical mask on the child is only needed during transport (the child is usually in isolation for the first 24 hours) and parents do not need to mask, choice C. Exposed family and close contacts may be treated with antibiotics; family and visitors are asked to wash hands before and after entering the patient's room.

Question 53
Answer: A, D
Review chapter: Psychiatry

There are many components and risks that may go into the development of an autism spectrum disorder. Family history has been shown to be one component, choice A. A developmental delay of not speaking by 2 years of age is another, choice D. Most children begin speaking long before 2 years of age. It is important to note that family history and speech delay are not independently indicative of autism; they are simply risk factors for further screenings. Therefore, choices A and D are correct.

There is no research showing a connection between vaccinations, choice B, and autism. This is a misconception by certain media. Smoking during pregnancy, choice C, is a risk and may lead to disability, diseases, and even death of the newborn, but it is not a risk for a psychiatric disorder. The same applies for diet, choice E; it can cause medical problems, but not autism.

Question 54
Answer: B
Review chapter: Critical Care

An increasing CVP displays a worsening condition, but depending on the value, it can also simply show a well-hydrated patient. However, this question states that heart failure is present, with a baseline CVP of 7 listed. Trend lab values whenever given. Are results moving in the right direction or the wrong direction related to patient status? Think about what CVP is measuring: pressure in the right atrium, which reflects right ventricular function and systemic fluid status. The normal range would be 2–6 mmHg. If the CVP was reading an outrageous number like 0, thinking about the technology itself may be appropriate (choice C), but you should always look at your patient FIRST. Is the patient hypovolemic? This patient at the moment is not showing any signs or symptoms of emergency, so the nurse should follow ADPIE; assess first. This rules out calling the physician, choice D. Choice A, an improvement of the heart failure is incorrect; increasing CVP is worsening. Therefore, choice B is correct.

Question 55
Answer: C
Review chapter: EKG Interpretation; Pharmacology

When bradycardia is symptomatic, it is not uncommon for the physician to order atropine to increase the heart rate. If that does not work and the patient's condition is worsening, pacing may be required. Therefore, choice C is correct.

Lidocaine, choice A, is used for ventricular dysrhythmias, not a sinus rhythm. Amiodarone, choice B, is also used for ventricular dysrhythmias and does not apply here. Sodium polystyrene sulfonate, choice D, is used for hyperkalemia. Refer to the cardiac dysrhythmia drugs to see each of these medications.

Question 56

Answer: B
Review chapter: Cardiovascular

The donor site is in the thigh where the greater saphenous vein was removed. Do not confuse the donor site with the chest where the surgical team cracked it open. If the patient was experiencing pain at the chest, it would be much worse. 8/10 pain is severe pain and would require a strong drug such as morphine. Therefore, choice B is correct.

Oxycodone, choice A, is not strong enough. Nitroglycerin, choice C, may be ordered if the pain was at the chest instead of at the donor site. The same critical thinking is used for splinting of the chest, choice D; this may be appropriate if the pain was at the chest and not the thigh.

Question 57

Answer: A
Review chapter: Cardiovascular

Nephropathy related to hypertension is common. The nephrons in the kidneys become damaged with chronic hypertension and the glomerular filtration rate (GFR) is reduced. Therefore, choice A is correct.

Cataracts, choice B, are not associated with hypertension. Retinopathy can occur due to hypertension, but that has to do with the retinal blood vessels in the back of the eye, not the lens. Diabetes, choice C, is a risk factor for CVD, the same as hypertension; however, they are independent of each other and treated as separate diseases. Raynaud's syndrome, choice D, is a vascular syndrome involving recurrent vasospasms of fingers and toes in response to stress or cold; it is not a result of an underlying blood pressure problem.

Question 58

Answer: B
Review chapter: Neurosensory

Cauda equina syndrome is a medical emergency that requires an immediate intervention. It is a complication of a pinched or damaged nerve that is only corrected surgically. Therefore, choice B is correct.

Giving morphine, choice A, just treats and masks the symptoms, not taking into consideration the cause of the pain. Ambulating, choice C, only helps if it is a vascular problem; cauda equina is a problem with the nerve. The same applies to choice D, maintaining respiratory function; this treatment does not have anything to do with the nerves.

Question 59

Answer: C
Review chapter: Leadership and Management

The patient should be assessed before the physician is called. Think about the first thing the physician is going to ask, and have the information ready before making the call. Therefore, choice C is correct.

Completing an incident report, choice A, is not likely to be performed for an issue such as this unless it became a sentinel event. Charting, choice B, will also be done after the problem at hand is taken care of. Patient safety is the main concern. As noted above, don't call the physician immediately, choice D; assess first, then call.

Question 60

Answer: B
Review chapter: Critical Care; Pharmacology

Maintaining a MAP above 60 is crucial to ensure proper circulation to the vital organs. This is the main reason for vasopressors in general. Therefore, choice B is correct.

WBCs, choice A, will not be affected by vasopressors. Consciousness, choice C, is not the main concern. If the underlying problem, blood pressure, is corrected first, consciousness will come after naturally. A decrease in cardiac output, choice D, is moving in the wrong direction; the goal is to increase it.

Question 61

Answer: C
Review chapter: Safety and Infection

Anthrax is not a communicable disease. Humans can be infected through contact with sick animals, eating contaminated meat, or inhaling the spores. Cutaneous anthrax can enter through an open cut or skin sore; this is the mildest form and is not fatal when treated. There is no evidence that anthrax is transmitted from person to person, therefore it does not require any isolation. Therefore, choice C is correct.

If a powder is inhaled, it can typically causes respiratory problems and flu-like symptoms, which can be fatal, so the patient's breathing should be assessed frequently, choice A. Open skin lesions may form, choice B, which may be contagious, so standard precautions should be taken. Anthrax is a bacteria, as stated in choice D.

Question 62

Answer: D
Review chapter: Respiratory; ADPIE (Nursing Process)

The best indicator of improvement is always to focus on the objective answer over the subjective ones. ABG lab values provide an objective measurement of the patient's respiratory status. Therefore, choice D is correct.

A normal pulse ox value is above 93% unless the patient has COPD, so an SpO_2 of 92%, choice A, does not indicate an improvement. The patient stating that she is experiencing a decrease in shortness of breath, choice B, is a subjective interpretation of improvement. While it is certainly a reassuring sign, it is not necessarily a sign confirming improvement, as people can "feel" like they're getting better only to quickly get worse again. The same applies to a patient who is sleeping, choice C. It is possible for a person to appear to be sleeping, but in fact be unconscious.

Question 63

Answer: A

Review chapter: Pharmacology; Neurosensory

The patient should absolutely not lose the gag reflex, choice A, as it is a sign of an unprotected airway. The patient is overly sedated if he is no longer protecting the airway and this is breaching into a more general anesthesia realm. Therefore, choice A is correct.

The levels of anesthesia are important to understand. Refer to the "Neurosensory" chapter where anesthesia is covered to brush up on anything you may not fully understand. Amnesia, choice B, is an expected goal of moderate sedation, as we do not want the patient to remember the procedure. The reversal agent for benzodiazepines is flumazenil, which may be ordered by the HCP if the patient was over-medicated, choice C. Remember, if the patient is "benzo naïve," the patient will not have a problem with this reversal agent; however, if the patient routinely takes benzodiazepines, there is a risk of seizure when using this reversal agent. Moderate sedation is administered by the RN, choice D, with continuous monitoring during the procedure and afterward.

Question 64

Answer: C

Review chapter: EKG Interpretation; ADPIE (Nursing Process); Prioritization

Following ADPIE strategy in situations such as this means saying to yourself, "Okay, something is wrong here, so what is nursing process?" Following nursing process (ADPIE), the first step is to assess the situation. You have already analyzed that the patient is in SVT, so the immediate risk is patient safety. If your patient is actively deteriorating due to the rhythm, such as dizziness and palpitations (indicative of a drop in blood pressure), THAT is the priority. Remember: "What can kill my patient the quickest?" Therefore, choice C is correct.

Looking at the remaining answer choices, choices A and B can both be eliminated because they are interventions, not assessments. Remember to assess first. While it is completely likely that this patient will receive a STAT EKG, choice D, assessing the EKG results is not your top priority. We are also already aware the patient is in SVT, so a follow-up EKG is generally considered more confirmatory than absolutely needed to address the problem right in front of you.

Question 65

Answer: D, B, C, A, E, F

Review chapter: EKG Interpretation

Here is the proper order:

> **D.** Ensure that the scene is safe to approach.
> **B.** Check to see if the patient is responsive by speaking to him, touching him, or shaking him.
> **C.** Have a nearby staff member or visitor call for help.
> **A.** Check for a pulse at the carotid artery.
> **E.** Begin CPR.
> **F.** Defibrillate the patient, if needed, by AED.

Question 66

Answer: B

Review chapter: Safety and Infection; Delegation

While LPNs can perform clean and sterile procedures such as dressing changes and catheterizations (both straight and indwelling), a central line dressing change must be performed by an RN. It has a high risk for a CLABSI (central line associated bloodstream infection). Therefore, choice B is correct.

An intubated patient receiving pantoprazole, choice A, is part of standard VAP (ventilator-associated pneumonia) protocol, along with elevating the head of the bed and frequent mouth care. The insertion of a straight cath is a sterile (aseptic) procedure often used for obtaining a urine specimen for culture directly from the bladder; a clean technique, choice C, should not be used for this. If a patient goes home on CIC (clean intermittent catheterization) for acute or chronic urinary retention, the patient is instructed on using a clean technique. An indwelling catheter placement is always a sterile procedure. Placing a trash can at the door, choice D, is acceptable in a contact or droplet isolation patient; we utilize the 4-foot rule.

Question 67

Answer: C

Review chapter: Gastrointestinal; Prioritization

This is a priority question. Remember to focus on ABCs and medical emergencies. What can kill your patient the quickest? In this case, typical Crohn's exacerbations involve diarrhea and potential blood loss. Therefore, the priority is to stabilize the patient hemodynamically by providing IV fluids. Therefore, choice C is correct.

The other answer choices—obtaining a fecal occult blood test (choice A), administering acetaminophen/oxycodone PO for pain (choice B), and drawing blood for a CBC and chem panel (choice D)—will likely be performed; however, they are less important than the initial priorities of ABCs.

Question 68

Answer: B

Review chapter: Gastrointestinal

Using ABCs as your guide, the first action would be to address the complications caused by the Sengstaken-Blakemore tube. The tube can be removed by using scissors to cut it and empty the air out. This is a difficult situation because you want to stop the bleeding, but that will not matter if the person cannot breathe. The breathing complication becomes the larger priority. Removing the tube and correcting the oxygenation and bleeding are the priorities in this case. Therefore, choice B is correct.

A nasal cannula at 2 L, choice A, would not be the appropriate intervention. The interdisciplinary team will assess the need for reintubation, choice C. Auscultating the lungs, choice D, sounds like a good answer since it is following ADPIE strategy, but the airway problem is understood without auscultating the lungs, making choice D redundant and, therefore, incorrect.

Question 69

Answer: B

Review chapter: Psychiatry

The NCLEX calls questions such as these "psychosocial integrity" questions. These are the questions that typically sound like "how does that make you feel?" or "I hear what you are saying." Respond in a therapeutic manner and you will likely select the correct answer. Therefore, choice B is correct.

Never be dismissive, such as telling the patient not to worry, choice A. The correct answer should be progressive in a movement that is trying to fix the issue at hand. If an answer choice does not address the initial problem from the patient in the first place, it is likely not the correct answer. It is like a patient in pain telling you that she is in pain, and you responding to her about the weather outside. Such a response is completely unrelated to the problem at hand. Asking the patient if she has any questions about the diagnosis, choice D, is on target with what is likely the problem here with the woman being sad about the diagnosis, but it is not therapeutic or kind. The same reasoning applies to choice C; it is not your job to inflict your own viewpoints or judgments onto the patient. It is their decision; not yours.

Question 70

Answer: B

Review chapter: Psychiatry; Pharmacology

Due to the repeated attempts to correct the depression with SSRI medications, it is likely the physician will order another type of antidepressant, such as a tricyclic antidepressant or an MAOI like phenelzine. It is not ideal to start patients on these medications before SSRIs because of the potential side effects and adverse reactions. This is especially true with MAOIs; this class of medication can interact with many things and must be taken carefully. Therefore, choice B is correct.

Choice A, sertraline, is an SSRI. As described above, these therapies have failed this patient; the physician is likely to move onto another class of medications. ECT, choice C, is considered a last resort. Clozapine, choice D, is an antipsychotic medication and is rarely used in people with depression unless the depression symptoms are related to schizophrenia or bipolar disorder.

Question 71

Answer: B

Review chapter: Pharmacology; Psychiatry

The immediate risk here is neuroleptic malignant syndrome (NMS), a medical emergency, due to the use of antipsychotic medications, such as haloperidol. If the patient presents with signs and symptoms of increased feelings of heat and muscle rigidity, it is important to hold these medications and call the HCP. In most cases, symptoms will resolve within 1–2 weeks after the oral medication is discontinued. Therefore, choice B is correct.

As long as the patient with anxiety, choice A, is breathing normally, feeling sleepy is a typical response to anti-anxiety medications. The patient on risperidone complaining of a sore throat, choice C, may potentially be showing signs of infection related to neutropenia induced by the medication. The patient will require follow-up treatment, but it is not the priority at this time. Remember, ABCs and medical emergencies are the priorities. Anorexia, nausea, and vomiting, choice D, are side effects of almost every medication available. It can be a problem if the nausea or vomiting is intractable (not easily controlled; hard to treat or cure). Regardless, these symptoms are not going to kill the patient. Remember, the priority to consistently focus on is "what can kill my patient the quickest?"

Question 72

Answer: C
Review chapter: Positioning

It is important to prevent any post-biopsy bleeding in this patient. The patient should be positioned on the right side to compress (tamponade) the organ against the abdominal or chest wall. This will reduce the chance of bleeding. Therefore, choice C is correct.

Refer to the "Positioning" chapter for specifics on all of these positions and when they should be used. Remember what you are trying to prevent or promote.

Question 73

Answer: C
Review chapter: Genetics

While questions like this are relatively uncommon on the NCLEX, it is important to understand the basics of genetics. Understand what the terminology means, such as *heterozygous*. From there, the best way of moving forward is to create a Punnett square to assess risk. This is a simple way to graph all the potential combinations of genotypes that can occur in offspring, given the genotype of their parents and odds of each of the offspring genotypes occurring. A recessive disease occurs when the patient has a homozygous recessive allele for the trait in question. The following Punnett square details the probability that these parents will have a child with CF:

	H	h
H	HH	Hh
h	Hh	hh

As you can see, there is a 25% chance that the child will have CF (HH). Therefore, choice C is correct.

Question 74

Answer: D
Review chapter: Pharmacology

There are many reversal agents or antidotes to medications; however, you cannot know if one may be of use without first assessing what type of medication the patient took. For example, if you know that the patient overdosed on benzodiazepines, it is possible that flumazenil will be used to reverse the overdose, but flumazenil may cause seizures. If the overdose occurs with SSRIs, MAOIs, or tricyclic antidepressants, the main concern may potentially be serotonin syndrome, a serious complication. The patient would require close monitoring for cognitive/behavioral changes, autonomic instability, neuromuscular changes, or even coma. Therefore, choice D is correct.

The amount of medication the patient took, choice C, certainly matters, but if the patient was already unconscious upon arrival to the ER, it is fair to assume that it was a lot. It is also important to assess for suicidal ideation, choice B, and risk for further self-harm. Psych should be called for consult, but, assessing the patient's feelings, choice A, while important, is not the priority. Addressing a patient's physical response to overdose and making sure your patient does not die is the priority.

Question 75

Answer: A, C, E, F
Review chapter: Pharmacology

There are long-term adverse effects of steroid medications that are very important to learn for the NCLEX. Steroids can induce hyperglycemia, so it is important to monitor the patient's glucose levels, choice A. Steroid use may also lead to immunosuppression, so it is important to monitor WBC levels, choice C, especially neutrophils. (Note: Symptoms such as a productive cough could be a sign of a serious infection. If a patient has taken steroids for over 2 weeks, it is important to taper them off slowly. It can take up to a year for the adrenal gland function to fully recover.) Steroids may cause weight gain, choice E. (Note: Steroids affect metabolism and how the body deposits fat, generally in the abdomen, back, or base of the neck. Reducing the dose can reduce the redistribution effect. Cortisone is also involved in water, sodium, and electrolyte balance, so fluid retention can also occur.) You may see your patient have increased edema, choice F; this also proves why choice E is correct. Increased water means increased weight. Therefore, choices A, C, E, and F are correct.

A wider antero-posterior diameter of the thorax, choice B, is associated with COPD patients; it is often called barrel chest. Bacteriuria, choice D, would be seen in the urine of a patient with a urinary tract infection (UTI).